Condition of the Workers in Asia

Studies in India, China, and Other Asian Countries

Update Study Group

AAKAR

Condition of the Workers in Asia
Edited by Suvro Mallick

First Published 2018

ISBN 978-93-5002-569-7

Published by
AAKAR BOOKS
28 E Pocket IV, Mayur Vihar Phase I
Delhi 110 091
aakarbooks@gmail.com
www.aakarbooks.com

In association with
Update Study Group
14B, BB Block, Salt Lake
Kolkata 700 064, West Bengal
(M) 94331 96728
suvro.mallick2@gmail.com
update.pub@gmail.com

Designed by
Limited Colors, Delhi 110 092

Printed at
Sapra Brothers, Noida

In memory of our teachers and guides

Sandwip Bagchi

Dipak Roy

Hence, in the history of capitalist production, the establishment of a norm for the working day presents itself as a struggle over the limits of that day, a struggle between collective capital, i.e. the class of capitalists, and collective labour, i.e. the working class.

—Karl Marx, *Capital*

Contents

Prologue

When we began our study in 2014 about the conditions of the workers in India, China, and other Asian countries, scores of startling facts were uncovered before us. We have found that all over the Asian countries the imperialist capital is making super-profits by super-exploiting the growing reserve army of labour. We have observed that the work-conditions are deplorable in all these countries. Workers are used to work under tremendous workload and work-speed where the employers will not let even a second to be lost. Working days are so long that in most cases workers have to work 12 hours in general—often for 16-17 hours—even 24 hours at a stretch. Wages are so low that they hardly touch the subsistence level. Workers are forced to work for longer hours to make ends meet in the name of overtime—often at a single rate—and confined in the workplaces till the production targets are met. Permanent or regular workers are gradually replaced by low-cost contract and casual workers who are hired and fired according to the demands in the market. Women and child labour are engaged in similar conditions as their male counterparts. Women labourers are preferred in many cases as they are 'docile', 'pliant' and 'reluctant' to join unions whose 'nimble' hands can do the delicate pieces of work. As the reserve army of labour is swelling rapidly, the bargaining power of the workers reduces to a minimum. In most cases workers are not unionized or are deprived of being unionized. Many of the workers are not even aware about the importance of unions. Workers are routinely denied access to the rights or the labour laws of the soil. They are forced to work in extremely dangerous and unhealthy conditions detrimental to their physical and mental health. In many cases they are even beaten by supervisors or thugs to make them 'obedient'. These are the very facts uncovered in this book that can stupefy one. In fact, these conditions remind us of the precarious conditions prevailing in the 'industrial age' of capitalism observed in England described by Marx and Engels in their works.

As our study progresses, we have to concentrate on the present stage of imperialism/capitalism which is operating globally to make the condition of the workers gravely precarious. It is uncovered before our eyes that workers in the said countries are more or less tied rigidly to the global supply chain well connected to the giant multinational corporations where intermediaries are numerous subcontracting firms. These facts have inspired us to study the present dynamics of the imperialist capital that are penetrating deeply into the Asian countries to reap the benefits of the cheapest labour. The imperialists are selling a model of 'development' to these countries in which only a minority section of the population thrives. On the other hand, billions of hapless workers, small peasants, and agricultural labourers are forced to toil hardest to earn wages or income which is far below the subsistence level. These facts make us more interested in studying further and thus we have taken a longer time to finish this venture.

We are indebted to analyses and survey reports made by many scholars, social-scientists, labour activists and labour organizations that have exposed the working conditions in these countries. Particularly several articles in *Monthly Review* and works/articles of John Smith, Surendra Pratap, and others have helped us to comprehend the functioning of the global supply chain in the present stage of capitalism. The works of Jenny Chan, Mark Selden, Pun Ngai, and Anita Chan have helped us in interpreting the working conditions in China. We are also indebted to Aakar Books for publishing this book with keen interest.

1

Workers in the Global Supply Chain in the Present Stage of Capitalism

> In its blind and measureless drive, its insatiable appetite for surplus labour, capital oversteps not only the moral but even the merely physical limits of the working day. It usurps the time for growth, development and healthy maintenance of the body. It steals the time required for the consumption of fresh air and sunlight. It haggles over the meal-times, where possible incorporating them into the production process itself, so that food is added to the workers as to a mere means of production, as coal is supplied to the boiler, and grease and oil to the machinery.
>
> –Karl Marx, *Capital*

The incidents of July 18, 2012 in the Manesar automobile factory shook the country. The Manesar factory is located in the Haryana state of India, owned by Maruti-Suzuki Company, a joint venture of the Government of India and the Japanese multinational Suzuki. The incidents not only expressed the anger building up among the permanent and contract workers of the company, but also it exposed the horrendous workplace conditions inside one of the 'state-of-the-art', and 'flagship' companies of modern-day capitalism. A labour dispute with the management was going on in the Manesar factory to regularize the contract workers (who are forced to do the regular nature of jobs till now), recognition of the newly formed union of the workers, and several other demands. Following this dispute, on that fateful day, workers were demonstrating against some racial comments made by a supervisor to a worker and on other demands. Then the 'bouncers' (goons) hired by the company management ransacked the factory premises and set the factory premises on fire in which a human resource manager lost his life owing to asphyxia. Immediately after this incident with a well-planned conspiratorial motive of the state apparatus and management nexus, a state-sponsored terror was orchestrated on the workers, 546 permanent and 1800 contract workers were terminated from their jobs, living places of the workers were hounded by the police, and security forces and criminal cases were filed against hundreds of workers, 147 workers were arrested. In May 2013, the Haryana and Punjab High Court refused to grant bail to the 147 imprisoned workers of the Maruti Suzuki plant, because "foreign investors are likely not to invest money in India out of fear of labour unrest". In March 2017, thirteen of the leaders of the workers weresentenced for life convicted for 'murder'.

Labour unrest has been developed in the factory from the day when the workers filed an application for registration of their newly formed union in the Manesar factory. During the last decade, a series of protests, demonstrations, and wild-cat strikes were observed in the booming automobile sector in India demanding regularization of the contract workers, reduction of huge wage-gaps between contract and permanent workers, recognition of unions or right to organize in unions, etc. Several reasons behind such continued unrest are precarious work-conditions, low-wage, extreme workload, long work-hours, engagement of contract or trainee workers in place of regular nature of jobs, snatching the right to organize in unions, and super-exploitation followed in the automobile industries in India where most of the operations are done integrated with the 'global value chain' (GVC) or 'global supply/production chain' (GSC/GPC). In fact, in the Maruti-Suzuki plants, the workers do not control machines, but machines control workers as the following:

> The car comes to the worker on the conveyor belt and depending on what your job is to add to it, it stops for 35-40 seconds on an average. So if a worker's task is to add a brake and pedal, then that's what you do all day, with 8-10 bolts in every car, car after car, 40 seconds per car. The result is a bit like a dance move, the same move, non-stop for eight hours. The screw gun in one hand, fix it, run back, pick up another bolt, move back to the car. A bit like aerobics.
>
> The Manesar plant is the world's fastest car production facility. The conveyor belt does not really stop, we move with it and rush back to the original position in time for the next car. We do not control the machine, the machine controls us. We dance to its tune. The result is that you could miss a car or two if you dared to drink water or scratch your back.[1]

This is the familiar picture of all the auto-clusters in India where a lead firm (essentially a multinational or big Indian corporate firm) does the main jobs of assembling and manufacturing main auto-equipment and different auto components, parts are supplied by several tier I, tier II, and tier III enterprises (which are joined or bound to form a single chain). It will be seen that the more we move below the tiers of these enterprises, the more precarious will be the conditions of the workers. In one of the factories of Honda (a Japanese multinational), in a bike-making factory, the conditions of the workers are no better: "The factory assembles various Honda two wheelers like Activa. Parts come from outside, and the cycle time to assemble one scooter is a mere 22 *seconds*.... There are no relievers and so except the half an hour lunch break and two tea breaks, we work continuously.... No safety equipment was provided and if a contract worker asked for it, he was immediately removed. If a permanent worker asked for it, he was warned of serious consequences and just asked to focus on his job."[2]

In the 'globalized' world, the above scenario is very similar—particularly in the developing countries—where most of the manufacturing jobs are performed now. In 1990, Asia accounted for 26.5 per cent of global manufacturing output. By 2013 this has reached 46.5 per cent. Out of these, China accounts for half of Asia's output today—surpassing the great economic powerhouse Japan and the 'Asian Tigers' like South Korea, Taiwan, Hong Kong and Singapore. Asia's share of the global trade in intermediate inputs—the goods that are eventually pieced together into final products—rose from 14 per cent in 2000 to 50 per cent in 2012.[3] In fact, the major developing and underdeveloped (apart from 'industrialized') countries of Asia become nerve-centres of global production/ supply chain. Millions of workers—mostly marginal, migrants, displaced, casual, part-time, contract workers are forced to toil in horrific work conditions at subsistence wages, and produce commodities that satisfy the global consumers.

In China, in the 'global workshop', a huge amount of electronic goods are produced. Among the foreign companies operating in China, there are Foxconn, a Taiwanese sub-contracting multinational company, which is the largest employer of the industrial workers with 1.4 million employees in China alone (more than the total employees of Indian railways). Foxconn has more than 30 factories across China located in eastern, central and western provinces, from Shenzhen to Guangdong, Chongqing, Shanghai, Tianjin, Beijing, Chengdu (so-called 'iPad city') producing for Apple, Microsoft, IBM, Samsung, Amazon, HP, Dell, Sony and other premium brands. In the 1990s, the monopolist barons like Apple, Lucent, Nortel, Alcatel and Ericsson sold off most, if not all, of their in-house manufacturing capacity—both at home and abroad—to a number of subcontracting firms like Foxconn, Pegatron, Flexitronics, etc. to cut labour-costs and other operating costs to reap super-profits. In 1982 Apple Computer President Mike Scott commented: "Our business was designing, educating and marketing. I thought that Apple should do the least amount of work that it could... *let the subcontractors have the problems*[4]."

Hence, to make super-profits and to bypass the 'problems' of handling production, operation, assembling, packaging, transporting and finally the 'problems' of tackling the labour, Apple has transferred the whole burden on to the Foxconn, and which in turn, to maintain sizable profits, pass the 'problems' on to the backs of the Chinese workers. In fact, Foxconn's production pivots on a flexible and abundant workforce which are super-exploited. Foxconn in mainland China relies entirely on the use of rural migrants who come from all over the country. Foxconn houses its migrant workforce in collective dormitories within or close to its factories so as to compress the workplace and living space and facilitate just-in-time, high-speed production. Foxconn's remarkable expansion throughout China gave rise to a mythology of corporate success until in 2010, 18 young workers, ranging in age from 17 to 25, *attempted suicide* jumping from multistoreyed workshops and dormitories. Fourteen died, whereas four survived with crippling injuries. One of them, 17-year-old Tian Yu, only after 37 days of employment, threw herself from the fourth floor of Foxconn's Longhua dormitory in Shenzhen, but miraculously survived with three spinal fractures, four hip fractures, and was left paralysed from the waist down. Her job at the Longhua factory had been her first, and probably will be her last. Immediately after joining the factory, Yu discovered,

> Each production line in my workshop had from a few dozen to more than 100 workers. I was responsible for spot inspections of glass screens to see whether they were scratched. I woke up at 6.30 am, attended an unpaid morning meeting at 7.20 am, started work at 7.40 am, went to lunch at 11, and then usually skipped the evening meal to work overtime till 7.40 pm.
>
> I attended compulsory unpaid work meetings every day. I reported to the line leaders 15 to 20 minutes earlier for roll call. Leaders lectured us on maintaining high productivity, reaching daily output targets and keeping discipline.
>
> There seemed to be no way for me to say 'no' to overtime... Toilet breaks during the working hours are also restricted. I had to swipe my staff ID card at electronic readers at the beginning and end of my work shift. I had to ask permission from the assistant line leaders to leave my seat....

> I was switched to the night shift in March. Checking the screens of the products made my eyes feel intense pain. Working twelve-hour days with a single day off every second week, there's no spare time to use the facilities like swimming pools, or to window shop for smartphones in the commercial districts within the enormous complex.[5]

So, under intense work-pressure and burden of captivity in prison-like dormitories, Yu tried to end her life. It will be seen later that almost all export-driven workplaces in China—which are making products for foreign investors in global supply chain—become prison-like factories where thousands of workers are competing with the speed of the conveyor belt and finally turn into 'machines' and have no pleasure in doing monotonous tenuous repetitive functions hour after hour, day after day. When the suicide attempts reached an appalling peak, Foxconn placed 'safety nets' around the roofs, on both sides of the corridors of the dormitories, and in all its manufacturing bases across China.

This has also been noted that the production process in Foxconn is simplified to an extreme degree so that workers need no specialized knowledge of training to perform most tasks. Technicians from the industrial engineering department regularly use stop watches and computerized engineering devices to test workers. If they are able to meet the quota, targets are increased to the maximum possible. On the iPhone assembly line, another worker described how her tasks were measured to precise seconds: 'I take a motherboard from the line, scan the logo, put it in an anti-static bag, stick on a label and place it on the line. Each of these tasks takes two seconds. *Every ten seconds I finish five tasks*[6].'

On April 24, 2013, Rana Plaza, a multistoreyed building at Dhaka in Bangladesh, housing a garment factory, a bank and some shops collapsed killing at least 1135 garment workers and wounding more than 2500 workers. It was known later that the structure of the building was not secure; it was unsafe to run a whole factory in that premise and local inspections suggested that the building should be evacuated and remain closed. Though the bank and shops were closed following the inspection, the workers of garment factories were ordered by the management to continue the production process threatening dismissal. When a generator at the top floor started operation, the whole building was shaken and collapsed like a house of cards. Many people were trapped inside the debris, killing hundreds and injuring more. Just a few months before, on November 24, 2012, a major fire engulfed the factory of Tejreen Fashion Limited, a sister concern of the Tuba Group in the district of Dhaka, Bangladesh. More than 111 garment workers died and around 300 were injured in that incident.

Bangladesh is the second largest exporter of ready-made garments. The clothing industry in Bangladesh is second only to China's in size and employs about four million people, mainly women, in approximately 3500 factories. Ready-made garments account for nearly four-fifths of the country's exports and contribute more than 10 per cent of the nation's GDP.[7] Bangladesh's garment exports turned into an industry with $25 billion in annual revenue. Sixty per cent of the clothes go to Europe, 23 per cent to the United States and 5 per cent to Canada.[8] Hundreds of small firms (including home-based enterprises) in Bangladesh stitch, manufacture and supply garments (through the global supply chain) to the foreign companies who are mostly located in the USA and Europe. The Who's Who of these companies are Gap, Old Navy, Nike, Patagonia, H&M Group, Primark, etc. But even after the four years of the worst industrial disaster of Bangladesh, the working and living conditions, pathetically low-wage working places, no-union regime of the Bangladesh garment sector have changed little. Most of the international buyers do not take responsibility for the disaster or do not force the suppliers to change the work-conditions. They have subcontracted most of the garment-making operations to the suppliers to make super-profits. They are not interested at all in the precarious working and living conditions, wage-level and deunionization problems in the workplaces of the supplier countries. As for an example:

> The Next Collections factory of Bangladesh, producing fashionable and costly garments for Gap and Old Navy have 3750 workers. They work seven days a week, including on Fridays, which is supposed to be their weekly day off. It is typical for the workers to toil from 8.00 am to 10.00 pm, 11.00 pm, 1.00 am, sometimes 3.00 am or even later. *Fifteen- to 17-hour shifts* are routine in the finishing section... In just 21 days in June, these workers were kept in the factory for a *stunning 334 hours*! When workers ask how long their shift will be, their managers always shout the same answer: "Keep working until it is done!"... Despite the mind-numbing mandatory overtime, if an exhausted worker arrives even a minute late to work, he or she will be docked their entire attendance bonus. If a worker punches his or her timecard out a minute early, he or she will be docked an entire hour's wages. Physical punishment is the norm at Next Collections. No matter how many hours a worker has toiled, if she makes an error in production, she will be slapped, shoved or even punched. Anyone who dares challenge the gross human, women's and workers' rights violations will be immediately fired.[9]

In the same report it is also observed that:

> On December 14, 2010, a fire broke out at the Ha-Meem Group's That's It Sportswear factory, killing 29 workers and injuring 100, 36 of them critically. Several workers jumped to their deaths so that their families could have their bodies to mourn. The majority of production in the factory was children's clothing being made for Gap. Workers told us that when the fire broke out, security guards deliberately locked several exit gates to prevent the garments from being stolen, trapping many of those who died.
>
> Senior sewers at That's It Sportswear earned just 28 cents an hour.
>
> In 1911—over 100 years ago—workers at the Triangle Shirtwaist factory in New York City were paid 14 cents an hour. Adjusted for inflation, that 14-cent wage would come to $3.18 an hour in today's dollars. *One hundred years later, workers at That's It Sportswear in Bangladesh are paid just 28*

> *cents an hour, earning just one-tenth of the real wages earned by New York City garment workers in 1911.*[10]

These garment workers are easy victims of the multinational corporations who buy the apparels through the global value/ supply chain and are marketing the products to the wealthy consumers in the advanced countries. One hundred years ago the workers in New York or London worked under subsistence wages. Their descendants are now found all over the Asian countries where millions of poor workers do almost the same type of jobs earning abysmal low wages, even far less than the wages received by the garment workers 100 years ago!

*****

Since the 1970s-80s, a structural change is observed in the global industrial production. During the last three-four decades a considerable number of industrial jobs are shifted to such regions of the advanced countries where labour-costs are cheaper. But a huge number of jobs are relocated to the developing and underdeveloped countries where labour-costs are the cheapest, raw materials and infrastructure are easily available at low prices and where the ruling classes of that developing and underdeveloped countries are prepared to provide huge tax-breaks and other financial sops to attract foreign investment.

In fact, since the 1970s and 80s, the capitalism in the advanced countries has dipped into stagnation and recurrent crisis. In the absence of new technologies or other stimuli to revitalize the economy, the imperialist capital or the multinational corporations have an urgent need to find new avenues of investing the surplus generated to maximize the profits. The 'globalization' drive of the imperialist capital is nothing but the aggressive search for new profitable investment opportunities around the globe. In the name of globalization the imperialist capital tries its best to break the barriers and restrictions made on the economy of the developing and underdeveloped counties. In fact, these barriers and restrictions were built under the era of Cold War waged between the imperialist countries and the Soviet bloc. Countries like India, dependent on the imperialist countries on the one hand, bargained for several concessions from both camps, and on the other hand, made possible to build some sort of barriers and restrictions on its economy. During the 1980s the barriers in these countries are beginning to be broken by the imperialist capital of the neoliberal era. Particularly during the late 1980s and early 1990s, with the demise of Soviet Russia (including the so-called socialist countries of Eastern Europe) and with the entry of China in the global capitalist market, the globalization drive of the imperialist capital gains a new momentum. The imperialist capital is now actually "battering" the barriers and restrictions made on the economy of the developing and underdeveloped countries. Capital is now circulated throughout the globe with utmost ease. All corners of the world are now actually opened before the capital as stated in *The Communist Manifesto* 170 years ago.

So, capital's push to move to profitable regions is in fact the search for low-cost labour and other low-cost facilities either in the backward regions of the advanced countries or in the developing and underdeveloped countries. There have been periods of time when union movements exist and/or 'pro-labour' political parties (especially in Europe) have allowed for improved working conditions, higher wages and social benefits. Although capital gave nothing away without a struggle by workers, the Cold War added a new dimension to it. Governments in the advanced countries needed to ensure the support of their workers as part of a Cold War compact and offered several concessions to the Western labour. Moreover, higher employment, particularly in the Korean and Vietnam War years, coupled with domestic repression in the United States, and a welfare state (especially in Europe where it was necessary to counter the challenge represented by the Soviet Union and Eastern Europe), created an era of relative 'peace' between monopoly capital and labour unions. Social benefits and concessions were given to the workers to maintain relative 'class peace'. In fact, beginning with the imperialist era in the last century (even the period before that when Marx was alive), a large section of the workers in the advanced countries (such as England) was bribed and corrupted giving them a part of the imperial loots. In the imperialist era and when multinational corporations emerged as major actors on the world stage, the upper layer of the workers in the advanced countries benefited indirectly from the world imperialist system and thus further degenerated and degraded. But some of these benefits were later reversed with the advent of neoliberalism and with the end of the Cold War period.

By the late 1970s, imperialist capital initiated the process of global economic restructuring resulting stagnation and/or reduction of real wages, cutbacks in welfare state spending, rise in prices of essential commodities, attacks on trade unions, and existing labour laws, and took other measures, commencing the heightened war against the working class ushering the era of neoliberalism. It had broken the resistance of the labour unions in the developed countries to relocate the production in cheaper locations or countries. Drives were taken for privatization and deregulation and cutting of social benefits enjoyed by the US and European workers. Enormous efforts have been made to break the strength of the workers' unions to accomplish this. US President Reagan's breaking of the PATCO (air traffic controllers') strike in 1981 struck a major blow to the power of organized labour. In Britain, the neoliberal policies of the Thatcher government dealt a heavy blow to the organized labour movement.

In Germany, corporations and government—attempting to increase capital's profitability—are changing the privileged position that labour has held since the Second World War. Chancellor Gerhard Schroeder boasted that "we have restructured the labour market to enhance its flexibility...With our radical reforms of the country's social security systems, most notably health care, we have paved the way for the *reduction of non-wage labour costs*"[11] In other words, German capital is weakening labour rights, making it easier to discharge workers, and at the same time reducing social benefits.[12]

In the USA, multibillionaire Warren Buffet declared in 2006: "There's class warfare, all right, but it's my class, the rich class, that's making war, and *we're winning*." With unions crushed to the point that they now account for only 6.6 per cent of private-sector employees of the USA, the lowest level in a century, the class war from above has shifted increasingly to attacking state and local government workers, including the private sectors dominated by the multinational corporations.[13] Moreover, there are lower frequency of major strikes (only a few per year compared to literally hundreds per year in the 1950-1980 period) in the USA. There is no doubt that the increased surrender of workers in the face of the assault by capital was due to the fact that they were understandably concerned that the bosses would either hire replacement workers or close the facility and move the jobs to some backward locations of the country or to developing and underdeveloped countries.

This retrogressive trend in the organized labour movement in the advanced countries is neither a sudden incident nor a surprising one. In fact, with the demise of the USSR (and 'socialist' countries of Eastern Europe) and the integration of 'socialist' China into the global capitalist market forces, it is established now that the international socialist movement (along with the international working class movement) has suffered a heavy and serious defeat. With this defeat the imperialist capital has increased its aggression not only on the workers of the advanced countries, but also on the workers of the developing and underdeveloped countries.

A prime important fact of this defeat is that it has occurred not at the frontal class war waged between imperialist and socialist camps, but it has occurred due to the internal weakness of the world proletarian movement at a certain point of its march when the leadership and control of the conscious section of the working class on the movement and organization slipped out of its hands. Notably, both in Soviet Russia and China the march along the path of transition to socialism was reversed without any resistance (and bloodshed) of the conscious section of the working class. This is enough in exposing that the socialist movements in these countries and other parts of the world have suffered a heavy and significant defeat the cause of which lie in the internal weakness of the international working class movement. The 'class peace' attained during the Cold War period is nothing but the capitulation of the leaders of the working class before the imperialist capital. These so-called representatives of the working class both at national and international level have sacrificed the working class interests in such a way that the strength of the working class movement has been squandered apart; in general the working class at national and international level are divided, dispersed and incapacitated enormously.

Following the defeat of the international working class movement the labour unions in both the advanced and developing/underdeveloped countries have become pro-business, bureaucratic, and conciliatory as the treacherous leaders sacrificed the interests of the proletariat on a global scale. Most of the unions have become 'company unions' or are busy in maintaining 'peace' at any cost. With this retrogression, in several countries of the Global South the remaining strength of the unions and workers was crushed with the might of the state atrocities.

Under the circumstances, the overall conditions of the workers, peasants and working people in the developing and underdeveloped countries have become more disastrous. In the neoliberal globalization, IMF and World Bank dictated structural adjustment programmes (privatizing the existing public sector enterprises, deregulating and liberalizing the economy, hire and fire of the workers and/or taking measures to end job securities of the workers, engagement of the low cost casual and contract labour in the perennial nature of jobs and so on), and imposed an export-oriented development model with the opening of foreign direct investment (FDI) on these countries. To gain economic 'growth', these countries have been engaged in fierce competition with each other to get more FDI and export orders in the booming export processing zones (EPZs). This competition ultimately took the form of offering multinational corporations (MNCs) cheaper natural resources and land, huge tax-holidays, cheaper infrastructure (often built by the debts taken from the imperialist donors and countries and thereby further tightening the hold of imperialist forces around the neck of the working people), and ensuring rock-bottom (somewhere, the cheapest) labour costs. Moreover, it is noted earlier that the opening of erstwhile 'socialist' countries, particularly the opening of China expanded the reserve army of labour on a huge scale.

Strikingly, most of these developing and underdeveloped countries have an enormous workforce attached in agricultural activities and maintained vast remnants of feudal exploitation and relations of production (apart from China). There are also scores of working people who are artisans, fishermen, tribal people dependent on forests and low-scale cultivation, and own-account workers (including petty shopkeepers and people dependent on several services). In the name of 'development' (and preserving the old feudal remnants to a large extent) a sizeable number of these workforces are uprooted, displaced and expropriated by setting up of booming EPZs/SEZs, industrial parks and corridors, glittering cities, and extravagant infrastructural projects—which are surrounded by an ocean of the poor and destitute. In fact, this model of 'development' is slated to maximize the profits of the owners; it is used to open opportunities to make quick bucks for the elite section of the society; whereas the vast majority of population—either engaged in agricultural activities or 'informal' nature of jobs (not barring the 'menial' works)—remain largely steeped in misery, poverty, ignorance and illiteracy. Constrained by increasingly harsh conditions and below poverty level throughout the developing and underdeveloped countries (including violence unleashed against the peasants and the landless poor, artisans, etc. in the name of 'development'), and finding no jobs or income sources in the rural areas, masses of people are forced to move from the countryside to the overcrowded urban centres which do not have sufficient jobs to absorb the newcomers. The result is a substantial increase in the number of people living a hand-to-mouth existence in slums and ghettos. These new recruits to the reserve army of labour are now easily available to imperialist capital. This massive workforce is prepared to do all sorts of jobs, even 'menial' ones, under any conditions dictated by the capitalists.

The presence of a large pool of workers living a precarious existence is nothing new. It is one of the basic characteristics of capitalism, described by Marx and Engels as the reserve army of labour. More than an underlying attribute of capitalism, the reserve army helps to keep costs down—permitting the market system to function profitably—and serves as a constant and effective weapon against workers. The unemployed, the underemployed, and those with only tenuous holds on their jobs, constitute the reserve army of labour, necessary for the functioning of capitalism. The reserve army is created and maintained as a means to capital accumulation, which requires that a surplus labour force be constantly available to facilitate expansion and at the same time to hold down the wages of workers and to make them 'docile' and 'pliant'.

The question of the reserve army of labour was discussed on numerous occasions since Marx and Engels used the term in their writings. But it becomes most important in the present-day capitalist economy and probably even more important in history because the reserve army of labour in not only the developed countries, but specially in the developing and underdeveloped countries is the main source of super-profits (and thereby opening the scope of super-exploitation of the workers) before the MNCs. Harry Magdoff and Fred Magdoff wrote in 2004 that,

> These are difficult times for workers. In the wealthy countries of capitalism's center, labor is struggling to maintain existing wages and benefits against a combined assault by corporations and governments, while conditions of workers in the periphery are even more difficult. The widespread acceptance and adoption of capital's agenda—"free trade," "free markets," greater "flexibility" regarding labor, and reduced social welfare assistance—has led to one group of real winners. Transnational corporations (and their owners

and top managers) now have more freedom to produce where labor and other costs are cheap, have their patents protected, and move capital in and out of countries at will. Many workers, unfortunately, are finding that their situation has become more tenuous.[14]

Chart 1: Distribution of Industrial Employment, 1980-2008

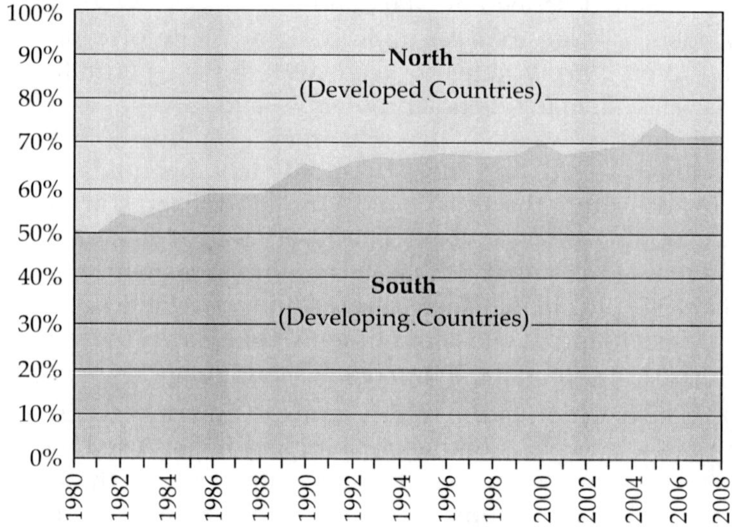

[*Source:* The Global Reserve Army of Labor and the New Imperialism, John Bellamy Foster, et al., *Monthly Review*, November 2011]

According to the International Labour Organization (ILO), the global labour force, between 1980 and 2007, grew from 1.9 billion to 3.1 billion, a rise of 63 per cent—with 73 per cent of the labour force located in the developing world, and 40 per cent in China and India alone.[15] In 2010, 79 per cent or 541 million of the world's industrial workers lived in "less developed regions", up from 34 per cent in 1950 and 53 per cent in 1980. In comparison 145 million or 21 per cent of the total industrial workers lived in imperialist countries. Among this industrial employment the manufacturing sector contributes the maximum employment—83 per cent of the world's manufacturing workforce lives and works in the Global South (i.e. in developing and underdeveloped countries).

Interestingly, these figures do not signify that the Global South becomes largely 'industrial'. Still a substantial percentage of labour are engaged in agricultural activities in these countries. In countries like India a sizeable workforce are engaged in the service sector which is more than industrial activities. In fact, as a share of global industrial workers, the South's growth of industrial workers are modest—rising from 14.5 per cent in 1980 to 16.1 per cent in 1990, 19.1 per cent in 2000 and then 23.1 per cent in 2010.[16] From Chart 1 it is found that most industrial workers are now located in developing and underdeveloped countries.

The free mobility of capital in and out of the countries, but the restrictions on the cross-border mobility of the migrant workers makes the conditions of the workers in the developing and underdeveloped countries more precarious. The industrial economy of the Global South cannot absorb the massive pool of burgeoning workforce coming from rural or less developed regions within the country. As a result, immense joblessness, underemployment, misery and poverty are observed in these countries which have exerted enormous downward pressure on wages and living conditions. In other words, the capital is "winning" everywhere in a war against the proletariat—won in the advanced and so-called socialist countries—they have won it in the developing and underdeveloped countries (formerly called the 'Third World') also.

It is noted earlier that the imperialist capital are relocating production facilities to low-wage regions and countries. In fact, a large part of the world trade is dominated now through the outsourcing and/or subcontracting by the MNCs. (One estimate put it at 40 per cent). In 1996, a single Nike shoe contained 52 different components produced by different subcontractors in five different countries.[17] Some economists rightly called these business companies *hollow MNCs*. They have no direct engagement in manufacturing operations at any level. In the garment sector all the major brands collect finished products from the suppliers or sub-contracting enterprises located in developing or underdeveloped countries. In many cases, the

MNCs are themselves the subcontractors such as Foxconn, Flexitronics, Kelon, Honeywell, Compaq, etc. International Trade Union Confederation reports in a review that the "top 50 MNCs only employ six per cent of people in a direct employment relationship but they rely on a *hidden workforce of 94 per cent*—a massive convenient workforce hidden in the shadows of global supply chains. Just a handful of these companies could recognize their workforce and change the lives of millions of working people... Working people pay the price of the scandal—slavery, informal work, precarious short-term contracts, low wages, unsafe work and dangerous chemicals, forced overtime, attacks by governments on labour laws and social protection, inequality—it's all part of a great global scandal that is today driven by corporate greed with an eternal quest for profit and shareholder value."[18]

John Smith has noted in his book *Imperialism in the Twenty-First Century* that according to the estimate of Kate Bronfenbrenner and Stephen Luce, each year from 1992 to 2001, between 70,000 and 100,000 production jobs are shifted from information and communication technology to high-end manufacturing of industrial machinery and electronics components to low-wage manufacturing in food processing and textiles from the USA to Mexico and China. In the new millennium the "total number of jobs leaving the US for countries in Asia and Latin America increased from 204,000 in 2001 to as much as 406,000 in 2004."[19]

In fact, in advanced countries fewer of jobs are created per unit of FDI stock, whereas the number of jobs created in developing and underdeveloped countries is more. Therefore, imperialist capital is moving to the low-wage countries more and more where the making of super-profits is easier. UNCTAD's 2007 World Investment Report writes that,

> [I]n 2003, 9.8 workers were employed for each $1 million of FDI stock owned by US TNCs in the manufacturing sector in the developed countries, whereas the same stock of FDI in developing countries employed 23.8 workers, or 2.4 times as many. As a result, a stock of $281 billion in US

> manufacturing FDI in developed countries employed 2.76 million workers, while a stock of $88 billion in developing countries employed 2.1 million workers. However, this data underestimates TNC employment, since UNCTAD does not count temporary, casual and subcontracted workers as employees, yet the US TNCs have led the way in casualizing labor of the developing and backward countries.[20]

Leading US MNCs, such as General Electric, Exxon, Chevron, Ford, General Motors, Proctor and Gamble, IBM, HP, United Technologies, Johnson and Johnson, Alcoa, Kraft and Coca Cola now employ more workers than they do in the USA—most of the vast number of these workers are employed through subcontractors in the global supply chain. Some major MNCs, such as Nike and Reebok, rely on developing country's subcontractors for 100 per cent of their production workforce—with domestic employees confined simply to managerial, product development, marketing, and distribution activities. The result has been the proletarianization, often under precarious conditions, of much of the population of the developing and underdeveloped countries, working in a massive number of EPZs and other zones under conditions dictated by the MNCs.[21]

Bourgeois economists called this outsourcing of capital to reap the benefits of low-cost wage-labour as 'Global Labour Arbitrage'. *The Economist* defines global labour arbitrage as "taking advantage of lower costs abroad, especially in poor countries". It is thus an unequal exchange process in which one country, as Marx said, is able to "cheat" another due to much higher exploitation of labour in the poorer country.

John Bellamy Foster, Robert W. McChesney, and R. Jamil Jonna write in *Monthly Review*:

> Dell, the PC assembler, purchases some 4,500 parts from 300 different suppliers in multiple countries around the world. As the Asian Development Bank Institute indicated in a 2010 study of iPhone production: "It is almost impossible [today] to define clearly where a manufactured product is made in the global market. This is why on the back of iPhones

one can read 'Designed by Apple in California, Assembled in China.'" Although both statements on the back of the iPhones are literally correct, neither answers the question of where the real production takes place. Apple does not itself manufacture the iPhone. Rather the actual manufacture (that is, everything but its software and design) takes place primarily outside the United States. The production of iPhone parts and components is carried out principally by eight corporations (Toshiba, Samsung, Infineon, Broadcom, Numonyx, Murata, Dialog Semiconductor, and Cirrus Logic), which are located in Japan, South Korea, Germany, and the United States. All the major parts and components of the iPhone are then shipped to the Shenzhen, China plants of Foxconn (a company headquartered in Taipei) for assembly and export to the United States.

Apple's enormous, complex global supply chain for iPod production is aimed at obtaining the lowest unit labor costs (taking into consideration labor costs, technology, etc.), appropriate for each component, with the final assembly taking place in China, where production occurs on a massive scale, under enormous intensity, and with ultra-low wages. In Foxconn's Longhu, Shenzhen factory 300,000 to 400,000 workers eat, work, and sleep under horrendous conditions, with workers, who are compelled to do rapid hand movements for long hours for months on end, finding themselves twitching constantly at night. Foxconn workers in 2009 were paid the minimum monthly wage in Shenzhen, or about 83 cents an hour. (Overall in China in 2008 manufacturing workers were paid $1.36 an hour, according to the US Bureau of Labor Statistics data.)

Despite the massive labor input of Chinese workers in assembling the final product, their low pay means that their work only amounts to 3.6 per cent of the total manufacturing cost (shipping price) of the iPhone. The overall profit margin on iPhones in 2009 was 64 per cent. If iPhones were assembled in the United States—assuming labor costs ten times that in China, equal productivity, and constant component costs—Apple would still have an ample profit margin, but it would drop from 64 per cent to 50 per cent.

> In effect, Apple makes 22 per cent of its profit margin on iPhone production from the much higher rate of exploitation of Chinese labor.
>
> Of course in stipulating a mere tenfold difference in wages between the United States and China, in its calculation of the lower profit margins to be gained with the United States as opposed to Chinese assembly, the Asian Development Bank Institute was adopting a very conservative assumption. Overall Chinese manufacturing workers in 2008, according to the US Bureau of Labor Statistics, received only 4 per cent of the compenzation for comparable work in the United States, and 3 per cent of that in the European Union. In comparison, hourly manufacturing wages in Mexico in 2008 were about 16 per cent of the US level.[22]

It is in fact, *super-exploitation* that lies behind much of the expansion of production in Global South, i.e. in the developing and underdeveloped countries. It should be noted that the term 'super-exploitation' appears to have two closely related, overlapping meanings in Marxist theory: 1) workers who receive less than the historically determined value of labour power, and 2) workers who are subjected to unequal exchange and overexploited, primarily in the poor and developing countries. In Samir Amin's framework, however, the two meanings are united. This is because the value of labour power is determined globally, while actual wage rates are determined nationally, and are hierarchically ordered owing to imperialism. In the developing and underdeveloped countries, therefore, workers normally receive wages that are less than the value of labour power. This is the basis of *imperial rent*.[23] The fact that this has been the basis of rapid economic growth for some emerging economies does not alter the reality that it has generated enormous imperial rents for MNCs and capital at the advanced and/or imperialist countries.

Strikingly, most of the 'super-exploited' jobs created in the Global South are 'informal' in nature signifying that these types of jobs are mostly vulnerable. According to an estimate the world's 'economically active population' grew from 1.9 billion in 1980 to 3.1 billion in 2006, a 63 per cent increase. Almost all of this phenomenal growth has occurred in 'emerging nations', now home to 84 per cent of the global workforce—out of which 1.6 billion are waged labour, the other billion are small and marginal peasants and another multitude of people working in the variegated 'informal' economy.[24] But the 'waged labour' does not mean that they are 'formal' workers. In fact, a significant portion of the waged labour is engaged in informal economy (other than self-employment). According to ILO documents informal employment as percentage of non-agricultural employment in 2004-10 is 82 per cent in South Asia and 65 per cent in East and South East Asia.[25] In Chapter II of this book it is observed that millions of informal workers are also engaged in the formal or organized sector. In fact, precarious working conditions, abysmally low wage-level, increasing working hours and work-pressure, are observed both at the formal and informal sector of the Global South (particularly in the global supply chains). It has been noted by the analysts that virtually everywhere today and especially in the Global South, the boundaries between the active and reserve armies of labour become even more fluid. The Swedish International Development Agency has noted that all segments of the informal workforce—self-employed, casual, sub-contract, temporary and part-time workers and micro entrepreneurs appear to be growing and the main reason for this growth is that the formal labour market cannot generate a sufficient number of jobs.[26] The following ILO comment depicts the modern aspects of global neoliberalism (called 'flexibilization'):

> As part of the cost-cutting measures and efforts to enhance competitiveness, firms are increasingly operating with a small core of wage-employees with regular terms and conditions (formal employment) ... and a growing periphery of 'non-standard' or 'atypical' and often informal workers in different types of workplaces scattered over different locations. These measures often include outsourcing or subcontracting and a shift away from regular employment relationships to more flexible and informal relationships.[27]

Therefore, flexibilization is a conscious effort of the imperialist capital. On the one hand, it is pushing for 'labour reforms' in the formal/organized sector to hire and fire at will or to cut social benefits enjoyed by the regular workers, and on the other hand, shifting an enormous amount of capital to flexibilized countries where the labour codes are either absent or minimal.

Another aspect of the shifting of manufacturing activities to the Global South from the advanced and/or imperialist countries is the huge engagement of women labour in the subcontracting enterprises. Particularly in the export-led industrialization in Asian countries the exploitation of low-waged and vulnerable women workers is massive. A report by the United Nations, the 'World Survey on the Role of Women in Development', commented, "Among the newly industrializing countries... none of [them] has increased its exports of manufactures without recourse to women workers. It is by now considered a stylized fact that the industrialization in the context of globalization is as much female-led as it is export-led". As a result, women workers now represent more than one-third of the manufacturing workforce in developing and underdeveloped countries and nearly a half in some Asian countries. The preference of women workers is particularly marked in export-processing zones where women workers make up the majority, reaching up to 90 per cent in some of them.[28]

Why have the women workers become so attractive to the investors? Primarily, everywhere in the Global South the wages of the women workers are considerably less than their male counterparts. Moreover, women labourers can be forced to work for more hours than the male workers; they are 'docile', 'flexible' (can be hired and fired at will) and in most cases they are 'reluctant' to join unions. Particularly in the EPZs/SEZs the conditions of the women workers are horrible including discrimination in wages, social benefits, protections, and career development, lack of accommodation and childcare facilities, dismissal if they become pregnant and absence of maternity leave, forced overtime and longer working hours, sexual harassment and exposure to violence in workplaces.

It is noted earlier that most of the outsourcing occurred in the developing and underdeveloped countries through a massive network of global value/supply chains. Most of these supply chains are operational both inside and outside the export processing zones of the developing and underdeveloped countries. In fact the imperialist capital turns the whole of these countries as export processing zones which are largely located in Asia. The number of workers employed in them nearly tripled between 1997 and 2006 (the latest year for which statistics are found), when 63 million workers were employed in EPZs located in 132 countries. In 2006, EPZs were responsible for 75 per cent or more of export earnings in Kenya, Malaysia, Madagascar, Vietnam, the Dominican Republic and Bangladesh, while Philippines, Mexico, Haiti and Morocco earned 50 to 60 per cent of exports from their EPZs. According to the ILO database, Asia's 900+ zones employed 53 million workers, 40 million of them in China and 3.25 million in Bangladesh.

In a survey of the ILO published in 2007, it is concluded that "despite the presence of EPZs—for over 30 years in some cases—there are very few cases where EPZs have played an important role in accomplishing… direct developmental goals". UNCTAD warned in 2004 that manufacturing EPZs were reproducing *colonial forms of "enclave-led growth"* in which "a relatively rich commodity-exporting sector, well connected to roads, ports and supported by ancillary services, exist side by side with large undeveloped hinterlands where the majority of the population live."[29]

In other words, the so-called 'development' model in the developing and underdeveloped countries is none other than an "enclave-like growth"—a latest form of colonial subjugation. In building such a 'growth-model', the capital in the developing and underdeveloped countries remains overwhelmingly dependent on the imperialist capital or big monopoly capital. The EPZ/SEZ model could not uplift the working mass from abject misery and destitution. When orders come from the host MNCs, they get jobs, and when the orders are poor or closed (as in the period of the 'great recession' of 2008-09), they become jobless. The suppliers and the sub-contracting firms operating in these zones thus, become de facto to the managers of the imperialist capital who are obedient to their masters in fear of flight of capital. It is a newer form of colonial subjugation in the period of globalization.

The global value/supply chains in developing and underdeveloped countries (particularly in Asia, on which we focus our attention) exhibit a classic example of this dependency on the lead MNCs in modern-day global capitalism:

> The global supply chains (GSC) of industries or companies are systems of resources, organizations, people, technology, information and activities spread across the globe and involved in the production and trade in goods and services. In other words, it is a worldwide network of suppliers of raw materials and other inputs, manufacturers (including component or other input manufacturers, assembly plants or final product manufacturers), warehouses, distribution centres and retailers, through which raw materials are acquired, transformed into the final product and delivered to the consumers. The supply chains of industries and companies have always existed in some form, but they were generally restricted in national boundaries and many times in particular regions of a country. The change that took place in the current phase of globalization is that now the supply chains are dispersed all over the globe. The relationship between the various parts of global supply chains varies greatly with the nature of the industry and company. The global value chains (GVC) of industries and companies are those parts of the global supply chains where value adding activities take place, including extraction and sourcing of raw materials, research, technological development and designing, manufacturing of intermediate inputs, and the manufacture of final products and services.[30]

This strategy of global supply/value chains has become dominant trend in the recent phase of globalization. Most of the labour-intensive, hazardous, pollution-prone industrial operations are shifted to developing and underdeveloped countries where Asia becomes the most important located. In short, the CEOs of the MNCs or the lead firms located mainly in the advanced countries (including Japan and so-called Asian Tigers) send orders, designs, technical know-how of the commodities to factories or sub-contracting enterprises in countries like China, Indonesia, Malaysia, Thailand, India, Bangladesh, Vietnam, Cambodia, Mexico, etc. They do not take any risks in running the industrial activities. They receive the final products and are involved only in marketing the products under a specific brand name. All the operational costs, labour costs, infrastructure, environmental costs, procurement of raw materials, packaging, shipping, taxes payable to the local government (if any), 'labour-trouble' and the 'problem' of social obligations are shifted to the suppliers.

Particularly in electronics, garments, toys, footwear, leather goods and agro-food industries such type of chains operate which are commonly called *buyer-driven supply chains*. Firms that fit the buyer-driven model, including retailers like Walmart, Sears and JC Penney, athletic footwear companies like Nike and Reebok, and fashion-oriented apparel companies like Liz Claiborne, Gap and The Limited Inc., generally design and/or market—but do not make—the branded products they order. They are "manufacturers without factories", with the physical production of goods separated from the design and marketing.

In the case of automobiles, aircraft, computers, semi-conductors and heavy machinery, this trend is almost similar, but here the lead companies bear the responsibility of assembling in their own plants due to the specific nature of the products and this practice is commonly known as *producer-driven supply chains*. In the automobile industry, in which the main assembly plants are required to be located close to the markets and a major section of supplier networks are required to be located in the vicinity of main plants, India has emerged as an important production centre other than China, Thailand, etc. Both in China and India, with their vast economies, large markets and huge regional disparities (inbuilt in the process of capitalist development) in the level of economic development as well as in wages, there is immense scope for retaining their position as production hubs for exceptionally longer periods by shifting the low ends of the value chains to low wage locations within the country. In fact, we will observe in the later section that China is already relocating the industries run on a subcontracting basis into the central and western part of the country where labour costs are cheaper. And in India the scope is wide open as a sizeable number of unemployed persons are joining the workforce every year.

Box: Global Supply Chain

In order to illustrate the effects of global supply chains it is useful to look at the famous example of Barbie and the world economy. A Barbie doll ("My First Tea Party Barbie") marketed in California in 1996 sold at a price of $9.99 and was labelled "Made in China." Nearly all of the raw materials and parts that made up the doll, however, were imported, while Chinese workers put together the final Barbie. (At the time there were two Barbie factories in China and one each in Indonesia and Malaysia.) Each factory in China employed around 5,500 workers. Most of the plastic resin in the form of pellets or "chips" was probably imported via the Chinese Petroleum Corporation, Taiwan's state-owned oil importer. The nylon hair came from Japan. The cardboard packaging and many of the paint pigments and oils used for decorating the dolls came from the United States. Only the cotton cloth for Barbie's dress came from China, which otherwise simply supplied labor to assemble the dolls. The workers operated the plastic mold-injection machines, painted the details on the doll (requiring fifteen different paint stations), and sewed the clothing. Workers were paid around $40 a month. The total labor cost for each Barbie was a mere 35 cents, or *3.5 per cent* of the final retail price.

[*Source:* The Global Stagnation and China, by John Bellamy Foster and Robert W. McChesney, *Monthly Review*, February 2012, Vol. 63, Issue 09

In fact, these subcontracting practices commonly include the use of smaller companies, informal workshops and home-based workers unknown to the lead firm itself. Small and medium-sized enterprises (SMEs) often supply intermediate goods to exporting firms in their country and are as such integrated into global supply chains. With SMEs constituting between 80 and 90 per cent of total employment in the developing and underdeveloped world, it is likely that a large part of employment generated in the lower tiers of global supply chains is in medium-sized, small and micro-enterprises. While this provides much-needed incomes to workers, it is in these enterprises where the precarious, casual, and super-exploitative nature of jobs is available. Of the estimated 420 to 510 million SMEs (excluding micro-enterprises) worldwide, only 9 per cent operate in the formal economy. These second- and third-tier firms often employ workers informally under unregulated terms and conditions.[31] Whereas wholly owned subsidiaries of MNCs have direct responsibility for employees, in global supply chains coordinated by such lead MNCs, where production is outsourced and subcontracted without ownership, the buyer is not the legal employer and has no formal responsibility for the employment relationship in the supplying company or further subcontracted firms, such as tier I, tier II or tier III enterprises.

This consolidation process at both the national and enterprise levels is most pronounced in the textiles and apparel, electronics, iron and steel, machinery and transportation sectors. It is noted earlier that Foxconn has grown to become the world's largest contract manufacturer of electronic goods, managing vast supply chains through the purchasing of parts and components around the globe. As for an example, Apple designed the product largely in the US, but does not manufacture it. The iPod's parts come from the US, Japan (hard disc drive from Toshiba), Korea (memory from Samsung), and China (small parts from anonymous companies). The manufacturing is overseen by Taiwanese companies (i.e. Foxconn, Pegatron, etc) with factories in mainland China. Similarly, Li & Fung, historically an intermediary trader in the apparel and toy manufacturing industry, has become the largest trading company in the world, sourcing from 15,000 supplier companies in over 40 countries. A further example is the banana trade, where three brands control 36 per cent of global exports and there is a high concentration of MNCs on the retail side, particularly supermarkets. ILO, a wing of the imperialist capital depicts the global value chains as the following:

A Night at the Movies

> Imagine that you are in a cinema watching a popular animated movie. Now imagine all the people that made the experience possible. The movie itself was made by a company in the United States, using subcontractors in India and the Republic of Korea. The popcorn you are eating was harvested by workers in Argentina, prepared with palm oil from a Malaysian plantation and produced in machines assembled in Italy. The seat you are sitting on was made in Poland. The car you drove to the cinema was assembled in Spain, with parts from Austria, France, Japan, Mexico and Thailand, and was transported on a container ship owned by a Greek national through a Liberian company, which was built in Japan and powered by Finnish engines. Indeed, the two hours you spend watching the film may have required the labour of thousands of people in dozens of countries in global supply chains.[32]

A major feature in global trade growth in the recent phase of globalization is the increasing participation of developing and underdeveloped countries, whose share in world trade rose from 33 per cent to 48 per cent between 2000 and 2012.[33] This growth in the share of global trade reflects the increasing engagement of developing and underdeveloped countries in trade through global supply chains. Whereas the growth of global supply chains was initially characterized by trade in manufactured goods, there has been a recent rise in trade in services, which are critical to the functioning and value added of global supply chains. Trade in agricultural goods and raw materials have also grown in developing and underdeveloped countries.

Owing to its specific characteristics of the global supply/value chains linked with the lead MNCs, where they have no direct or indirect responsibility for the well-being of the workers in the sub-contracting firms, in most cases the subcontractors squeeze local suppliers, small manufacturers (SMEs), distributors, retailers, etc. for 'just-in-time' supply of commodities. It is often seen in the chains that the lead MNCs change the designs at the last moment, or increase the volume of orders to keep in line with the global demands. In such cases, the local manufacturers, suppliers and subcontractors shift the whole burden on to the workers increasing work-speed and workload. This translates into excessive work-hours, increasing motion of the conveyer belt maximizing production, long hours of unpaid overtime, no rest or leisure, almost no breaks during work (even no toilet-break), no rights to be unionized—workers are turned into machines, sometimes non-human 'animals'. In fact, the system of global value/supply chains is operated in such a way that makes the working conditions more precarious. Due to the pressure of global buyers, employment in global supply chains is insecure, unprotected, even labour laws (if any exist) are often violated. Engaging temporary, casual, contract, seasonal, women ('cheapest'), migrant workers are the common strategy of the subcontractors. To employ workers at paltry wages are made possible due to the presence of the huge reserve army of labour which are continuously increasing as more and more people join the workforce each year. Moreover, forced labour, child labour, forced overtime, hazardous and polluted workplaces, unhealthy work-conditions, unpaid wages, and absence of any social benefits or protections including robbing the rights to organize in unions and collective bargaining are common in such supply chains. In a word, the conditions of the workers becomes highly precarious.[34]

Under this perspective, the precarious working conditions in the global production (or value/supply) chains are discussed. For better convenience we have concentrated the discussion on the work conditions in India, China and selected countries of Asia focusing on several sectors.

Notes

1. The Maruthi Way, Shyam Vij, FountainInk, September 5 , 2012, http://fountainink.in/?p=2660&all=1; quoted in Remembering Manesar, doccentre.net/cc/cc_labour_strikes.pdf, retrieved on 09.05.16.

2. Make in India: Carrots to the Corporate—Lathis to the Workers, 11. 03. 16, http://sanhati.com/articles/16509/, accessed 23.04.16.
3. The Future of Factory Asia, 14.03.15, http://www.economist.com/news/briefing/21646180-rising-chinese-wages-will-only-strengthen-asias-hold-manufacturing-tightening-grip, accessed 25.05.16.
4. Quoted from 'The Politics of Global Production: Apple, Foxconn and China's New Working Class', Jenny Chan, Ngai Pun, Mark Shelden, http://onlinelibrary.wiley.com/wol1/doi/10.1111/ntwe.12008/full, accessed 28.06.16.
5. A Suicide Survivor: The Life of a Chinese Migrant Worker at Foxconn, Jenny Chan, retrieved from http://onlinelibrary.wiley.com/doi/10.1111/ntwe.12007/full, accessed 13.04.14.
6. Interview, October 15, 2011, quoted in above.
7. Bangladesh Garment Workers Suffer Poor Conditions Two Years After Reform Vows, 22.04.15, http://www.theguardian.com/world/2015/apr/22/garment-workers-in-bangladesh-still-suffering-two-years-after-factory-collapse, accessed 23.04.16.
8. Three Years After Rana Plaza Disaster, Has Anything Changed? 22.04.16, https://www.reuters.com/article/us-bangladesh-garments-lessons-analysis/three-years-after-rana-plaza-disaster-has-anything-changed-idUSKCN0XJ02G, accessed 26.10.17.
9. Gap and Old Navy in Bangladesh, October 2013, http://www.globallabourrights.org/reports/document/1310-IGLHR-GapOldNavyinBangladesh.pdf, accessed 29.05.16.
10. Ibid.
11. *Wall Street Journal*, December 30, 2003; quoted in 'Disposable Workers, Today's Reserve Army of Labor', Fred Magdoff, Harry Magdoff, *Monthly Review*, April 2004.
12. 'Disposable Workers, Today's Reserve Army of Labor', Fred Magdoff, Harry Magdoff, *Monthly Review*, April 2004.
13. 'The Plight of the US Working Class', Fred Magdoff and John Bellamy Foster, *Monthly Review*, January 2014.
14. See Note 12.
15. 'The Global Reserve Army of Labor and the New Imperialism', John Bellamy Foster, Robert W. McChesney, R. Jamil Jonna, *Monthly Review*, November 2011.
16. *Imperialism in the Twenty-First Century*, John Smith, Dev Publishers and Distributors, New Delhi, pp. 101-02.
17. 'Internationalization of Monopoly Capital', John Bellamy Foster, Robert W. McChesney, R. Jamil Jonna, *Monthly Review*, June 2011.
18. Scandal: Inside the Global Supply Chains of 50 Top Companies, 2016, http://www.ituc-csi.org/IMG/pdf/pdffrontlines_scandal_en-2.pdf, accessed 12.01.17.
19. *Imperialism in the Twenty-First Century*, John Smith, p. 42.
20. Ibid., p. 75.
21. See Note 15.

22. Ibid.
23. *The Law of Value and Historical Materialism*, Samir Amin, pp. 11, 84; quoted in 'The Global Reserve Army of Labor and the New Imperialism', John Bellamy Foster, Robert W. McChesney, R. Jamil Jonna, *Monthly Review*, November 2011.
24. *Imperialism in the Twenty-First Century*, John Smith, pp. 113.
25. http://www.wiego.org/informal-economy/statistical-picture, accessed 12.01.17.
26. Quoted in *Imperialism in the Twenty-First Century*, John Smith, pp. 118.
27. Decent Work and the Informal Economy, ILO, 2002, http://www.ilo.org/public/english/standards/relm/ilc/ilc90/pdf/rep-vi.pdf, accessed 12.01.17.
28. *Imperialism in the Twenty-First Century*, John Smith, pp. 125.
29. Ibid., pp. 55-56.
30. Emerging Trends in Factory Asia, Surendra Pratap, Asia Monitor Resource Centre, http://www.amrc.org.hk/sites/default/files/Emerging%20Trends%20in%20Factory%20Asia.pdf, accessed 12.01.17.
31. See Note 27.
32. Ibid.
33. Ibid.
34. *Monthly Review* in the editorial column writes and quotes the following: The working class's general condition thus can be described in terms of precariousness, where the constant threat of being thrown into the "surplus population" of the unemployed and underemployed only intensifies over the course of capital accumulation. For Engels, this was an integral part of the theory of an "unemployed reserve army of labor" that constituted the whole basis for bourgeois exploitation of the proletariat. In *The Communist Manifesto*, Marx and Engels followed this same line of thought, stating, "The growing competition among the bourgeois, and the resulting commercial crises, make the wages of the workers ever more fluctuating. The unceasing improvement of machinery, ever more rapidly developing, makes their livelihood more and more precarious." 'Marx's Theory of Working-Class Precariousness: Its Relevance Today', R. Jamil Jonna, John Bellamy Foster, *Monthly Review*, April 2016.]

2
Working Conditions in India

In an era of excess supply, companies lack pricing leverage as never before. As such, businesses must be unrelenting in their search for new efficiencies. Not surprisingly, the primary focus of such efforts is labor, representing the bulk of production costs in the developed world… [O] ffshore outsourcing that extracts product from relatively low-wage workers in the developing world has become an increasingly urgent survival tactic for companies in the developed economies.

–A senior economist at Morgan Stanley

We see then that, leaving aside certain extremely elastic restrictions, the nature of commodity exchange itself imposes no limit to the working day, no limit to surplus labour. The capitalist maintains his rights as a purchaser when he tries to make the working day as long as possible, and, where possible to make two working days out of one. On the other hand, the peculiar nature of the commodity sold implies a limit to its consumption by the purchaser, and the worker maintains his right as a seller when he wished to reduce the working day to a particular normal length. There is here therefore an antinomy, or right against right, both equally bearing the seal of the law of exchange. Between equal rights, force decides. Hence, in the history of capitalist production, the establishment of a norm for the working day presents itself as a struggle over the limits of that day, a struggle between collective capital, i.e. the class of capitalists, and collective labour, i.e. the working class.

—Karl Marx, *Capital*

In the neoliberal period of global capitalism and since the inception of the structural adjustment programme, liberalization and economic reforms in India, partly under the dictate of the imperialist organizations like the International Monetary Fund (IMF), World Bank, World Trade Organization (WTO), etc. and partly under the compulsion of the capitalism in India, significant structural changes have occurred in the Indian economic policies. In fact, after the dismantling of the former USSR and subsequent demise of the so-called socialist bloc of Eastern Europe (and with the end of the Cold War), coupled with the march of 'socialist' China along the road of capitalism (and particularly because of the retrogression in the working class movement both at the national and international level due to its defeat), the gamut of global capitalism has changed substantially. In this globalized era, and with the aggressive march of neoliberalism all over the globe, the dependent countries like India cannot maintain former bargaining tactics with the imperialist forces and Soviet bloc (that has been observed in the 1950s to 1970s) like before. For this reason and owing to the compulsion of the inner dynamics of capitalism in India, the ruling classes of India earnestly follow the prescribed path of the imperialist capital.

Accordingly, new industrial policies have been taken, import policies are liberalized leading to easier flow of imported goods, regulation on the investment of foreign capital is lifted, the policy of taxation is revamped to serve the foreign and Indian big capital, large-scale privatization have been initiated, natural sources are opened before both the foreign and Indian capital, subsidies for the poor are withdrawn on a massive scale, the agricultural sector is increasingly corporatized (though maintaining alongside vast remnants of feudal productive forces and relations), a sizeable amount of farm-land, forest-land, coastal land are acquired for the setting of power stations, ports, mines, cities, infrastructure, special economic zones (SEZs) and economic corridors, etc. in the name of 'development'. Along with these measures the labour policy has been changed substantially. In the name of golden handshake, continuous and systematic attacks on the job-security of the workers in both public and private sectors have been launched. Millions of jobs are lost in both the public and private sector enterprises. According to an estimate, around 18.5 lakh (1.85 million) jobs have vanished only in the public sector of India in the period of 1995 to 2012.[1] Moreover, during this period millions of job seekers were added to the existing workforce.

In fact, during the last twenty years or more, in the name of 'development', large-scale foreign investment is invited, several sectors are opened up for the foreign and Indian business magnets, hundreds of SEZs have been set up offering enormous subsidies, tax-breaks, and with the exemption from any labour laws. Under the guidelines of the World Bank and to make business 'easier', a substantial amount of money has been invested in the infrastructure projects much of which are borrowed from the imperialist countries or organizations magnifying debt burden on the people of India. Under the slogans of 'Shining India', 'New Manufacturing Policy' or 'National Manufacturing Investment Zones', 'Make in India' or 'Digital India', etc., all colours of governments run by several mainstream parties or coalitions have followed the same model of 'development' prescribed by imperialist capital.

The liberalization policy taken by the ruling classes of India and reforms of the Indian economy along the prescribed path of globalization are not only an aggressive search for profitable investment opportunities and subsequent profit maximization, but also it is a concerted effort of the capitalist class backed by imperialist capital to perpetrate an offensive against the working people of the country. Particularly after the defeat in the international working class movement these attacks became more atrocious and all pervasive. This march of liberalization, privatization and commodification of every aspect and sector of life is going on all over the globe. In India it takes a form of ruthless exploitation and oppression of the working people along with the suppression of any kind of protests or resistances of the workers.

The attacks unleashed on the workers can be summarized as follows:

- Gradual transfer of all natural resources, land and public property to the hands of private and foreign capital. This takes the form of privatization of the public sector and services, deregulation of existing hurdles before private and foreign investment, opening of the entire economy before private and foreign investors offering huge concessions, subsidies and tax-breaks.
- Acceleration of the setting up of Special Economic Zones (SEZs), National Manufacturing Investment Zones (NMIZs), Industrial Corridors and other projects for export-led 'development'. These zones become like "foreign enclaves"—a newer form of colonial subjugation. This measure is translated into large-scale acquisition of the farmland, forest-land and coastal zones displacing millions of people from these lands which are the main source of their income and survival.
- Financialization of the finance, banking, and real estate sector along the path taken by the global capital. This is not only pillage of the resources but also a well orchestrated attempt to grab and privatize the provident funds and pension funds of the workers.
- Gradual withdrawal of the benefits and subsidies offered to the poor. These measures have been taken under the dictate of the World Bank and IMF which dismantle the public distribution system, and withdraw assistances and reformative measures to a large extent both at the central and state levels.
- As part of the global supply chain and imitating the export-led economies of the East and South East Asia, many labour-intensive industries in India are integrated to the global economy in such a way that on several occasions these enterprises become sub-contracting firms supplying manufactured goods and services. Giant MNCs place orders for manufactured goods before these firms for just-in-time delivery and will not take the

responsibility for the plight of the workers. To facilitate these operations the subcontracting enterprises owned by either foreign or Indian capitalists transfer the whole burden to the workers who are super-exploited and forced to work under subhuman conditions, massive workload and hazardous workplaces at below subsistence wages. It is also easier to repatriate profits to host investor MNCs.

- All pervasive concerted attacks are carried out on the labour laws which were once enacted to minimize the conflicts between the workers and capitalists. These labour laws though in the main served the interests of the capitalists of India, they nonetheless were the fruits of the struggle between labour and capital creating some protections for the workers. With the defeat of the working class movement and with the aggressive march of the globalization drive undertaken by the imperialist capital several protections under the labour laws are attacked with sinister designs.
- A systematic and well-planned attack was perpetrated on the efforts of the workers (both organized and unorganized) to organize into unions. During the last decade wherever the workers tried to organize into unions, well-designed attacks have been launched on behalf of the governments of all colours, administration, police and judiciary to break the efforts and resistances of the workers signifying that these armies of the state machinery are like appendages of the capitalist class.

Overall, the country witnessed a caricature of 'development' in which billions of working people are excluded and cornered. It is a 'jobless growth' in the economy developing a colossal reserve army of labour; jobs created are mainly 'informal' in nature which are super-exploitable; more and more contractualization and casualization of available jobs means increasing vulnerability; suppression of real wages and income of the working people leading to extreme poverty and destitution; availability of 'surplus' labour who are prepared to do any kind of jobs at any wages; reforming the labour laws robbing several protections and rights to organize and thus cornering the workers more and more; promoting export-led zones or corridors where the labourforce are denied any benefits and protection. The details of this onslaught are discussed below.

'Jobless Growth' and Unemployment

Ironically, though the economic or GDP growth of the Indian economy is 'sky-rocketing' breaking previous records, the growth of employment remains almost flat and inequality among people has grown markedly. Many economists like to call this type of 'growth' in India as 'jobless growth'. During 2004-05, India's GDP grew by 8.43 per cent on average. Since then it maintains the rate more or less at 6-8 per cent on average. Sometimes it touches as high as 9 per cent. Though in recent times there are signs of a plummeting growth rate, it nevertheless remains at 5.7 per cent in the first quarter of 2017. It is to be noted here that several questions are raised time and again regarding the method of measuring the GDP of the Indian economy and many analysts have argued that the growth projected in the government publications are largely overestimated. Since no other recognized data are available to us, we have no option other than following the data of the Government of India (GoI). Though the Indian economy shows some sluggishness in recent times, it is ironic that this growth rate is one of the 'fastest' in the world (second only to China)—particularly in the context of global economic stagnation—which cannot achieve momentum of the great pre-recession period of 2008-09.

During the tenure of the United Progressive Alliance (UPA)-led government of 10 years (2004-14), the economic growth rate has touched its apex notwithstanding the slow rate of job-growth. Particularly during this period the term 'jobless growth' debate appears in the limelight. *Livemint* writes:

> It was during UPA's tenure that the first serious debate on jobless growth came to a head.... 66th round of the National

> Sample Survey Office (NSSO) data on employment in 2011 ... showed that between 2004-05 and 2009-10, only 1 million jobs were added per year; in a period when the economy averaged a record 8.43 per cent growth annually. In this period, 55 million people joined the labour force. So, another way of looking at it is that a *staggering 50 million failed to find employment.*[2]

Therefore, in the five-year period between 2004-05 and 2009-10, only 5 million (i.e. 50 lakh) jobs are created and 50 million (5 crore) people 'fail to find' any jobs when the growth rate of the Indian economy touches its zenith. In fact, an additional 150 million people will join the workforce in the next 15 years. Currently the country's labour pool is growing by more than 1 million workers each month.[3]

If we look into this joblessness from another angle, a few glaring facts will be revealed:

> *Economic Survey 2014-15* showed that during the last decade (2001-11), the growth rate of the labour force (2.23 per cent) was significantly higher than the growth rate of employment (1.4 per cent), which itself was several-fold less than the growth rate of the economy. According to Census 2011, the average growth rate of the economy was 7.7 per cent per annum, when it was only 1.8 per cent for employment.[4]

If we count the historical data, i.e. the data of the pre-reform and post-reform period, it is observed that "the average annual employment growth was about 2.4 per cent in the 1970s. In the 1993-94 to 2009-10 period, it averaged around 1.65 per cent."

Table 1: Employment Growth in Pre-Reform and Post-Reform Periods

Sector	*1972-83*	*1983-93*	*1993-2009*
Primary	1.7	1.4	0.7
Secondary	4.4	2.8	4.3
Tertiary	4.2	2.0	1.7

[*Source:* http://www.business-standard.com/article/opinion/abheek-barua-india-s-jobless-growth-story-113010200119_1.html, accessed 22.06.16]

Chart 2: Jobs Created and GDP Growth Rate During Six Years (2009-15)

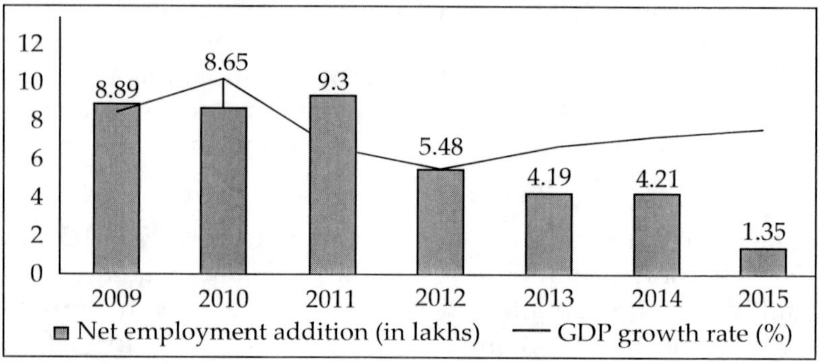

[*Source:* Ministry of Labour; quoted in http://www.bloombergquint.com/union-budget-india/2017/01/06/government-schemes-to-generate-employment-have-not-borne-fruit-says-cmies-mahesh-vyas, accessed 02.02.17]

This pathetic picture of job-creation does not alter during the present National Democratic Alliance (NDA) regime. The Labour Bureau, under the present government said in its latest employment-unemployment survey (published in April 2016) that top employment generating manufacturing sectors like textiles, leather, metals, automobiles, gems and jewellery, transport, information technology and the handloom sectors together created *only 135,000 jobs* during 2015. So job addition in the first full year of this government fell to just a fourth of 2014 and was only a tenth of the growth seen in 2009, when the UPA was in power.[5] Ironically, at a rally in Agra in 2013, the present Prime Minister said that the BJP would create 10 million jobs: "If the BJP comes to power, it will provide one crore jobs which the UPA government could not do despite announcing it before the last Lok Sabha polls".[6] Moreover, adding more punch, the Centre for Monitoring the Indian Economy (CMIE) estimates that "about 1.5 million jobs were lost during January-April 2017" probably due to the demonetization drive taken by the government.[7]

An analysis presented by a recent article published in *Economic and Political Weekly* (EPW) depicts striking figures compiled from government sources. According to this article:

> From about 2 per cent per annum between 1999-2000 and 2004-05, employment growth declined to around 0.7 per cent per annum between 2004-05 and 2009-10, and further slowed down to around 0.4 per cent per annum between 2009-10 and 2011-12.... [F]or the age group 15 years and above, total employment in India shrunk by about 0.4 per cent per annum, during the period 2013-14 to 2015-16.... This corresponds to an estimated reduction in employment for about 37.4 lakh persons during the period 2013-14 to 2015-16. If we consider the total employment based on sectoral estimates then the drop would have been to the tune of 53 lakh jobs.... It seems that the deceleration of employment growth during the period 2004-05 to 2011-12, has not reversed, but has worsened during the period 2013-14 to 2015-16. Perhaps this is for the first time in independent India that we have an absolute decline in employment, though there had been phases of employment growth being low at around 1 per cent during 1993-94 to 1999-2000 and below 1 per cent during 2004-05 to 2011-12.[8]

Therefore, the jobs created in the recent past are abysmally low. In fact, the data presented above does not include the job losses due to retrenchment or downsizing of the enterprises during the last three decades. This astronomical increase in workforce with little scope of creation of new jobs increase the reserve army of labour enormously who are available to do any kind of jobs at any wages and under any precarious working conditions. In other words, they are the most vulnerable section of the population who are super-exploited and are languishing under sub-human conditions.

Moreover, regular (or direct/permanent) kind of jobs is created on a meagre basis. Most of the jobs created in this dismal job-market are of self-employed, casual, contract and seasonal nature. A mainstream business paper shows:

> Joblessness in India is running at a five-year high of 5 per cent of the 15-plus-years workforce. Over a third of working people are employed for less than a year....

> What do 5 per cent unemployment and 35 per cent underemployment mean in hard numbers? Projecting from Census 2011 figures 5 per cent is a whopping *2.3 crore persons*. In addition, there are those who work but not for the whole year, signifying hidden unemployment. This works out to nearly *16 crore* persons....
>
> The labour bureau survey also found that about 47 per cent of the working population was self-employed. This would be mostly farmers (mostly poor and small peasants), [petty] shopkeepers, and enterprise owners. But the low economic level of this section is revealed by the fact that *85 per cent of such households had a monthly income of less than Rs. 10,000*. Another 33 per cent of households earn their living through *casual* employment. Regular wage or salary earning households make up just 17 per cent of all, although this is the kind of work that pays more with 43 per cent of people earning more than Rs. 10,000.[9]

Therefore 2.3 crore people are jobless and another 16 crore people do not find work the whole year. They (18.3 crore people, according to official data) are totally out of the ambit of the so-called 'development' policy followed in India.

In India the size of the labour force is 381.1 million in 1993-94, which increases about 104 million (on an average, 6 million per annum) to reach 487.7 million in 2011-12. During the ten-year period ending at 2011-12, about 5 million workers leave agriculture per annum. To be more precise, during the 2004-05 and 2009-10 period, *24 million workers leave agriculture* (4.8 million per annum). This happens for the first time in the history of the Indian economy which indicates a 'structural change in employment' during the high economic growth period. Moreover the additional 13 million workers (6.5 million per annum) leave agriculture during 2009-10 and 2011-12.[10] Almost the same figures are presented by the above-mentioned article published in *EPW*. The writer, quoting some authors shows that there was "an absolute decline in employment in the rural agricultural sector by about 200 lakh between 2004-05 and 2009-10." It was in decline by "130 lakh during 2009-10 and

2011-12. Much of the decline in employment during this period was due to a decline in female employment in the sector and shifting of male employment to non-farm sectors."

That means there is a sizeable decline in agricultural employment in recent times. But, where does this huge workforce go? Do they manage to find any work in other sectors? Do they manage an income to make ends meet? According to the above analysis these jobseekers have managed to find work mainly in the construction sector. Others have gone to either the manufacturing or service sector. Since the level of job-creations is abysmally low it may be said that most of these uprooted and displaced people are forced to do any type of 'menial' jobs or remain dependent on the doles (such as 50 to 100 days' of work under NREGA) delivered by existing meagre schemes of the government. The data presented earlier clearly states that in the last five years a 'staggering 50 million (5 crore) failed to find employment'.

The subject may be somewhat clearer if we count the number of internal migration. *The Economic Survey 2015-16* reports that net out-of-state flows of migrant labourers across India peaked at almost 9.4 million in 2013-14, before falling to 9.1 million in 2014-15 and just over 8.4 million in 2015-16. Much of this migration has entailed movement of labour from relatively poor states such as Uttar Pradesh, Bihar, Rajasthan, Madhya Pradesh, Odisha, West Bengal and Assam to more prosperous states like Maharashtra, Delhi-NCR, Gujarat, Tamil Nadu, Kerala and Karnataka.[11] Therefore, in each year approximately 80-90 lakh people from backward states migrate to other states searching for any type of jobs. Understandably, these huge internally migrated people manage to find work in the mainly 'informal' sectors (majority in the construction sector as has been reported) at abysmally low wages, with no job security and virtually have no statutory benefits.

In fact, from the data of the Government of India hazy impressions emerge from the picture of job-creation and job losses. We may have a less hazy picture if we study some data on the 'formal' and 'informal' sector and/or workers.

Informal Sector and Informal Worker

In India, the concepts of 'organized' or 'formal' and 'unorganized' or 'informal' are used interchangeably. In fact, the terms 'formal' and 'informal' are popularized by the imperialist organizations like the World Bank and IMF in the globalization period. The mainstream media run by the ruling classes of India took the catchwords showing on a number of occasions that the informal sector and informal workers are placed in a disadvantageous position vis-à-vis the formal sector and formal workers and thus need special attention and policy to 'uplift' them. It is nothing but shedding crocodile tears for the 'informal' sector and 'informal' workers which remain and grow together with the 'formal' sectors and workers with the development of capitalism in India. The 'informal' sector in fact serves the formal sectors and through this process capitalists subjugate 'informal' workers under super-exploitative conditions for profit maximization. The automobile giants like Maruti-Suzuki, Hyundai, Honda, Toyota, etc. required informal sectors to outsource its ancillaries, parts and spares production. They needed 'informal' workers in their main plants also, i.e. casual or contract workers who can be hired and fired at will, who are used to being paid paltry wages and who are denied several protections like social security benefits, insurance, provident funds, etc. In fact, with the development of global supply chains informal workers and informal sectors become an integral part of the capitalist production process and for this reason the capitalist class of the modern day, either in India or in Asia, have a keen interest to maintain their downtrodden condition and status.

But what is meant by 'informal' sector and 'informal' workers? Which belong to the 'formal' sector and 'formal' workers? To comprehend the above terms we take the definitions provided by the Government of India in a Survey released by the National Commission for Enterprises in the Unorganized Sector (NCEUS). According to its definitions,

> *Informal Sector*: The unorganized sector consists of all unincorporated private enterprises owned by individuals

> or households engaged in the sale and production of goods and services operated on a proprietary or partnership basis and with less than ten total workers.

Clearly, this 'unincorporated' sector is not covered under any of the Factory Acts and the social security legislations like Employee's State Insurance Act and Provident Fund Act, etc.

> *Informal Worker/Employment*: Unorganized workers consist of those working in the unorganized sector or households, excluding regular workers with social security benefits provided by the employers and the workers in the formal sector without any employment and social security benefits provided by the employers.
>
> *Informal Economy*: The informal sector and its workers plus the informal workers in the formal sector constitute the informal economy.[12]

Still, from these definitions true pictures of 'formality' and 'informality' do not emerge clearly. In fact, the vast agricultural sector in which millions of marginal, poor peasants and agricultural workers cultivate the land, enterprises run by 'self-employed' persons on their own account (owner him/herself is the sole worker), casual workers and/or contract workers either in the 'formal' or 'informal' sector have different problems and crisis which cannot be discussed or addressed under a single policy or approach. Though confusing to a certain extent, we have to take make a note of these definitions and data as no other data-source and definitions are available which are recognized. Nevertheless, according to the definitions cited above four categories of workers can be comprehended. These are:

(a) formal workers in formal/organized sector,

(b) informal workers in formal/organized sector,

(c) formal workers in informal/unorganized sector, and

(d) informal workers in informal/unorganized sector.

According to the definitions of the Government of India the *non-agricultural* informal workers (if we exclude the vast masses of agricultural workers, poor/small peasants in this discussion) work in enterprises employing less than ten workers or work in the formal sector. It is not surprising that all of them are not protected by any social and workplace law; they are seasonal, casual, contract, or internally migrant workers; gravely low-paid, poverty-ridden, and super-exploited as the employers (including public sector) hardly pay their wages according to the minimum wage scale fixed by the governments (the scale itself is questionable as 'living wage' or 'subsistence wage').

According to NCEUS 2007 data, the informal sector (including agriculture, forestry, etc.) gives jobs (however insecure and poor quality the jobs may be) to 84 per cent of the workforce and informal workers constitute about 92.3 per cent of the total workforce. Agricultural workers (including peasants, workers, plantation and forestry workers, fishermen, etc.) are 64 per cent of the total informal workers. In absolute terms, others, i.e. non-agricultural workers were 204.03 million in 2011-12.[13] Interestingly, this informal sector, though engage 84 per cent of the workforce, contributes 50 per cent of India's GDP.[14]

From Table 2 several conclusions can be drawn:

1. In the formal/organized sector, both the formal and informal employment is increased in absolute terms between 2004-05 and 2011-12. But in percentage, the share of formal employment in the organized/formal sector has declined from 52 per cent to 45.4 per cent, whereas that of informal employment has climbed from 48 per cent to 54.6 per cent.
2. Moreover, in 2011-12, it is to be noted that in absolute terms, the number of informal workers in the organized sector has crossed the number of formal workers. Now in the formal/organized sector, *54.6 per cent* of jobs are *informal* in nature, while the percentage of formal jobs is 45.6. Hence generation of employment in the organized sector during the last 8 years is *mainly informal in nature.* Moreover, it is for the first time in history that the formal/ organized sector employs more informal workers (in the

Table 2: Formal-Informal Employment Across Organized-Unorganized Sectors (in million)

2004-05			
Workers	*Organized/ Formal Sector*	*Unorganized/ Informal Sector*	*Total*
Formal	32.6 (52)	1.35 (0.3)	33.41 (7.3)
Informal	29.54 (48)	396.66 (99.7)	426.20 (92.7)
Total	61.61 (13)	398.01 (87)	456.61 (100)
2011-12			
Formal	37.18 (45.4)	1.39 (0.4)	38.56 (8.1)
Informal	44.74 (54.6)	390.92 (99.6)	435.66 (91.9)
Total	81.92 (17.3)	392.31 (82.7)	474.23 (100)

Note: Computed using unit level data of NSSO various rounds. Population projected for year 2004-05 and 2011-12 using decadal population growth rate between Census 2001 and 2011
Figures in brackets indicate per cent share

[*Source:* An Analysis of the Informal Labour Market in India, A. Srija and Shrinivas V. Shirke, Confederation of Indian Industries (CII), www.ies.gov.in/pdfs/CII%20EM-october-2014.pdf]

form of casual and contract workers who are mainly out of the purview of most of the labour laws) than the formal (regular or direct) workers. This is nothing but steps towards 'informalization' of the workforce in the name of 'growth'/'development'.

3. Though the total (formal+informal) employment in the formal/organized sector has increased between 2004-05 and 2011-12 (from 13 per cent to 17.3 per cent; in absolute terms, from 61.61 million to 81.92 million, i.e. by 20 million), and the total (formal+informal) employment in the informal/unorganized sector has decreased by 5.7 million, it is interesting to note that during the same period the percentage of informal jobs in the total (formal+informal) sectors/economy has decreased microscopically (from 92.7 per cent to 91.9 per cent). In fact, in absolute terms informal workers in the economy has increased by 9.46 million.

According to the *Economic Survey 2015-16* of GoI, informal firms account for most employment growth and nearly all the increase in the number of establishments since 1989. Of the 10.5 million new manufacturing jobs created between 1989 and 2010, only 3.7 million—about 35 per cent—were in the formal sector. This pattern is even starker when looking at growth in establishment counts: total establishments increased by 4.2 million from 1989-2010, but the *formal sector accounted for only 1.2 per cent of this growth.*[15]

> Such is the informality of the Indian economy that almost *three-fifths* of its enterprises operate either out of home or without a fixed structure. It is a stark reminder of just how informal the economy really is, how the vast majority manage to scrape out a living.... The average number of persons per establishment is 2.18, according to the 2013 census. *Enterprises are getting smaller and smaller and average employment per establishment has steadily come down from 2.88 in 1990 to 2.75 in 1998, further to 2.41 in 2005 and now to 2.18!*[16]

Therefore, the incidence of informality is predominant in the Indian economy even after the 'spectacular' growth rate experienced in the post-reform era. It will be seen later that this trend is maintained or climbing upwards in the last five years. Therefore, it is not only a 'jobless growth' of Indian economy, but also it does not 'uplift' the vast mass of labour force out of the informal nature of work, i.e. most of the 'employed' labour force are steeped in abject misery, poverty and destitution, and of course constitute the reserve army of labour in the main.

CII reveals several more facts about the incidence of informality in the Indian economy. If we exclude agricultural workers from the purview of this discussion, it is found by CII that informal employment in the non-agricultural sector has increased from 160.83 million in 2004-05 to 204.03 million in 2011-12, i.e. an increase of 27 per cent. And out of this non-agricultural sector,

- The manufacturing sector employs 52.49 million informal workers in 2011-12 which is 4.57 million more than the 2004-05 level.

- One of the biggest 'job-creators', i.e. the construction sector employed 24.94 million informal workers in 2004-05. In 2011-12 this amount was nearly doubled to 48.92 million—a whopping 100 per cent increase. In fact, most of the workers who left agriculture after 2004 have joined this sector as informal workers.
- In trade, the hotel and restaurants sector 50.17 million informal workers were employed in 2011-12, which is 4.15 million higher than 2004-05.[17]

This vast sea of informal workers in India is the real reserve army of labour which is increasing by leaps and bounds. Capitalism needs a reserve army of labour. But under the present circumstances this reserve army in India is surpassing all the previous records documenting the super-exploitative nature of 'growth' and 'development' of the Indian economy.

It was pointed out earlier that the informal sector is necessary for the formal sector as it manufactures components, parts, spares for the formal/organized sector. In fact in many cases the entire major operations of manufacturing are outsourced to the informal enterprises. In our discussion it will be revealed that most of the garments, footwear, leather products, electronic goods and automobile component industries are dependent on the small-scale suppliers or contractors who overwhelmingly employ informal workers as casual, contract or seasonal workers and even home-workers. Moreover, service jobs show an upward movement engaging mainly informal workers. As for an example, to make the software industry of India competitive globally the owners rely crucially on the very cheap supporting services in the form of logistics, security, transportation, cleaning and catering that are provided by companies or individuals that use workers on informal contracts that are well beyond the pale of labour protection. This is equally true for other formal sectors.[18]

In the automobile sector of India, mostly dominated by the multinationals, and due to its specific nature of automobile manufacturing, the main assembling is still done in the assembly plants of lead firms. Moreover, the value chain of the automobile industry is more organized nationally or regionally close to the larger markets to reduce the transport costs. A section of component suppliers, particularly those producing bulky, heavy and model-specific parts, are concentrated close to final assembly plants. Others are distributed in different auto-clusters and ranked as different tiers such as I, II, III, etc. The tier III suppliers are generally small-scale informal sector enterprises. Some specific operations are also outsourced to own-account workers who work in home-based settings.

This is a typical structure of the value/supply chain in the automobile manufacturing in India, in which the informal sector is systematically integrated in the value chain as part of profit maximization strategies. Similar operations are seen in electronics and other electrical and engineering industries in which a significant part of the value addition is done by informal sector enterprises.[19]

Contractualization and Casualization

The conditions of the contract workers in the organized/ formal and informal sector become one of the most important issues particularly in the post-reform period. In fact, all over the world, particularly during the globalization period, the majority of the manufacturing, mining, construction industries and service sector employ contract (or temporary) workers in the main plants/firms (along with supplier firms) for profit maximization. Particularly in India, the MNCs and the Indian corporate houses employ contract workers in formal/organized nature of operations to bypass the labour laws, take recourse to hire and fire at their will and deny the contract workers the protections and social benefits enjoyed by the direct/regular workers. Even the government-owned public sector firms are no exception.

In a report, one of the leading organizations of the Indian businesses, ASSOCHEM pointed out in 2014 that "There was a steep rise of 39 per cent in the number of contract workers across sectors last year... In contrast, the growth in the number of regular workers nearly halved to 25 per cent... [There was a] steady rise in the number of contract employees 32 per cent in 2012, 28 per cent in 2011 and 22 per cent in 2010." ASSOCHEM found that "the trend [is] more prevalent in sectors such as automobiles, manufacturing, telecom, IT, BPO, FMCG, healthcare and education."[20]

It also states that,

> Apart from being paid less than regular employees on corporate payrolls doing similar tasks, contract workers have virtually no job security and no benefits like medical aid, gratuity, provident fund, educational funds, pension and health insurance and leave benefits." It further shows that "the telecom sector [is] scoring the worst with up to 60 per cent of its staff on contract, followed by automobiles (56 per cent) and other sectors such as education (54 per cent), manufacturing (52 per cent), FMCG (51 per cent), IT, BPO (42 per cent), hospitality and travel (35 per cent), pharma and healthcare (32 per cent). Contract labour is increasingly being used in smaller and larger Indian companies as well as multinationals.[21]

Chart 3: Contract Workers in Registered Manufacturing

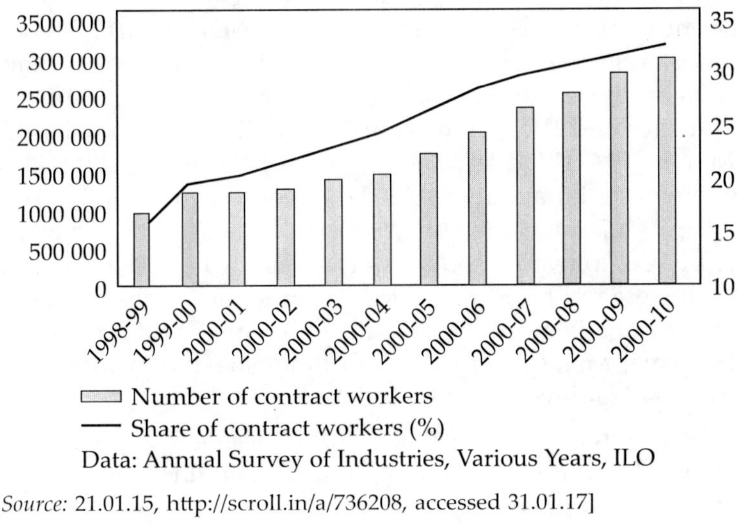

Data: Annual Survey of Industries, Various Years, ILO

[*Source:* 21.01.15, http://scroll.in/a/736208, accessed 31.01.17]

Chart 4: Percentage of Contract Workers: Major States

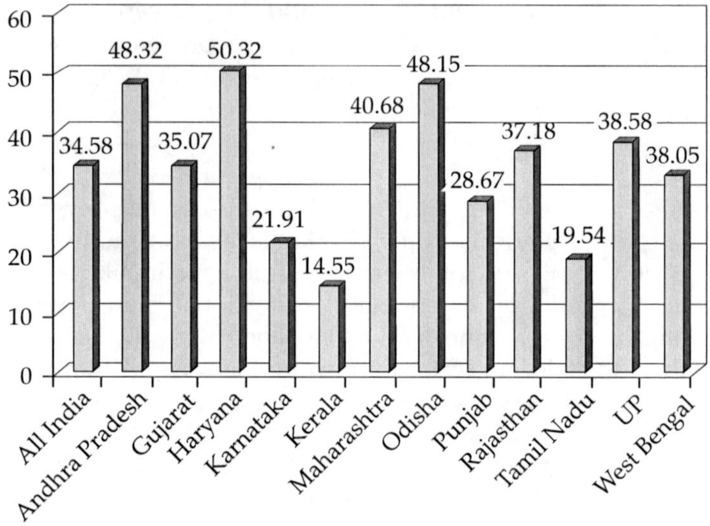

[*Source:* https://counterview.org/2014/03/28/with-workforce-in-agriculture-shifting-to-industry-contractualization-of-labour-becomes-a-major-factor-both-in-gujarat-and-across-india/, accessed 31.01.17]

In fact, in the 1980s, in manufacturing industries, only 7 per cent of the workers are temporary, *while by 2012 it rises to 35 per cent.*[22] Even in Gujarat, the show-piece of Indian capitalists, the situation is similar. Data given by the Ministry of Statistics and Programme Implementation report, released in March 2014, titled "Annual Survey of Industries 2011-12", have suggested that out of 10.60 lakh workers in the industrial sector in Gujarat, 3.72 lakh workers, or nearly 35 per cent, have been employed through contractors.[23] Chart 4 shows that the percentage of contract workers in some 'industrialized' states of India is more than the all India average. Particularly in Haryana, Maharashtra, Andhra Pradesh—the incidence of contractualization is steeper.

A recent report shows that in 2014-15, *almost 94 per cent* of the jobs added in the formal/organized manufacturing sector are hired through contractors:

> In 2014-15, the latest year for which the numbers are available, as much as 93.9 per cent of the addition to the workforce in the formal manufacturing sector was hired through contractors. That means these people weren't directly employed by the manufacturing companies. At a time when the government is talking of the benefits of formalizing the informal sector, what we're seeing is the increasing informalization of the workforce in the organized sector.... [T]he number of contractual employees is growing by leaps and bounds—they accounted for 16 per cent of the total manufacturing workforce in the formal sector in 1998-99 and by 2014-15 they were 35 per cent.... The compound annual growth rate for direct employment of workers in the organized manufacturing sector in this century has been 2.17 per cent. For workers employed through contractors, it has been 7.76 per cent. The trend towards the casualization of labour is well established and *certain to continue*.[24]

It is interesting to note that in central government enterprises also the incidence of contractualization and casualization is increasing. A business newspaper, quoting from a non-government source has noted that "About 43 per cent of the 28.8 million formal-sector workforce with the central government is either on contract or are casual labourers with virtually no social security cover... The Indian Staffing Federation ... estimated temporary workers dependent on government at 12.3 million, of which 10.5 million are casual workers engaged in sectors such as mining and construction and are without any formal job contract." Share of contract and casual workers in the public sector was barely 6.4 per cent in 2001, 11.65 per cent in 2009 and *in 2013 it is a whopping 43 per cent*![25]

A report titled as 'Contract Workers in India's Organized Manufacturing Sector', prepared by A.K. Panigrahi of the Central Statistics Office states that during 2000-01, the ratio of direct workers to contract workers was 80:20; whereas in 2012-13 the ratio changes to 66:34—almost collaborating the data furnished above (see Chart 3 also).[26]

Moreover, such is the level of insecurity of the jobs that at the all India level, 64.9 per cent of the regular wage/salaried workers, 67.8 per cent of the contract workers and 95.3 per cent of the casual workers do not have a written job contract. Only 27 per cent of the regular wage/salaried workers and 11.5 per cent of the contract workers had written job contracts of more than three years.[27]

Wages and Income

> Instead of the conservative motto, "A fair day's wage for a fair day's work!" they ought to inscribe on their banner the revolutionary watchword, "Abolition of the wages system!"
>
> —Karl Marx, 'Value, Price and Profit'

In the production process the worker creates value greater than that of his labour power. Consequently, wages are a part of the newly-created value although, on the surface of the bourgeois society, it is represented as payment for all the labour. In fact, the wage (or nominal wage) is the monetary expression of the value of labour power. The price of labour power can be expressed as the costs for reproduction of labour power. The reproduction of labour power, consequently, boils down to maintenance of the life of the worker him/herself. To restore and preserve his/her capacity to work, a worker must satisfy his/her needs for foods, living place (shelter), clothing, footwear, furniture, maintenance of good health, proper education of his/her children, maintenance of his/her family and so on which he/she buys in the market. Expenditure on training of workers, and on their acquisition of specific skills, is also included in the value of labour power. Marx showed that "in contradistinction therefore to the case of other commodities, there enters into the determination of the value of labour power a historical and moral element."[28] Thus the value of labour power is determined by the value of the means of subsistence necessary for the reproduction of labour power, i.e. for maintenance of the worker and his family. It can be said that the value of the goods needed for the reproduction of labour power is determined by a complex process of social evolution and the level of class struggle. "The local and national determinants of this continues to be predominating over the global dimension, yet workers' demands and needs are being transformed at an accelerating pace by heightened economic, political, social and cultural interaction across borders of all kinds"[29] and the needs and desires are determined by the class struggle developed at the national and international level. Hence the term 'living wage' used by several international organizations (even by the ILO) and its determination cannot be uniformly accepted globally. Still, we have used the term as no other better standard is available.

Without going into the details about relative and absolute surplus values, it can be said for simplicity that the greater the number of unemployed in the given society, i.e. more the volume of the reserve army of labour, the wages face a pressure to fall. In fact, capitalism means existence of a reserve army of labour and consequently the wages feel a downward pressure. When this reserve army swells in the Global South and the production processes are outsourced more and more to the Global South to reap the benefits, it is paving ways for super-exploitation and low wages in backward countries. John Bellamy Foster and Robert McChesney write:

> New realities dominate labour at the world level today. One is global labour arbitrage, or the system of imperial rent. The other is the existence of a massive global reserve army, which make the world system of extreme exploitation possible. Labour arbitrage is defined quite simply by *The Economist* as taking advantage of lower wages abroad, especially in poorer countries. It is thus an unequal exchange process in which the one country, as Marx said, is able to cheat another due to the much higher exploitation of labour in the poor country.... It is such super-exploitation that lies behind much of the expansion of production in the Global South. The fact that this has been the basis of rapid economic growth for some emerging countries does not alter the reality that it has generated enormous imperial rents for multinational corporations and capital at the centre of the system.[30]

Under this perspective, the wages of the overwhelming numbers of workers in India are far lower than the advanced countries and in most of the cases it is lower than the subsistence level (or 'living wage'). With the defeat of the international working class movement, and subsequent retrogressive trend in the working class movement in Asia, and with the 'informalization' of the workers, more downward pressure on wages is observed in the countries of the Global South (including India). Though the workers in the organized industries of India are able to achieve some rise in the nominal (i.e. minus the inflation) wages, as more and more contract and casual workers have been engaged in the regular/permanent nature of jobs, the wages overall face a downward pressure.

Chart 5: Real Wage and Real Productivity

[*Source:* Higher Productivity Equals Higher Wages? Not for the Indian Industrial Worker, 22.01.15, http://www.livemint.com/Opinion/Vxmd5HHO8qeLuqYUiobbpM/Higher-productivity-equals-higher-wages-Not-for-the-Indian.html]

If we count real wages, during the last three decades, it remains almost flat though the real productivity has increased significantly. According to the Annual Survey of Industries (ASI) data, real wage for workers is observed as stagnant in the three decades to 2013, while real productivity has increased at an annual average rate of 7 per cent (see Chart 5).[31]

Even in comparison of profits gained, the wages felt a downward movement in the last three decades as observed in Chart 6.

Chart 6: Profit vs Wages

[*Source:* Higher productivity equals higher wages? Not for the Indian industrial worker, 22.01.15, http://www.livemint.com/Opinion/Vxmd5HHO8qeLuqYUiobbpM/Higher-productivity-equals-higher-wages-Not-for-the-Indian.html]

In India the average wage (nominal wage) rate per day for direct workers is Rs. 164 in 2000-01. However, the wage rate has increased during the last decade and reached Rs. 404 in 2012-13. But the average wage rate per day for contract workers is Rs. 90 in 2000-01 and increased to Rs. 221 in 2010-11 and

Rs. 156 in 2012-13. *Therefore, the wages of contract workers per day is only 54.7 per cent of that of direct workers in 2010-11, and in 2012-13 it is only 38.6 per cent.*[32]

The income of most of the working households portray a dismal picture. It is reported that *67 per cent* of the households of India have average monthly income which *does not exceed Rs. 10,000*. In a country like India, where the population in 2016 is estimated at 1.324 billion (or 132.4 crore), these 67 per cent of households shows that a massive number of people are dependent on the paltry income of their earning members of households. Interestingly, if we take *average monthly income of regular wage/salaried workers*, it is found that as much as *57.2 per cent* of the households have monthly income *not exceeding Rs. 10,000*. These data on income level is not at all surprising as the NCEUS has given an astounding data that *77 per cent of Indians are living with an expenditure of Rs. 20 per day per capita in 2009.*[33]

'Employment-Unemployment Survey' of GoI (2015-16) depicts that:

> At the All India level about 77 per cent of the households were reported to be having no regular wage/salaried person.... It is estimated that at the All India level a little more than 67 per cent of the surveyed households had average Monthly Earnings not exceeding 10,000 only. In the rural sector such households constituted about 77 per cent, whereas the corresponding proportion was about 45 per cent among urban households. The state of Madhya Pradesh recorded the highest proportion (35.8) percentage of households with average monthly earnings not exceeding to Rs. 5,000 followed by West Bengal (34.5 per cent), Uttar Pradesh (30.1 per cent) and Odisha (29.8 per cent)....
>
> At the All India level, a majority 67.5 per cent of the self-employed workers had average monthly earnings up to Rs. 7500. Similarly, 57.2 per cent i.e. more than half of the regular wage/salaried workers had monthly average earnings up to Rs. 10,000. At the All India level 38.5 per cent of the contract workers and 59.3 per cent of the casual workers had monthly earnings of up to Rs. 5000.[34]

Therefore, almost three out of four households in India have no regular waged/salaried person. Moreover, one-third of the households have monthly income not exceeding Rs. 10,000. Almost four out of ten contract workers earn less than Rs. 5000 in a month; nearly six out of ten casual workers are forced to live by monthly income of Rs. 5000.[35] Another painful fact is that the *women workers* have received only *48 per cent wage of the male counterparts* on an average![36] Therefore, most of the workers in India are living with wages below the subsistence level, i.e. most of the workers cannot find ways to reproduce his/her working capacity after toiling hard at the workplaces. This is obviously translated into a position which is nothing but destitution, ultra-poverty, and undernourishment and absorbing in a precarious state.[37]

Reforms of Labour Law

The efforts to liberalize the existing labour laws are one of the most discussed issues in recent times. First it takes the form of 'golden handshake' measures to reduce the workforce in both public and private sectors. Millions of jobs have been lost during the last three decades. Moreover, a massive amount of newcomers in the 'job-market' each year increases the reserve army of labour manifold. But still now, owing to the compulsion of electoral politics, the governments at the centre run by mainstream parties have not overhauled or liberalized the labour laws to that extent when hire-and-fire of the permanent workers from the factories (where more than 100 workers are working) will be unrestricted and legal. So the capitalists of India take another route to reduce regular/direct workers by engaging contract and casual workers (and apprentices) in the perennial type of jobs. With the help of the law-enforcement wings of the government and judiciary and due to the weakness of the workers' struggle (though in some cases, contract and permanent workers are able to forge unity and struggle against these measures, particularly in the automobile sector) these efforts of the capitalist classes are increasing rapidly.

In recent times, the governments in the states run by the Bharatiya Janata Party (BJP) become active in changing the labour laws. It is interesting to note that the forerunner in this case is the state of Rajasthan which is not an industrially forward state. To make it a 'potential labouratory' for changing labour laws, this state has been chosen. Some of the important changes in the labour laws of Rajasthan are:

Industrial Disputes Act

- Firms employing up to 300 workers can retrench or shut shop without the government's permission (against the former limit of 100).
- In case of retrenchment, a worker should raise an objection within 3 months (there was no time limit before the changes in the labour law).
- A trade union can be formed only if it gets 30 per cent of the workers as members (15 per cent condition formerly).

Factories Act

- The Act will apply to factories with 40 workers, if without electricity; and 20 workers, if with electricity (the former condition respectively was 20 and 10).
- Complaints against an employer about violation of this Act would not receive cognisance by a court without prior written permission from the state government.

Contract Labour Act

- The Act will apply to companies employing more than 50 workers (against 20 workers before).
- The industries will be able to hire more temporary workers without passing on to them the benefits contract workers are entitled to.[38]

Following the footsteps of Rajasthan, the governments of Madhya Pradesh, Haryana and Maharashtra became active in rewriting the labour law to test the fathom of water. It is now clear that the governments are making amendments to make hire-and-fire of workers a legal one. It is also clear that the measures taken at the state level will be implemented country-wise in an opportune time. It is notable that being a backward state in terms of industrialization, 7,252 factories employing less than 300 workers each, out of a total number of 7,622 factories (i.e. 95 per cent) in Rajasthan will now come under the 'hire and fire' regime. Moreover, "all the contract workers numbering more than two lakh will be thrown out of the coverage of all labour laws including Contract Labour (R&A) Act and at least 70 per cent factories and their workers will go out of coverage of the Factories Act."[39]

Similar amendments are in the pipeline in Maharashtra where factories employing up to 300 workers will come under the ambit of 'hire and fire':

> If approved by the state cabinet, 3,426 industrial units, which employ 100 to 300 workers, will be exempted from the legal bindings of seeking permission from government authorities. This also means the 5.84 lakh workers employed with them will lose protection from lay offs, retrenchments and closure of the units.
>
> Of about 37,000 factories, governed under the Act, 32,000 are with less than 100 workers, while 1,365 are with more than 300 workers.[40]

Therefore the government in Maharashtra is proposing to bring 35,635 factories (i.e. *more than 96 per cent*) employing less than 300 workers under the proposed labour law to give industrialists a free hand to hire-and-fire lakhs of workers.

Now, the BJP-led NDA government at the centre is going to make reforms in the labour law. A panel, headed by Finance Minister Arun Jaitley, is attempting to convert 44 labour laws into four simplified codes and released a draft of Industrial Relations Bill, 2015. The codes relate to 'industrial relations, wages, social security and safety'. A website writes: "Among the major proposals are introducing fixed-term employment—which was made applicable in the textile and garment industries last year—in all the sectors, allowing units employing up to 300 people to retrench/lay off workers and/or close down without government approval, making trade unions with negotiating powers more representative, barring outsiders from being office-bearers of unions in the organized sector and reducing such persons' role in union activities in the unorganized sector. Also, an industrial strike would be defined afresh by including concerted casual leave by 50 per cent of more workers while the provision for prior notice of strike would be extended to "all activities similar to existing public utility services."[41] In order to apply for registration of a trade union, the Labour Code requires disclosure of the names and addresses of workers applying for registration to the registrar. Without confidentiality and other protective measures, this disclosure clause opens the door for retaliation against workers who attempt to form a union. With regard to unorganized sector trade unions, under the Trade Unions Act, 1926, up to half the office bearers may be persons not actually engaged or employed in the establishment or industry. Under the Labour Code on IR Bill, 2015, all office bearers of a registered union must be people actually engaged or employed in the establishment. Thus unprotected, semi-literate and illiterate workers may have limited avenues in forming their unions once this outside support vanishes.

If we take the changes in the Factories Act (enacted by the Rajasthan government), it will be observed that the definition of factory is radically changed. This measure will have far-reaching effects since workplaces having 20 workers with electricity and 40 workers without electricity will now be recognized as 'factories'. Others, which are employing fewer workers per enterprises and are overwhelming in number, will not be treated as factories resulting in the jobs of the workers being severely vulnerable (as they are thrown out of the purview of factories act). If it is implemented all over the country significant numbers of factories will come out of the purview of the Factory Act as follows:

> Data from the Annual Survey of Industries—the most comprehensive official exercise on the industrial sector—reveals that about 1 lakh, or 58 per cent, of the 1,75,710 factories reported to be operating in the country in 2011-12 employed up to 30 workers. While 63,568 units employed 0-14 workers, another 18,763 factories employed 15-19 workers and 20,541 units had 20-29 workers on their payrolls.
>
> This is backed by the Labour Ministry's data based on returns submitted by factories under the Factories Act, 1948. The statistics reveals that in 2010, of the 67,508 factories that submitted returns (except from Orissa), 52.5 per cent, or 35,208 units, had employed less than 20 workers. However, the number of workers employed by these units was just 3,78,970 workers, as compared to the total 44.96 lakh workforce in factories.[42]

The newspaper which published these figures also notes that:

> The move is expected to ease the labour law burden on most of the existing factories by *freeing* them from complying with the numerous provisions of the Act that relate to safety, working conditions and welfare of the employees, as well as filing lengthy compliance reports to the government.[43]

It is to be noted that the data on the number of factories employing 30-39 workers is not given by ASI. If it is counted then more factories (probably more than 60 per cent) will not be recognized as factories where the Factories Act will not be implemented.

By amending the Contract Labour (Regulation & Abolition) Act (CLRA), owners of the factories now will have a free hand to engage contract workers as the ceiling of contract workers is increased to 50. Therefore most factories will employ contract workers denying them the meagre rights enjoyed by the contract workers. In fact, the CLRA becomes almost meaningless with respect to the question of absorption of the contract workers as permanent labour after a judgment of the Supreme Court which ruled in 2001 that:

> CLRA Act does not provide automatic absorption of contract labour on issuing a notification prohibiting employment of contract labour and the principal employer cannot be required to absorb those contract labour.[44]

Moreover, the central government ruled by NDA has amended the Apprentice Act which will have a serious consequence as more and more apprentices/trainees now will be engaged in perennial nature of jobs offering them a paltry sum of money. In fact, this, along with the enhanced flexibility allowed to the employer, may encourage replacement of the contract/casual/temporary workers and even regular workers with comparatively lower paid apprentices (minimum 70 per cent of the minimum wage) in production work, thereby reducing the overall labour cost. The ground reality is that in many establishments including companies like Maruti-Suzuki, the practice of using the apprentices/trainees in regular production jobs, year after year is widely prevalent.[45] It is to be noted also that the government will now share the cost of apprenticeship. If a company having less than 250 workers hires apprentices, the state will absorb half the cost, and if it has more than this number, the government will absorb a fourth of the cost. And under the act in no cases will the employers have the liability to absorb trained apprentices as regular workers. After the completion of training, apprentices will be left high and dry.[46]

To please the corporate houses, the central government has passed relaxed norms for overtime work in the Lok Sabha in 2016. Now the amended act permits increasing the overtime limit of factory workers from 50 hours to 100 hours in a quarter. It also permits to increase the overtime working hours for factories with "exceptional" workload from 75 hours to 115 hours in a quarter. Further, the centre or states may increase this overtime limit to 125 hours in a quarter in the "public interest."[47] In the name of 'public interest' foreign and Indian corporate houses now have the power to increase the overtime work to 125 hours in a quarter along a 'legal' course; in fact, we will see later that enterprises integrated in the production chain have already increased the overtime jobs surpassing the 'legal' binding. In addition, under the proposed amendment in the Factories Bill of the central government, it is stated that women can work in night shifts on the condition that their employers guarantee their occupational safety.

One of the most atrocious attacks on the workers' rights in recent times is non-recognition of the newly formed unions of the workers by the labour departments of several state governments (one of the most glaring examples of which is the reluctance of recognition of Maruti-Suzuki workers' newly formed union by the Haryana government), unleashing state terror on the workers joining the unions or making the process of the formation of unions so stringent that most workers cannot join the unions. Particularly in the SEZs, the formation of unions is made almost impossible by the SEZ acts. Other than this, several draconian acts (such as Essential Services Maintenance Act or ESMA) and judicial verdicts against the workers make the exercising of 'rights to organize' or 'rights to strike' extremely difficult. In 1998 the Supreme Court of India had upheld a 1997 verdict of the Kerala High Court directing that the bandhs (general strikes) are illegal and violate the Indian Constitution. In 2002, the State of Kerala issued an order stating that all general strikes were illegal when they involve a complete close down of all activities, and later when it was challenged, the Supreme Court also upheld this order as legally justified. The Calcutta High Court in 2004, the Kerala High Court in 2006 and the Supreme Court in 2007 reiterated that the general strikes were illegal and not constitutional.[48]

Thus, in the liberalization era, all-pervasive attacks have been unleashed on the working people on behalf of the ruling classes of India. In fact, the national and international capitalists want a 'docile', 'obedient' workforce who will be forced to work under the worst work conditions and lowest wages.

Special Economic Zones (SEZs) and Economic Corridors

It is noted earlier that all over the world, since the 1970s and 80s, a shift occurred in large-scale industry based on mass production to disperse and widely spread assembly line production operations by subcontracting to small, very small and even to home-based enterprises. This drastically brings down the cost of production and works towards an absolute exploitation of surplus. The process of 'lean production' promotes the development of export-oriented manufacturing bases in the developing and underdeveloped countries, the majority of which are located in Asia. Export Processing Zones (EPZs) have mushroomed in Indonesia, Thailand, Malaysia and thereafter in China, Bangladesh, Sri Lanka, Myanmar, etc. to exploit the cheapest labour, infrastructure and tax-holidays and thus the EPZs become the major powerhouse of exports destined to be the advanced countries' markets. It is already noted that more than 900 EPZs (or SEZs) are operating in Asia alone. According to the World Bank, EPZs exhibit the following characteristics: duty-free imports of raw and intermediate inputs and capital goods, red tape is streamlined, labour laws are often more flexible than in the domestic market, generous and long-term tax concessions, infrastructure more advanced than in other parts of the country, etc. Actually the labour laws are not only flexible, but also the authorities of the EPZs are hostile to any type of union or organizing activities.[49] Moreover, the wage-level in these zones are enormously cheaper compared to the advanced countries, working hours are stretched to so long that it reminds us of the Dickensian age England. Working conditions are extremely hazardous and polluted and in most cases women workers are engaged as the cheapest source of labour. It is also noted by UNCTAD that these EPZs/SEZs are in fact "foreign enclaves" or a newer form of colonial subjugation extracting super-profits repatriated to the host countries of the giant MNCs.

In 2006, 130 countries have established over 3500 EPZs within their borders, with an estimated 66 million workers employed in those EPZs. China is now estimated to have 40 million people working in EPZs or EPZ-like operations, an increase of 10 million since 2002. Bangladesh had 3.25 million working people in 2005-06. In many countries, EPZ exports continued in 2006 to account for 80 per cent or more of exports.

Bangladesh saw its EPZ exports rise from 3.4 per cent in 1990 to 21.3 per cent in 2003.[50]

The Government of India has notified 583 SEZs till October 2011. Out of these, 143 are functional SEZs. Almost 24 per cent of these SEZs are in the IT and ITES sectors. In 2010-11, exports from SEZs have been growing and are to the tune of US$14.7 (Rs. 722.55) billion, indicating a growth rate of 23 per cent over the previous year. In the three quarter period of 2010-11 (April-December), exports from SEZs have climbed to 29.7 per cent of total exports. By June 2011, the total investment in SEZs had reached US$42.3 (Rs. 2129.143) billion. SEZs provided direct employment to about 714,412 persons. Total land required for approved SEZs is about 670,676 hectares, and for the notified SEZs, it is about 45,897 hectares.[51] It is to be noted here that the share of India's exports out of the total export volume of the world is still a mere 1.7 per cent in 2016-17[52] rising from 1 per cent in 2006.

The ruling classes of India have developed EPZs long before the inception of New Economic Policy. In 2000, during the tenure of the NDA government, existing EPZs are transformed into SEZs when the Government of India has formulated the SEZ policy. The real great SEZ rush started after the SEZ Act 2005 was passed and the SEZ Rules 2006 were notified. To boost the SEZs the government has provided a series of fiscal concessions and rebates to the developers of the SEZs and to the enterprises operating in the SEZs. In almost all cases 100 per cent of FDI has been granted through an automatic route. Water, electricity and other services are provided as required. A Development Commissioner (DC) is appointed as chief of the SEZ who will be an officer not below the rank of Deputy Secretary and is appointed by the central government. The DC also regulates the entry of the persons to the processing area of the SEZ by issuing identity cards. No one can enter the zones without the permission of the DC. The SEZs are within the area of village panchayats and municipalities, but for all practical purposes they are out of ambit of any of these public bodies. The SEZs will consume a large part of natural resources including water, natural resources and will affect the local population adversely by polluting the environment, but there is no scope for any democratic dialogue between the local people and the SEZ investors. There is no space for local people's representation in any decision-making body for approving SEZs or units within the zones.[53] In fact, the Act on SEZs clearly states that "An SEZ… is like a foreign territory within a country."

It is noted earlier that a sizeable amount of land has been acquired either forcefully or by dangling carrots and sticks or treacherously by the developers with the direct involvement of several governments at the centre and states displacing and expropriating lakhs of peasants, agricultural workers, labourers dependent on agricultural activities and allied services, forest workers, artisans, adivasis, fishermen, etc. It is observed that:

> Let us once more remind ourselves that the total area under SEZ across India is … predominantly agricultural and typically multi-cropped land capable of producing close to one million tons of food grains. The land acquisition for SEZs will result in mass destruction of livelihoods of not only farmers, agriculture labourers, but also forest workers, cattle-rearing communities, artisans and fish workers. It is estimated that more than 10 lakh people dependent on agriculture (114,000 farming families and 82,000 families of agriculture labourers) will be displaced. If we include those of artisans, fish workers, forest workers and cattle-rearing communities who may not face displacement but their livelihood may be largely destroyed; then the figure may be close to 15 lakhs.[54]

By the revamped SEZ Act, a minimum 50 per cent of SEZs is fixed for the 'processing area' of the development of industries/factories/projects including infrastructure. The remaining 50 per cent area is provided for developing housing complexes, hotels, restaurants, hospitals, shopping malls, entertainment centres, multiplexes, playgrounds, and even golf courses. Thus the SEZs are turned into lucrative destinations even before the real estate barons. It is also estimated by the Finance Ministry that the revenue loss on account of SEZs could be over $25 billion for 2007-10; this would be nearly 4-5 per cent of total tax revenues of the government. Revenue forgone due to SEZ-related activities has gone up phenomenally from $281.1 (Rs. 13,830) million in 2006-07 to $1,279.3 (Rs. 62,940) in 2009-10 (including both the corporate and non-corporate sector). Moreover, with all the incentives that are given to SEZs, there is every chance that industries already operating in the country may shift to the special economic zones and they will not create any new jobs. It is natural that most of the IT and ITES companies operating in the country may shift to the SEZs. On the contrary, de facto, no new job is created in the country only resulting in uprooting and expropriation of lakhs of working people.[55]

In these SEZs all the units are declared as 'public utilities' where existing 'mainland' labour laws will not act. Besides this, the state governments have enacted new labour laws for the respective state-SEZs as observed in states like Maharashtra, Gujarat, Tamil Nadu and UP. With the exemption of labour laws, indiscriminate hire-and-fire policy is permitted in the enterprises operating within the SEZs, employment of casual and/or contract labour are allowed and the workers/employees are stripped of the rights to strike. Workers of Brandix Apparel city (in Madras SEZ) have reported that the police are not entertaining the complaints related to the incidents inside the zone. Workers mentioned that they tried to file a complaint regarding sexual harassment inside the zone, but the police refused to entertain it; saying that the police are not authorized to file a complaint for incidents happening inside the zone.[56] Therefore, the SEZs are a de facto 'foreign enclave' within the country.

It is a matter of grave concern that due to the preventive measures framed by the SEZ Act prohibiting entry of the outsiders in the zones without written permission of the Development Commissioner of the SEZs, even the academic survey within the SEZ premises are restricted and thereby very few reports about the working conditions in the SEZs come out to the 'mainland' India. Still, the reports sneaked from these well cordoned fortified zones and a very few trade unions and NGO surveys observe that the working conditions in the SEZs are pathetic and reminiscent of Dickensian England. A survey reports about the garment workers in Madras SEZ show:

> [M]any workers were not getting the minimum wages; contract labour was employed in large numbers. Majority of women workers in Madras zone were getting less than the minimum wage. The women did not get maternity leave; in fact women generally lost their jobs if they got pregnant. Some companies employed women on the condition that they would not get married or pregnant in the near future. As per the Factories Law, employers were prohibited from allowing women to work in night shifts, but women were found working in night shifts in many places in MEPZ.
>
> The garment workers said, 'supervisors treat us as dogs. They hurl lot of abuses at us. Physically hitting the workers is not common but it also happened sometimes.... They physically hit one of our friends when she failed to meet her target on two consecutive days due to illness. She is not given leave in the first place.... One of my friends was singled out for bad behavior and made to run 10 rounds in the company.'
>
> The company runs two shifts of 8 hours each. Within 8 hrs working time there is only one break of 30 minutes for lunch. There are no tea breaks, however tea is provided to the workers of morning shift. The workers reported that it took not less than 10 minutes to go from the production department to the locker room and then to reach the lunch room; therefore in real terms the lunch time was only 10 minutes. Moreover, the workers also reported that they had to take permission for going to the toilets...
>
> Many co-workers report coughs and asthma due to dust. While cutting and sewing lot of dust is generated.... [M] any workers got ill. The workers standing can't sit and vice versa. Lot of workers experience back pains, especially during periods.[57]

ILO reports that,

> Existing studies on SEZs reveal that the Minimum Wages Act is implemented on paper but workers never get it. Only permanent workers get minimum wages, and rest of the workforce, which forms a significant majority, are denied their minimum wage. Payment of wages could be in the form of daily, monthly, and piece rate. Piece-rated wages are common in the SEZ garment units. The wages of contract labour are paid by the labour contractors and remain concealed. Overtime is not properly recorded and calculated. In effect, workers get the minimum wage after working for 10-12 hours. Provident fund, ESI, and bonus are also limited to the regular workers.... Overtime is also apparently paid at a premium rate (double wages). But workers reported that the number of overtime hours worked is grossly misrepresented in the salary statement—company pays overtime of a maximum of 25 hours per month, though workers record overtime of about 40-50 hours per month.
>
> In the NOIDA SEZ, workers from a garment unit reported that they worked for 10 hours every day. In addition, they had to put in 2-6 hours of overtime for most of the days in the week (for all six days during the peak season, which is for 6 months a year). Compensation for the overtime (over 10 hours of work) was paid but not at a premium rate. The production targets for workers are very high and pressure is such that they are not easily permitted to even go to toilets. Contract and casual workers do not get paid leave. There is always a fear of retrenchment due to the high turnover.[58]

In essence, these SEZs are 'special exploitative zones' (super-exploitation, of course) where thousands of workers bear the brunt of 'export-led development'. This happens although several of the SEZs are not operational till now. Moreover, the performances of these zones as export powerhouses are not very impressive. In fact, the massive drive for the promotion of 'export-led development' in India through the routes of SEZs has not achieved the 'desired' goal for several reasons. One of the foremost reasons is the global recession in the world economy since 2008 (from which the economy of advanced countries can recover only partially till now). The *Economic Survey 2016-17* says that "exports" of India "need to grow at 26.5 per cent annually for the next five years for India to reach a 'respectable' 5 per cent share in world trade."[59] This projection is utterly ambitious in face of the fierce competition among the other low-cost countries like China, Bangladesh, Sri Lanka, or Myanmar, and the tiger economies of South East Asia, etc.[60] and due to the ongoing stagnation in the advanced countries. In addition, the lands acquired for the proposed SEZs become a minefield to the 'developers' and help to make a super bonanza for the corporate realty houses.

Under this backdrop, the ruling parties or coalitions in the governments—representing the interests of the capital—have opened another route for 'development' with variegated projects like National Manufacturing Investment Zones (NMIZ), 'Make in India', 'Industrial Corridors', etc. In fact, the UPA government at the centre led by the Congress Party has finalized the 'New Manufacturing Policy' in 2011 stating that the goal of the initiative is to increase the share of manufacturing in India's economy to 25 per cent by 2022 from the present 15-16 per cent.[61] To fulfil the goal, the UPA government has announced to develop several NMIZs across the country to attract foreign and national investment and assured the hapless unemployed that at least 100 million jobs will be created through this venture.[62]

After the change in batons at the central government in 2014, the new NDA government led by Narendra Modi has declared with much fanfare that the new motto will be 'Make in India', 'Digital India', 'Skill India', 'Smart Cities', etc. which will spearhead the country along the path of development of manufacturing and that will create *10 million new jobs per year*. In fact, Modi serves the old wine of the UPA government in a new bottle as the development of NMIZs is finalized well before he was sworn into power. The corridors (integrated to NMIZs) under construction or yet to be constructed are: Delhi-Mumbai Industrial Corridor (DMIC); Bengaluru-Mumbai

Economic Corridor (BMEC); Chennai-Bengaluru Industrial Corridor (CBIC); Visakhapatnam-Chennai Industrial Corridor (VCIC) and Amritsar-Kolkata Industrial Corridor (AKIC).[63] It is stated that the minimum size of the NIMZs will be 5000 hectares (50 square kilometres) wherein the processing area has to be at least 30 per cent. Out of these mammoth projects the DMIC projects are developing with full swing acquiring large stretches of land:

> The process of DMIC, which is the biggest industrial project undertaken by India so far, started in 2008. As part of the project, 1483 km long freight corridor called Dedicated Freight Corridor (DFC) will be developed parallel to the existing railway track to join Delhi and Mumbai for industrial transport and development. DFC will also run parallel to the National Highways which are part of the Delhi-Mumbai link. The influence area of DMIC will cover 100 per cent of Delhi, 60 per cent of Haryana, 58 per cent of Rajasthan, 62 per cent of Gujarat, 18 per cent of Maharashtra, 12 per cent of Uttar Pradesh and some areas of Madhya Pradesh and Uttarakhand. 11 investment regions (IR) with minimum 200 sq km area, and 13 industrial areas (IA) with minimum 100 sq km area, within 150-200 km both sides of DFC will be developed.[64]

The industrial regions (IR) and industrial areas (IA) connected with the DMIC are: Dadri-Noida-Ghaziabad IR in UP, Manesar-Bawal IR in Haryana, Jodhpur–Pali Marwar IA in Rajasthan, Khushkhera-Bhiwadi-Neemrana IR in Rajasthan, Ahmedabad-Dholera IR in Gujarat, Pithampur-Dhar-Mhow IR in Madhya Pradesh, Shendra-Bidkin IA in Maharashtra and Dighi Port IA in Maharashtra.[65] The DMIC website states that:

> [T]wo power plants, 24 smart cities, 23 industrial hubs, six airports, two ports and a six-lane expressway stretching 1,500 kilometres [will be developed] along this corridor.... It usually takes 13 or 14 days to transport goods manufactured near Delhi to the ports on India's west coast.... This [DFC] would cut down the travel time to about 16 hours.... The Government of India owns 49 per cent stake in the DMICDC,

> the Japan Bank for International Cooperation owns 26 per cent and other government-owned financial institutions share the remaining 25 per cent equity. Even though the government owns the largest chunk of shares, the DMICDC is deemed to be a private company.... The whole project is estimated to cost $100 billion. Of this, $4.5 billion is being initially funded by the Japanese government as a loan for a period of 40 years at a nominal interest of 0.1 per cent.[66]

It is interesting to note that the Japanese government will take 'only' a nominal interest of 0.1 per cent on their loan for a period of 40 years. Identically, for the 'dream-project' of running the bullet train between Mumbai and Ahmedabad the Japanese government offers a loan at 0.1 per cent interest. In the 40 years' period the debt-burden will magnify if we take into account the probable depreciation of the Indian rupee with respect to the Japanese yen in the next 50 years.[67] Moreover, the NMIZs, the 'largest industrial project' in the world will be a lucrative destination to the speculators, developers and real estate magnets that has occurred in the case of the SEZs. The real price for these mega projects will be paid by the working people and the peasants, agricultural workers, Adivasis, artisans, etc. who are expropriated earlier by the pillage meant for building SEZs. Moreover, they will increase the reserve army of labour which pushes down the wages, as well as the displaced workforce will be engaged in 'menial' jobs under any work conditions pointing out once again that this type of 'development' is not for the millions of hapless people.

One of the largest NMIZs will be the Manesar-Bawal industrial region located in Haryana which will be developed as a single industrial zone covering 354 sq kms. It is interesting to note that this region is a major hub of automobile and auto-parts industry in India which is integrated to the global supply chain of automobiles. It is stated also that the region has the potential to attract nearly 30 industries, with major clusters like Engineering Cluster (automobile, engineering, downstream iron and steel), Consumer Product Cluster (food processing, readymade garments, downstream plastics, building materials),

Technology Clusters (IT/ITES, telecom equipment, consumer durables), Service Clusters (education, healthcare, hospitality) and Future Technology Clusters (nuclear equipment, pharmaceuticals, research and development, biotechnology).

But these rosy and optimistic projections cannot conceal the oppressive and exploitative work conditions in the manufacturing zones. The National Manufacturing Policy clearly states that in the NMIZs there will be limits on the right to form trade unions, workers with salaries higher than a certain level will not be allowed to form trade unions, Contract Labour Regulation (and Abolition) Act will not be implemented here, hours of work per shift will not be fixed, women workers can be employed on a shift basis including the night shift, the rules and conditions to retrench workers and reduce the workforce as per requirement will be made easier and flexible, the amount of any retrenchment payable will be flexible and will depend on the affordability of the company, temporary status can be assigned to the workers and it will be easier for the company to stop production and exit from the zones.[68] Invariably, the impact of all these measures will ensure draconian assaults on the workers in the name of 'development', 'Make in India', 'export-oriented growth', etc.

In fact, the automobile and auto-parts manufacturing clusters (now integrated with the developing NMIZs) near the National Capital Region (NCR) has become one of the centres in which regular as well as casual and contract workers are exploited and oppressed by the MNCs and national business houses in the lead company and the sub-contracting enterprises. As a part of the Global Value/Supply Chain, these zones show the degree of exploitation and precariousness operating in 'shining India'.

Working Conditions in the Automobile Sector

> Speed of assembly lines has gone up a great deal in the last six years—from 42 seconds per motorbike to 28 seconds, resulting in 1,028 two-wheelers being produced daily. Many of the young workers suffered from kidney stones because of

> the unrelenting pace and a fall in the number of "relievers'. From the five to seven relievers needed for every 75 workers (so that the latter can go to the toilet or to drink water), the number has come down to three.
>
> —A Bajaj two-wheeler plant worker of Chakan, Pune, Maharashtra

The automobile production in India is structured in such a way that the main manufacturing and assembling jobs are accomplished in the lead firms and the other assembling and production of auto-parts, components, basic production from raw materials are outsourced to several subcontracting firms which are mainly located close to the lead firms. The several operations are performed in distinct tiers: a) Lead firms or original equipment manufacturers (OEMs), b) The tier I suppliers (mainly assembling the subcomponents), c) The tier II suppliers (manufacturing/assembling subcomponents), d) The tier III suppliers (manufacturing the basic parts). Most of the tier III firms are generally small sector unorganized/ informal enterprises, even home-based settings mainly operated by own-account workers.[69]

The major automobile manufacturing clusters in India are located in the NCR of Delhi, Pune-Chakan region (Maharashtra), Chennai-Bangalore region in the states of Tamil Nadu and Karnataka, Udhamsingh Nagar-Haridwar region (Uttarakhand), Sanand-Halol region (Gujarat). The auto-component manufacturing clusters are located in Delhi (one), Haryana (three), Gujarat (five), Karnataka (two), Maharashtra (five), Tamil Nadu (one), Andhra Pradesh (one), Jharkhand (one), Punjab (four).[70] A sizeable percentage of the auto-component manufacturing and assembling enterprises are MNCs, the others are domestic companies, and tier III firms are predominantly small manufacturing or home-based enterprises. A report by the National Skill Development Corporation (NSDC) has cited that the state of Haryana currently leads in the production of passenger cars, motorcycles and tractors, contributing 50 per cent of the total passenger cars and two-wheelers produced in India.[71]

The Indian automobile sector is fully integrated to the global value/supply chain and records strong growth during the liberalization period. It has posted an impressive growth of around 20 per cent per annum since 2000.[72] India is currently the sixth largest producer of automobiles in the world with an average annual production of 24 million vehicles, of which 3.64 million are exported. Moreover, India is the second largest two-wheeler manufacturer, and the fifth largest commercial vehicle manufacturer in the world.[73] According to a CII report, the sector accounts for 7 per cent of India's GDP, 45 per cent of manufacturing GDP. Further, the sector contributes around 4.3 per cent to India's total exports and 13 per cent to the country's excise revenues.[74] With the 100 per cent FDI under automatic root in the automobile industry, the industry has attracted FDI worth US$ 17.40 billion during the period April 2000 to June 2017, according to data released by the Department of Industrial Policy and Promotion (DIPP).[75] The total number of auto parts producers is over 2500, out of which 500-600 are in the organized sector and contribute to 70 per cent of production (including exports). Moreover, even though India is the world's sixth largest auto producer by volume, and auto exports increased at 18 per cent per year over 2009-2013, India owns less than 1 per cent of global export markets. This is attributable to India's large domestic market, as it is easier for auto firms to fulfil domestic demand than export.[76]

A total of 19.1 million people are employed in the Indian automobile sector directly or indirectly. This includes manufacturing in OEM, auto components enterprises, raw material factories, automobile dealers, service centres and other enabling sectors. Among the auto component suppliers, 70 per cent of which constitute SMEs, a majority of the workforce is employed in tier III firms and raw material manufacturing companies.[77] It is an open secret that most of these (around 70 per cent) workers are casual, contract, temporary, and trainees. The more we go down the value chain to the tier II or tier III enterprises, the more we get the incidence of casualization and contractualization even up to 100 per cent. Overall 48 multinational and domestic auto-companies are operating in India as lead firms or tier I firms. There are hundreds of enterprises operating as tier II and tier III firms.

The leader of these firms is the 'renowned' company Maruti-Suzuki which occupies 47 per cent of the passenger vehicles market of India at the end of 2015-16.[78] Other front-runner companies are Hyundai, Mahindra, Honda, Tata Motors, Ford, GM, Hero, TVS, Bajaj, etc. The working conditions are more or less the same in all these companies. But the most notorious of these is Maruti-Suzuki (MSIL). MSIL operates its production from three factories in India—two in Haryana (one each at Gurgaon and Manesar) and one in Gujarat. According to a business newspaper: "During the period between April 2016-February 2017 the company manufactured a total of over 14.28 lakh units and is attempting to … cross the 15-lakh production mark.... Currently, the annual capacity of Gujarat plant is 2.5 lakh units.... [While the] Gurgaon plant manufactures 7 lakh units and Manesar plant rolls out about 8 lakh units annually."[79] It is stated by a member of the management staff of the company that Manesar firms produced 1200 cars per day in 2012 which will be increased to 1500 cars.[80] Another manager proudly proclaims that "we make one car every 12 seconds. In fact, one more is ready just as you finish reading this line."[81]

One of the distinctive features of all Maruti-Suzuki plants is the horrible work-line speed. In the absence of any declared daily target the assembly line continues no matter how many cars are produced. The assembly line is supposed to meet the target of *one car in 42 seconds*. After the registration of the union in the Manesar plant the pace of work is reduced somewhat to one car in 50 seconds. High speed production is not just a feature of the assembly line but also of the other shops—casting, welding, painting, etc. In the Gurgaon plant also a similar process of work-speed is followed. When the demands are climbing the output of one car engine takes just 45 seconds instead of 60 seconds in the low demand period. *A worker reported that he used to do the work of checking 142 parts of a car (more or less in different cars) in just 42 seconds.*

Apart from the speed, a relentless and continuous schedule of work characterizes production at Maruti-Suzuki. Workers have to work in shifts of eight and a half hours, in which they get a lunch break of thirty minutes and two tea-breaks of seven minutes each. Going and coming from the canteen takes about 10 minutes as the canteen is at a distance of 500 metres from the workplace and there are long queues for lunch. The lunch also becomes a rushed affair with workers actually getting about 10 minutes to somehow finish their food. There is no time to relax even slightly. The same applies to the tea break. Such is the dehumanization of the production process that the workers sometimes cannot even take a break for going to the toilet when required.[82]

A worker narrates the inhuman speed that they are forced to follow:

> You catch a bus at 5 am for the factory. Arriving a second late to punch in your card means a pay cut, but you can't leave the premises once you've entered. At 6.30 am, you exercise and supervisors give you feedback on your previous output. Start work at 7 sharp. Everyone does his one task—assembling, welding, fixing—for a minimum of 8 continuous hours. A car rolls off the line every 38 seconds, which means you can't budge from your position, ever. You get two breathless breaks during the day. At 9 am, a 7-minute break to drink tea or go to the loo, or both. After a while you might, like many of your friends here, end up taking your hot tea and kachori to the bathroom with you. Then a lunch break of 30 minutes, in which you walk about a half kilometre to the canteen, wait in line with everyone, eat and walk back. Returning even a minute late from any break, or leaving the assembly line for any reason even for a minute, means half a day's pay cut.[83]

In fact, the Maruti-Suzuki company regularly increases the speed of the production to super-exploit the workers (both permanent and casual/contract or trainees) in maximizing the profits. A commentator describes how every second matters in the production process of making cars which satisfy the desires of the 'great' consuming class of India and abroad:

> Maruti is all about speed and control, like the ads say. To that we could add stealth and influence. Speed, stealth, control, influence.
>
> Inside Maruti's sprawling new factory in Manesar, its all about speed and control too. Maruti's ads talk about 'Class Power'. Inside the Manesar factory, class power means something very specific. It means what it always does in factories—speed and control.
>
> Videos or images of what a Maruti factory looks like from the inside are hard to come by on the internet. Not because there are no images of them. Every inch of a Maruti factory is photographed and recorded by surveillance cameras. Cameras keep a precise record of how long a worker takes to complete a task. How long they take breaks for. Do they talk to each other sometimes? Do they breathe more than necessary? There are even cameras in the washrooms. Speed and control win over privacy, anytime. That's class power. Ultimately, the power that capital has over labour is a matter of speed and control.
>
> No, we do not have a video of the interior of the Manesar factory. But you do not need to see a video from the inside of the factory. All you need to do is to see a clip from *Modern Times*, by Charlie Chaplin on Youtube....
>
> The production targets set by the management ratchet the number of cars that each worker handles up to six hundred per shift. Six hundred cars multiplied by forty five seconds, makes twenty-seven thousand seconds, or four hundred and fifty minutes, or seven and a half hours. In an eight hour working day, with a twenty minute lunch break (in a canteen that is a distance from the main plant) and a seven-minute tea break, the respite from continuous control and speed (control over movements, speed of operations) that an average worker gets is something like three minutes. One hundred and eighty seconds of breathing space stolen from twenty-seven thousand seconds of labour. If we distribute these one hundred and eighty instants across these twenty-

> seven thousand moments of labour, we get a figure that looks like this. In each second, a worker in the Maruti Suzuki Manesar Plant gets to move like a human being for something like one hundred and fiftieth of that second. That is his time. The rest of each second, each minute, each hour belongs to Maruti-Suzuki. That's class power. That's control and speed. In one of its ads, Maruti tells its customers—'You're the Fuel'. That's the kind of tag line that always sounds good in an ad. Sounds hot, sounds cool. But what is really burning up is the life of every young worker at Manesar.[84]

The oppressive work-conditions do not end here. The management takes such policy on leave to make workers frightened not to 'waste' any seconds, minutes, hours or days of his/her work schedule. In fact, the workers in the factory have effectively no paid leave. Even subsequently every leave a worker takes means a percentage deduction from his/her salary. If a worker takes one day's leave even after informing the supervisor, then a sum ranging from Rs. 1,200-1,500 (depending on the salary of the worker) was deducted from his/her salary. The amount increases proportionately for every day of leave taken. If a worker has to take 4 or 5 days of leave in a month, even for entirely valid reasons such as illness, he/she has to forego effectively about half of the salary. If he/she takes leave without informing the supervisor, even for an emergency, then the deduction will be about double the amount.[85] Interestingly, the workers are paid for eight and a half hours of work, even though the management forced the workers to arrive at the workplace 15 minutes earlier for pre-work unpaid meetings.

This working schedule is valid for all types of workers—permanent or casual or the contract. In fact, not only in Maruti-Suzuki factories of Gurgaon and Manesar, but along all the organized factories in the Manesar-Dharuhera-Bawal industrial belt of Haryana, contract, casual workers and apprentices are engaged in regular or perennial nature of jobs which is not legal. Each of the independent sources, even some mainstream media have reported that in the Gurgaon or Manesar factories around 75 per cent of the workers are contract, casual and trainees who work along with the permanent workers. The only difference is in their uniforms and wages. Some workers have been on contractual jobs for a decade or more, and several thousands have been contractually employed for four years or more and the tactics of the management shows that these workers are deliberately retained as *permanently temporary* in clear violation of law and labour rights.

Box: Human Robots: Block Lines in the Engine Shops
Tasks to be Completed in 46 to 52 Seconds

The following tasks are completed by a worker in one of the Block lines in the Engine Shop in Gurgaon unit within 46 seconds to 52 seconds, depending on the target.

1. Get the housing and sealant for the engine block.
2. Place the housing on top of the engine block (as it comes up on the conveyor belt in front of the worker).
3. Place 6 bolts between the block and the housing. These are tightened mechanically.
4. Torque 6 bolts.
5. Mark them as done.
6. Place the baffle plate stud in the space made for it in the engine block.
7. Move the block with a pedal.
8. Place the oil scan jet on top of the engine block.
9. With three blows of the hammer push it into the appropriate space.
10. Fix two water pumps by attaching and tightening them on the grooves made for them.
11. Lift the piston gauge.
12. Match the block and piston gauge.
13. If the two match then let the belt move the block ahead.

In case they do not match and the bearing of the piston gauge does not fit, the block cannot be moved forward till this problem is fixed by another worker.

[*Source:* Driving Force: Labour Struggles and Violation of Rights in Maruti Suzuki India Limited, PUDR, May 2013, http://pudr.org/content/driving-force-labour-struggles-and-violation-rights-maruti-suzuki-india-limited, accessed 14.10.16]

After the pre-planned incidents of July 18, 2012, a new category of contract labour is engaged in the Manesar unit which is called 'Company Temps', but not 'contract workers'. These 'temps' are hired directly by the company and not through agents. This company temps, would work for seven months and then be laid off for five months. After the lay-off, some workers could be recalled for another seven-month stint if the demand arose. The 'company temps' would be paid Rs. 14,000 monthly—about half the salary of permanent workers, who earn Rs. 35,000 and more. "A contract worker cannot possibly have any commitment," Maruti Suzuki India Limited chairperson R.C. Bhargava told *The Economic Times*. "He does not see a future for himself in the company. Instead of motivation and accountability, we have suspicion and witch-hunting." Direct hiring of temporary workers, Bhargava and other senior managers argue, would promote loyalty, offer labour flexibility in months of shifting demand, and give the company greater control in determining who gets hired.[86]

Chart 7: Real Wages of Auto Workers (in 2000-01 Rs.)

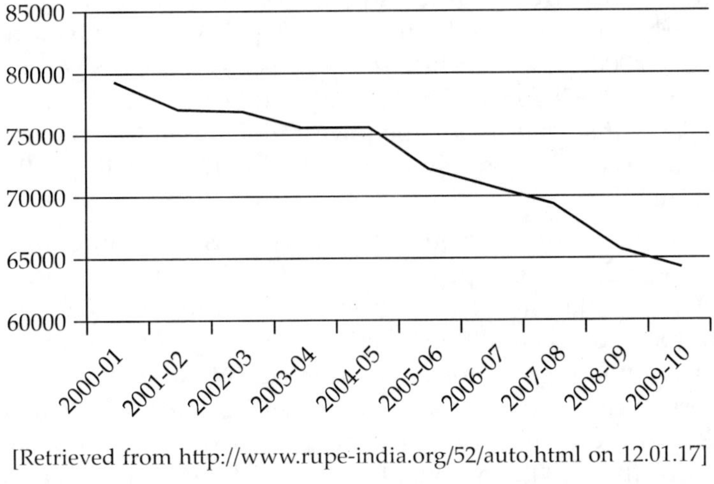

[Retrieved from http://www.rupe-india.org/52/auto.html on 12.01.17]

It is noted earlier that Maruti-Suzuki has outpaced its rivals acquiring 47 per cent of the market share of passenger vehicles in 2015-16. Therefore, it is the most 'valuable' automobile company of the country now. The net sales of the company have increased from Rs. 43,587 crore in March 2013 to Rs. 68,034 crore in March 2017, i.e. an increase of *56 per cent*. Net profit in March 2013 was Rs. 2,392.1 crore which is increased to Rs. 7,337.7 crore in March 2017, i.e. an increase of *207 per cent*![87]

On the contrary, the workers, particularly the contract, casual and trainees get half or one-third of the wages paid to the permanent workers. Understandably, the major source for the cost-cutting of the company comes from the engagement of contract, casual workers and trainees at low wages. It is reported by mainstream media that the wages of the workers in the auto sector have risen in the last decade. But an economic journal ('Aspects of India's Economy', see Chart 7) calculates that the real wages of the auto workers have declined in 2009-10. Then after, a rise in real wages is observed in the auto industry which is achieved by the workers' struggle and unrest. A business magazine reports that the overall cost of labour for auto companies has fallen from 7.95 per cent of their total expenses in 2000-01 to 5.54 per cent in 2015-16, according to the Centre for Monitoring Indian Economy (CMIE). Similarly, the cost of labour constituted 8.31 per cent of net sales in 2000-01, which in 2015-16 was *down to 5.28 per cent*. Even after the 2015 wage increase, Maruti's *labour cost is a mere 0.96 per cent of its net sales*, the lowest global cost for its parent Suzuki Motor Corporation (SMC). Before the hike, it was 0.74 per cent.[88]

Accidents are common at the workplaces in the automobile sector—both in lead firms and lower tiers. A study conducted by SafeInIndia and NGO Agrasar has estimated that every year 1500 contractual workers in the Gurgaon-Manesar belt meet with accidents mostly crush injuries that lead to loss of fingers or hands particularly in the tier III enterprises. About 80,000 workers, most of whom are contractual, are employed in more than 600 component makers. These makers supply to Maruti Suzuki, Hero MotoCorp, Honda Motorcycle and Scooter India, etc. Nineteen out of 20 victims are from tier II and tier III factories highlighting the lack of safety protocols and infrastructure. Sixteen out of 20 workers are not provided any training; 15 out of 20 victims are below 23 years of age; Only 8 out of 20 workers have ESI cards.[89]

Lokesh Kumar, an auto worker narrates: "I am lucky. I pulled out in time." Half a centimetre of his thumb had been shaved off by a machine. "In every factory, you will find at least ten boys with broken fingers," he said. "About half the boys who have come from Uttar Pradesh and Bihar to work in Haryana have lost their fingers." Another worker said, "with a hourly production target at 240 pieces, I had to complete four work cycles in a minute, or one in 15 seconds. I thought it is 11 pm, let me hurry up, finish the work and get some rest. I might have pressed the pedal too fast. Or the machine slipped..." Before he could remove the piece and his hand out from harm's way, the machine's arm came crashing down, crushing the top half of his right thumb. But why was he working till so late? "The supervisor said a work order has to be completed. On such days, you cannot slip out even if you want to." Dr. Pankaj Bansal, the orthopaedic surgeon of the orthopaedic hospital run by the central government's Employee's State Insurance Corporation said, "We see about 20 cases of crush injuries every day. In most cases, the fingers are auto-amputated, which means they have been lost even before the worker has come to us. In some cases, the entire hand is lost."[90]

Not even at the workplace, the workers are vulnerable at their living places as well. In fact they have to struggle to reproduce their labour power in a pathetic condition:

> The workers of Maruti Suzuki generally live nearby villages of the industrial area of Manesar. They live in small, dark and unhealthy rooms. Three to four people are forced to stay together. The workers cannot spend time with their families or friends; in fact, they cannot even indulge in recreational activities. Their children cannot receive proper education. They spend their lives under pressure from and surveillance of supervisors and landowners. Lack of balanced diet causes malnutrition and various diseases. Also, there is not sufficient money for proper treatment. So, the reproduction site is in a dismal condition for majority of the workers in the automobile sector.[91]

Bawana Industrial Area, Delhi

[There are] over 3 lakh labourers at Bawana industrial area, where 17 workers were killed in a blaze at an illegal firecracker packaging unit last week...

With no labour union office in Bawana, workers rarely know whom to approach when they face problems—from breathing fumes all day to drinking water with more than 700 'total dissolved solvents', a measure of the inorganic and organic substances in a liquid.

Take, for example, Mohammad Hashim, a 27-year-old press machine operator at a glass frame factory, who has cuts across his palms. "The factory owner would provide new gloves every two weeks, but then stopped. You never get used to the pain, but where do I report this?"

The answer lies in the labour department office at Nimri Colony. But the 20-km journey takes two hours and requires changing two buses. "Many do not know about the office. There are no trade unions in Bawana, and most labourers are illiterate, with no idea about their rights," an official said. Most workers in Bawana are landless peasants who come to the city when there is no work at their village. They stay either in three villages around the industrial area, Metro Vihar or in JJ colonies.

At a utensil-making unit in Sector 8, Deepak does not blink as the metal is pressed into shape. "The last worker who got distracted had his right hand amputated. You barely have a minute to take the utensil out of the machine," he said. None of them are aware of Section 23 of the 1948 Factories Act: "No young person shall be required or allowed to work at any machine unless he has been fully instructed as to the dangers arising with the machine."

In most factories *The Indian Express* visited, owners had not designated the 10 per cent safety buffer around a machine. They reasoned that the factories are "too small" to take such precautions. The space crunch also means there are no provisions for drinking water or toilets. Often, many units share a common bathroom—violating Section 19 of the Factories Act.

In factories that produce auto and machine parts, workers are not given helmets and welders do not have eye protection. "Every time I breathe, my chest hurts," said 32-year-old Mohammad Imran, a dye operator in a 200 sq m factory for the last three years. Windows are opened only thrice a day and workers are not provided masks...

Many workers *The Indian Express* spoke to were also oblivious of minimum wage. The average salary is around Rs. 9,000, though a machine operator who puts in overtime and works seven days a week can make up to Rs. 12,500. The minimum wage, as per the Delhi government, is Rs. 13,584. And as per the law, no labourer should be made to work more than 48 hours in a week, and should get twice the ordinary wage for overtime.

[*Source:* Bawana Fire: For the Labourer, No Masks, No Helmets, No Minimum Wage and No Options, 03.02.18, http://indianexpress.com/article/cities/delhi/bawana-fire-for-the-labourer-no-masks-no-helmets-no-minimum-wage-and-no-options-5049541/, accessed 04.02.18]

It is noted earlier that the workers of the Maruti-Suzuki plant and of the several factories located in the Manesar-Dharuhera-Bawal industrial region of the National Capital Region (NCR) are seething with discontent on various grounds. The grievances of the workers are common in most of the firms: overwhelming engagement of contract and casual workers in perennial and regular nature of job, huge wage gap between the regular and temporary workers, least job-security, hire-and-fire at any time or utter flexibilization, poor working conditions and long working hours, forced overtime, low payment for women and child labour, lack of or near absence of social security, medical benefits, etc. and absence of pro-labour honest unions. In fact, in the Manesar factory of the MSIL, the workers are struggling for regularization of the contract workers, poor working conditions and recognition of workers' newly formed union. But in the last few years, there have been numerous cases of repression of workers in this belt—whenever the workers stood up against the unjust and illegal activities of capitalists and came together to form their union. The managements in most of the factories have a tacit understanding with the labour administration of Haryana state (in fact, with all the states of the country) and thereby in reality, no union can be formed without a green signal from the management in this belt. In the automobile sector, in 2005, when workers at Honda stood up against the exploitation and oppression of the management and demanded to form a union, they were brutally lathi-charged by the police. In 2009, when the workers of Rico,

Gurgaon, went on a strike for 44 days demanding their right to form a union, the hired goons of the management killed Ajit Yadav, a striking worker, at the site of *dharna* outside the factory gate. Similarly, in 2010 in Denso, a strike demanding the formation of a workers union was met with repression. There are many such examples like suppression of workers' protests in Sunbeam, Bosch, Napino, Senior India, Bajaj Motors, Suzuki Powertrain, Suzuki Motorcycle, Daikin, etc. The most glaring example is that of Maruti Suzuki's Manesar plant. While they were successful in forming a union, they had to face the July 18, 2012 conspiracy of the management to smash the union. After the incident the entire plant was turned into a fort with heavy deployment of police forces and production in the plant flows from the barrel of the gun, as workers were forced to work under heavy police presence inside the plant.[92]

In fact the complicity of the management and the state administration is so obvious that when the PUDR team interviewed the DCP Maheswar Dayal on the phone, the DCP said candidly that,

> It has been a model investigation and will see a model conviction. I can tell you that Manesar will not see violence in the future. The Maruti management has decided to stay on because of the police presence there. There is a special battalion, the Indian Reserve Battalion (IRB) there—500 persons, and 150 PSOs and staff and also the HQ of the ACP has been shifted to Manesar from Pataudi.[93]

When asked about the MSIL hostility to the contract workers organizing into a union, Anupam Malik, the Joint Labour Commissioner of Haryana state unequivocally declared in an interview that 'It is not illegal to refuse to negotiate with an outsider. It is the management's wish. It is the right of the employers to refuse to negotiate."[94] The public prosecutor of the Haryana government, who pleaded against the arrested workers of the MSIL Manesar factory and wanted death sentences for their 'crime', stated in an interview that they deserved death because theirs was a crime against capital, against "industrial growth", against "Foreign Direct Investment

(FDI)" and against "Make in India jo Modi ji keh rahe hain" (Make in India that Mr Modi speaks of). Thus the class character of the government and state machineries are clearly exposed.[95]

If the working conditions in one of the lead firms like Maruti-Suzuki are so horrid, it is not difficult to estimate the conditions in the tier I, tier II and even tier III firms integrated in the GVC.[96] In fact, the tier I and some tier II firms in many cases are MNCs and frontline domestic companies in which the working conditions are almost the same or worse than the lead firms. In tier III firms it is more precarious. To reduce the bargaining power of suppliers and to put consistent downward pressure on the prices of the parts, the tier I and tier II companies generally maintain multiple suppliers for most parts, promoting intense competition among them, and causing orders to particular suppliers who can deliver the parts at the lowest possible cost. In these situations, the tier III companies are never in a position to invest in improving infrastructure, machineries and skills. In fact, overcrowding of enterprises in the sector led to a cut-throat competition for supply orders leading them to fall into a continuous crisis which results in tremendous pressure on the workforce engaged in these enterprises. Hence precarious working conditions, extremely low wages and intense exploitation of the workforce are very common in these firms. Almost all the tier III firms run the production operations by informal (mostly casual) workers and in general the overwhelming majority of them are migrants, including women.[97]

In the majority of tier I and tier II companies' wages are so low that the workers are forced to do the overtime of 2-4 hours per working day. In most cases the workers are denied premium rates for overtime or double the rate of hourly wages, particularly in the case of contract workers who form the majority of the workforce. But the conditions in tier III enterprises are far worse. There is no limit of working hours in general. Moreover, the workshops are generally 50-60 sq m in area with no proper lighting and ventilation. In most cases, there were only ceiling fans, only few had coolers, and none had air-conditioning units. The lack of safety standards is glaring. Hot metal forgings are done by hand without any safety equipment while workers turn molten steel into moulds, also by hand, in largely dark and unventilated workshops. These casual and/or migrant workers cannot demand any labour rights legally, they have no rights to complain to the labour department about the labour conditions. They do not have any job security; they are hired and fired easily and smoothly without any having to follow any legal procedure. Social security schemes like ESI and PF are not applicable in their cases. Their wages are generally less than the statutory minimum wages that also depends on the availability of overtime work. Most are 19 to 48 years old as anyone beyond 50 cannot expect to meet the strength and stamina demanded in the line of work. They live in slum-like conditions, in small and unventilated rooms overcrowded with workers and unhealthy surroundings, with no facilities like toilets, bathrooms, drinking water, etc. Under such conditions, it becomes hectic and tiring to get ready for work in the morning and reach the factory in time, especially since they almost regularly do overtime work two to four or more hours. Unionization in the tier III stage is almost absent.[98]

Garment and Textile Sector

> Aakriti says: "I had to stand all the time and the tasks that I needed to carry out required a lot of walking. I had to climb on a bench to tie the thread, because the machine was located too high. There was no chair for us to sit on. All eight hours and overtime hours I had to stand, walk and climb."
>
> —A female worker in the garment industry in India

The garment industry is now one of the most proliferating export-driven manufacturing sectors of the developing countries in Asia. Moreover, it is one of the most labour-intensive manufacturing sectors which employ more than 25 million workers worldwide estimated by ILO in 2005. But if we add footwear to the garment and textile sector, a recent publication of ILO estimates that only in developing Asia does the garment, textile and footwear (GTF) industry employ more than 43 million women and men.[99]

In India, several sub-sectors like jute, cotton and artificial yarn production are included in the broad category of 'textile' industry. Therefore, it is difficult to measure the number of workers engaged in the garment (or apparel) sector. Moreover, most of the employment in the garment sector is informal in nature which complicates the exact measurement. According to one source, the textile industry as a whole employs about 45 million people directly and 20 million people indirectly,[100] second only to agriculture as the largest employer. According to another estimate, the readymade garment sector provides employment to 12 million workers in India.[101]

The textile production in India contributes about 14 per cent of the industrial production, 10 per cent of the manufacturing production, 2 per cent of GDP, and 13 per cent of total exports. The industry attracted FDI worth US$ 2.55 billion during April 2000 to June 2017.[102] The readymade garment industry in India constitutes 44 per cent of the country's entire textile and apparel industry.[103] The largest garment manufacturing centre is located in Bangalore (Karnataka), Tirupur and Chennai (Tamil Nadu), and in the National Capital Region (NCR) where millions of workers are engaged in formal and informal firms (including the household enterprises). There are somewhat smaller clusters of leading exporters in other states (Madhya Pradesh, Maharashtra, Andra Pradesh, Gujarat) and clusters of small and medium-sized garment factories dispersed across the country that make up to 2.4 million workers.[104]

It is noted earlier that the garment production in the world is predominantly integrated to the global value chain (GVC). Gary Gereffi and Olga Memedovic on behalf of the United Nations Industrial Development Organization showed that,

> In this buyer-driven value chains large retailers, marketers and branded manufacturers play the pivotal roles in setting up decentralized production networks in a variety of exporting countries, typically located in developing countries. This pattern of trade-led industrialization has

> become common in labour-intensive, consumer-goods industries such as garments, footwear, toys, handicrafts and consumer electronics... Firms that fit the buyer-driven model, including retailers like Walmart, Sears and JC Penney, athletic footwear companies like Nike and Reebok, and fashion-oriented apparel companies like Liz Claiborne, Gap and The Limited Inc., generally design and/ or market—but do not make—the branded products they order. They are "manufacturers without factories", with the physical production of goods separated from the design and marketing... In buyer-driven chains profits come from combinations of high-value research, design, sales, marketing and financial services that allow the retailers, designers and marketers to act as strategic brokers in linking overseas factories and traders with product niches in their main consumer markets.[105]

In these buyer-driven chains, in most cases the brand owners become speciality retailers and open their own stores to sell and promote the goods manufactured. Most of the global brands are from the USA, EU and Japan which enjoy monopoly on these goods—apparel, footwear, toys, etc—selling items while transferring, as much as possible, the rest of the production activities to the contract manufacturers of the exporting countries where the labour and other costs are the cheapest. It is in the interest of the suppliers to offer a 'full package' service including upstream and downstream activities. In case of the garment sector, 'upstream' means taking responsibility for sourcing fabric and trim; 'downstream' means organizing the logistics and transportation, and delivering the items to the retailer's (i.e. brand company's) warehouse or even stores in a 'ready to sale' packaged state. The brands are thus perfectly called "manufacturers without factories".

The big brands sourcing garments from India are Gap, Liz Claiborne, Polo Jeans, Tommy Hilfiger, JC Penney, Macy's, Van Heusen, Walmart, etc. Indian exports to the United States, Canada and European Union comprise 80 per cent of the total garment exports; the remaining 20 per cent goes to the rest of the world. In India, Delhi's (NCR) contribution towards garment exports stands highest at 30 per cent and then Tirupur (in Tamil Nadu) with 25 per cent. Mumbai and Bangalore come next with 20 per cent and 15 per cent respectively and lastly Chennai with the contribution of 10 per cent.[106]

In most cases the spinning, weaving, bleaching, dyeing and garmenting take place in separate, specialized plants. Additionally, there are around a dozen manufacturers that combine all these activities within their plants. These vertically integrated manufacturers perform all stages of textile and garment production; from processing the raw cotton to finishing the garments. Entrepreneurs have created a web of smaller units all networked among each other to such a degree that each unit supplies another. Horizontal integration is also found among Tamil Nadu garment producers. This means that the same type of production takes place in many different units under a single firm. For example, one company may operate various garmenting units, under different names. The different production facilities are registered as separate units, despite common ownership. Small units with 100-200 machines are more agile and able to handle both small-batch orders and large orders, and even a small unit can fulfil larger orders by utilizing the hundreds of other units to subcontract.[107] Such is the extent of subcontracting that when the lead company has to place an order, the sourcing team takes costing from 10 and 15 different factories from (say) five locations. Whoever quotes the lowest price, the brand will go to that factory. Similarly the contractors will go even to homeworkers who are prepared to work at a lower cost. According to the National Sample Survey (NSS) estimate around 45 per cent of the country's 37.5 million home-based workers make clothes or textiles, and about 33 per cent of those are subcontracted homeworkers. WEIGO, an NGO finds in its own survey that 71 per cent of home-based workers are subcontracted themselves. In Ahmedabad, in particular, all the workers surveyed are subcontracted.[108] Undoubtedly, the living and working conditions in these home-based operations are the worst in the highly competitive garment market of the world. They have to deliver the products at minimum prices of what they are offered by the subcontracting firms.

In fact, the condition of the workers in the garment industry in India is more precarious than their counterparts in the automobile sector. In Tamil Nadu, one of the major garment exporting states, around 40 per cent of the workforce resides in hostels (like the dormitories in China) and are referred to as 'camp-coolies'. It is in the interest of the manufacturers to have a substantial part of their labour force residing on the factory grounds (or in hostels near the factory) so that they are ensured of a constant supply of labour. Spinning mills operate *24 hours a day* and workers are needed around the clock to keep the machines going. It is estimated that around *80 per cent of these workers are women* which means that the manufacturing in these small to medium sized subcontracting enterprises are largely feminized. After all, the female workers are generally 'pliant', 'docile', non-inclined to unionization, and cheapest. A sizable section of these workers are migrant labour coming from Andhra Pradesh, Bihar, Jharkhand, Odisha, West Bengal, Manipur and Meghalaya.

Horrific exploitation is observed in the Tamil Nadu garment enterprises where thousands of women and child (girl) labour are recruited from the hinterlands luring them with advertisements posted in billboards or leaflets: 'We request you to bring us the lovely girls you know and make their lives prosperous as a lighthouse'. This process is called 'Sumangali' (Tamil word for 'happily married woman') system by which the parents of the young girls of ages between 14 to 21 years are attracted by the 'agents' (who earn Rs. 500 to 1000 per recruits) to earn up to Rs. 40,000 to 60,000 in three years to meet the expenditure of dowries at the time of marriage. The parents of these hapless families, most of them are Dalits, are promised a well-paid job, comfortable accommodation, three nutritious meals a day and opportunities for training and schooling for their children. Clothes and household articles are also given to attract the parents. The real ordeal begins after the recruitment. The stipend/wages received by the young girl workers vary in different enterprises. If the lump sum (money to be received after the end of the contract) is added to the monthly wages, the total amount earned in the contract period in most cases does not equal the amount a worker would have earned had she received the minimum wages for an apprentice in the garment industry. Strikingly, the lump sum payment is denied if a worker leaves the factory before the end of the contract period. Many workers do not reach the three or five-year mark as they fall sick due to the unhealthy and unsafe working conditions and the extremely long working days. Sometimes the workers are fired just before the end of the period under any pretext. A 2011 study by a local NGO with the support of KFB Austria showed that among 1,638 'Sumangali' workers only 60.74 per cent of the workers had signed a contract, and that an overwhelming majority of these workers (96.1 per cent) did not receive a copy of the contract.[109]

At the workplace these young female workers are forced to do exhausting work. In fact, in Tamil Nadu, extremely long working days and forced overtime are the general phenomena. The survey report writes:

> *Four hours of compulsory overtime work a day* is common, irrespective of the season of business. During production peaks, workers are forced to complete two shifts (16 hours) or *even three shifts (24 hours) in a row*. Workers also reported that *they are frequently woken up in the middle of the night* to complete urgent orders. Many of the interviewed workers said that working night shifts is one of the most difficult aspects of their job. Workers have difficulties staying awake and errors are more easily made which may lead to abusive treatment by the supervisor or work-related accidents.
>
> Hostel workers in particular are extremely vulnerable to be subjected to excessive and forced overtime work. Refusing overtime work is not an option as the supervisors put pressure on the workers to keep working. Threats used by supervisors include that part of the wage will be withheld if workers do not continue working or that they will call the workers' parents and inform them about their daughters' bad behaviour. In addition, Sumangali workers fear that they will lose their lump sum amount if they do not do as the supervisors tell them. Workers who stay in dormitories outside the factory are simply not physically able to get out

of work, as buses will not be permitted to leave until the work is finished.

Workers who stay in dormitories are severely restricted in their freedom of movement. In their free time female workers are not allowed to leave the hostel accommodation freely.... Outside working hours men are free to leave the factory/ hostel grounds. In most cases, when female workers leave the hostel they are accompanied by a guard.... Parents and other family members are allowed to visit their daughters on free Sundays, but only if a photograph of these family members has been submitted to the factory management.

The use of telephones is restricted. Sometimes workers are not allowed to use mobile phones. In most hostels there is a common phone, often in the warden's room, which can be used by workers to speak with their parents. Workers can make calls to their parents with the permission and in the presence of the warden....

Workers are physically and verbally abused by male higher-caste supervisors. This occurs if they fall asleep or if their work pace is going down after having worked long hours. Sexual harassment is reported as well.... The girls, who have no freedom of movement and very little contact with their families, are forced into the sex trade. They work during the day and are sold as prostitutes during the night. Clients are international buyers, company owners, senior management, supervisors and mid-level management.

The combination of extremely long working days, the abusive behaviour of supervisors towards the workers, lack of free time and scarce opportunities to interact with family and friends causes fatigue and physical breakdowns of the workers. Over the last years, alarming reports about workers *committing suicide* have come to the fore... [M]ore than 100 female workers have taken their lives in the past two years [in Tirupur alone] because they could not face the hardships of working and living in the factory any more...

Trade unions are not allowed on the premises of the factories and organising workers is very difficult because workers are not aware of their rights. In addition, no

> independent and effective grievance mechanisms are accessible for the workers.[110]

Another testimony of a woman worker narrates a harrowing experience in one of the garment factories of Coimbatore in Tamil Nadu when she was contracted for the 'Sumangali' system:

> When Aruna arrived at the factory, about 40 miles from her home, she found a vast facility where close to 1000 girls, many in their teens, lived 10 or 15 to a room. From 8 am till 10 pm every day, including weekends, she fed and monitored rusty machines that spun raw cotton into yarn. Her bosses often woke her in the middle of the night because, she recalls, there was "always some sort of work, 24 hours a day." Aruna made just a quarter of the $105 a month she was promised, about $0.84 a day.
>
> Aruna shows me a scar on her hand, more than an inch long, where a machine cut her. She often saw girls faint from standing for too long. One had her hair ripped out when it got caught in a machine. Others were molested by their supervisors. "They said we would get less work if we slept with them," Aruna says. Sometimes girls would disappear, and everyone would speculate whether they had died or escaped. Still, she needed the money, so she worked there for two years.[111]

Not only duped by the so-called 'Sumangali' offers, but also these workers are forced to stay in virtual captivity in the dormitories and to work longer than even 24 hours at a stretch. Another 2011 report by the Dutch watchdog groups Centre for Research on Multinational Corporations and India Committee of the Netherlands has found that 'Sumangali' factories employed an estimated 120,000 workers, some as young as 13, and supplied dozens of international companies, including Gap (which denied the allegation), H&M, American Eagle Outfitters, and Tommy Hilfiger.[112]

It is estimated that in Bangalore alone there are 500,000 workers in the garment industry in 1200 factories spread across the city. Up to 80 per cent of these workers are believed to be migrant workers. Many do not speak the local language and struggle to find housing, so garment factories fill the gap by offering company accommodations. The only catch: some residents are treated like prisoners. A 'National People's Tribunal for living wages and decent working conditions for garment workers' was convened in 2012. Sakamma, a 42-year-old mother-of-two working for Gap supplier Texport in Bengaluru, told the tribunal she earned *just 22p an hour* and that when she finished at the factory she had to work as a domestic help to top up her wages. "It hurts us to be paid so little. I have to do this and they sell one piece of clothing for more than I get paid in a month," she said. "We cannot eat nutritious food. We do not have a good life; we live in pain for the rest of our lives and die in pain." Like many of the women giving evidence, she said workers faced abuse if they failed to meet quotas. "The targets are too high. They want *150 pieces an hour*. When we cannot meet the targets, the abuse starts. There is too much pressure; it is like torture. We cannot take breaks or drink water or go to the toilet. The supervisors are on our backs all the time," she said. "They call us donkey, owl [a creature associated with evil], dog and insult us ... make us stand in front of everyone, tell us to go and die."[113]

Another report prepared by labour rights NGO India Committee of the Netherlands writes that at a hostel run by Arvind in Banaglore, which supplies to H&M, men slept on three-tier bunk beds in large, divided halls. There are no kitchens, the water supply is irregular, and one bathroom serves 12 to 14 people. "Nothing is good," one Arvind worker said. "But we are staying here because we have to live and there is no other way." Workers also had to pay to stay there. Interestingly the global brands who make supplies from these firms are H&M, C&A, Gap, Tommy Hilfiger, and Inditex, the owner of Zara.[114]

A woman worker of Bangalore says that: "My salary gets cut if I take even a day's holiday. All of us feel that there is no job security; we are under constant threat of being fired by our supervisors," says Banu, a garment worker in the Hosur Road area of Bangalore. "Minor mistakes in the work, or non-completion of targets could trigger the management to ask us to leave the job," she adds. The work of garment workers is physically demanding, calling for impossible targets of *100-120 garments an hour as against the normal rate of 60-70 pieces*. And this is made more punishing by the verbal harassment employed to goad women to work faster and longer hours, often skipping lunch to meet their targets. "I have experienced verbal abuse when I do not meet the production targets. Cloth pieces are thrown at my face," says Shyla, a garment factory worker in Bangalore. The workers complain that women are prevented from leaving the factory during work hours even for genuine medical reasons. One woman says that a garment worker who developed labour pains was not allowed to leave work. She lost her child because she did not reach the hospital in time.

Another worker says that: "I suffer from backache, leg and knee pain due to constant bending over the table to see the needle and running the machine with my leg." Injuries are common, especially puncture wounds from needles on the fingertips and nails as the cloth is passed through heavy vibrating mechanized machines. A worker can ill afford to report this as she may be declared unfit and removed from the job. Very few workers get masks to wear during work. They are constantly engulfed in the fluff of cut pieces of cloth. Women complain of tightness in the chest, breathing difficulties, allergic sneezing, persistent coughs and runny noses. Illnesses like asthma and tuberculosis are frequently reported. Long hours of sitting, very little water intake, and the fear of going to the toilet causes constipation and piles. In some sweatshops, supervisors keep a check on the number of times a worker takes a toilet break. If it is frequent the worker is asked to leave the job as it is believed speed of production is hampered. As a result, many workers do not drink much water.

The triple burden of household work, looking after children and being productive in the job has a longstanding effect on women's health. They skip their morning meal to rush to the factory, they miss their lunch if there is pressure to meet targets at work, and, when they get home in the evening, the responsibilities of cooking, cleaning and caring take precedence. Shyla says: "We are always on the run; we eat just to satisfy our hunger pangs. It is so difficult to sit down and eat peacefully."[115]

In the National Capital Region (NCR), the garment factories, which export the maximum to the lead brands, and where the majority of workers are male—the working conditions are also precarious. The suppliers employ mainly contract workers hired through contractors. *These contractors often supply 'supervisors' and 'bouncers' to 'control' workers.* The contract workers are illegally engaged in core and perennial production activities. In fact, the idea of regular or permanent employment in the garment sector is vague in the NCR, actually non-existent—even for a worker who is working in a single company for 10-12 years. *They are discharged whenever it is felt as 'required'*. Their salaries are equivalent to the minimum wages, overtime is compulsory; generally workers have to work for *12-14 hours a day*, including Sundays. Sometimes, in case of urgent delivery (as required by the lead brands) they have to work for *36 hours at a stretch*. In almost all cases, workers are illegally given overtime at single pay rate. Workers are denied leave or absence. Most of the workers have no identity proof. Moreover, the jobs in the garment sector are too monotonous, repetitive, and tiresome that demands closest attention by the eyes of the workers resulting in damages. There is no union and any such attempts are brutally crushed.[116]

A worker of the garment industry in Okhla in the NCR describes the work stress at the workplace in the following words:

> At the moment I work at the Anand Internationals D-3 factory in Okhla Phase One. Right from the beginning of the shift at 9 am you are immersed in trying to meet the target. Nowadays I make ties—when starting this work the company gave you *12 minutes to finish a tie, then after three days it was 11 minutes, then 10-9-8 and now it is 7 minutes per tie*. Because the target was too high I left the Anand Internationals A-185 factory

> after two months of work. There you got 20 minutes per skirt at the beginning, then 19 minutes the next day and the target time kept on dropping; by the third day it was *down to 10 minutes*. You have to increase the work speed so much that the body cannot keep up, the work is consuming the body...
>
> Then at D-3 factory of Anand International you had to work from 9 in the morning to 12 at night. Official working hours were from 9 am to 9 pm but if a worker finished work at 9 pm then the company would only count working-time till 8 pm, meaning that in order to save one hour paid working time for which you had already worked, which is 16 and a half rupees, you work till 12 at night...
>
> In the factory the target becomes an obsession; if you go for a piss, you get minus (meaning that they cut your wage), if you go to drink water, you get minus. Only when it becomes unbearable do we go for a piss or to get water. Only for the lunch break at 1.15 pm do we get up from the machines....
>
> In the factory there are 300 sewing machines, they are in the basement where it is very hot; even in winter you sweat. One always feels suffocated. Out of the 300 workers there will be 10 who are healthy, the rest of us suffer from this or that illness. No one has been given an ESI card, we pay privately for our treatment and if you are too ill you get fired from the company. On the first floor of the D-3 factory of Anand Internationals there is the office, on the second and third floors the finishing department—cutting threads, removing stains, ironing and packaging. On the fourth floor there are people who earn 15,000 to 25,000 rupees, they do not talk to us. On the fifth floor, next to the canteen, chemicals are prepared for washing the clothes. For 500 men and women working in the factory there is only one latrine each in the basement, there is always a queue.[117]

Another worker of 'Gaurav International' of Gurgaon of the NCR tells his story:

> Working times are from *9 am till 11 pm*—the thread cutting and packing department starts as soon as 8 am. The management locks the gates in order to enforce over-time.

> The female workers have a lot of stress because of that. In the factory 600 female and 1,000 male workers are employed—the male workers are forced to work till 2 am. The company will not even give you a cup of tea during the *14 to 17 hours of work*. They swear at us, they swear at the female workers, too. An official inspection was announced to visit the factory on 28th July, so the personnel manager told us to say that we do 10 to 12 hours over-time per month…—when we actually do *more than 150 hours*. The tailoring of velvet (makhmal) produces a lot of dust, this is why till last year they gave us free sugar molasses, but this has stopped now. Only on the day of the inspection on 28th July they distributed the sugar molasses again…. If you take two days off they will take the company pass away from you.[118]

A worker of Richa and Company:

> [W]e fabricate garments for GAP. There is one shift in the production department, which starts at 9 am and finishes at midnight. Women workers are called to work at 7.30 am, they are sent home at 9 pm or 10 pm, if they refuse to stay that long, they are immediately sacked. On 27th March some male workers said that they would refuse to work till midnight. *The in-charge and some men gave those workers a beating and made them stay till midnight*. The company pays only the first two hours overtime at double rate. If you are five minutes late for work, they close the door in your face, if you want to take a day off, they swear at you. If you take two or three days off, they keep your company card and say: "Pay us Rs. 500 and then you will get your card back."[119]

One of the most notorious sectors in the garment industry is zari work, intricate embroidery that is immensely popular in American and European fashion stores. Enterprise owners prefer to employ children because their *thin, nimble fingers* can work *quicker* on intricate ethnic designs. It is estimated that 100,000 children work for more than 14 hours a day in the illegal sweatshops in and around Delhi. But the zari (child) workers are spread across all the garment hubs of India. By the time the youngsters engaged in the zari sector reach their mid-teens, their fingers and hands often are badly damaged and their eyesight weak from long hours of tedious work in dark rooms. Their growth is often stunted by years of sitting in uncomfortable, hunched positions at the bamboo framed workstations. Child workers have no fixed hours of work, nor is there any trade union to fight for their cause. For those children 'lucky' enough to get paid, the combined wages of five unskilled child workers is less than that of a single unskilled adult.

Most work around 12 hours a day, with only small breaks for meals. Most of the child workers start work at dawn and work till the evening. Mal-nourished, the children are very often fed only minimal staples. The vast majority of migrant child workers, who cannot return home sleep at the workplace, further inviting sickness and poor health. There are cases of exploitation followed by no or minimum medical aid. The children are seldom, if chronic taken to the doctor. At many places it has been found that children are punished by not provided meals for the day. Also subjected to bullying, children often lose the bare minimum of food that they get.

Jivaj, who is from West Bengal and looks around 12, informs us that some of the boys in the workshop had been badly beaten. 'Our hours are hard and violence is used against us if we do not work hard enough. This is a big order for abroad, they keep telling us that. 'Last week, we spent four days working from dawn till about one o'clock in the morning the following day. I was so tired I felt sick,' he whispers, tears streaming down his face. 'If any of us cried we were hit with a rubber pipe. Some of the boys had oily cloths stuffed in our mouths as punishment.'[120]

One of the most scandalous parts of the exploitation of the workers in the global value/supply chain of the manufacturing of garments is abysmal low wages across all the Asian countries. Though there are some differences in the wage-level of the garment workers in the Asian countries and in some of the countries the wage level is increased to a certain extent in recent times to quell the protests of the workers, still the wages of these countries are extremely low compared to the advanced countries. In fact, the garment workers are not only ill-paid, but also they cannot earn the minimum subsistence wage required for the reproduction of their labour power. Even the mainstream international media now acknowledge the fact that the workers in the poor and developing countries (including the advanced countries) will not get the required payment by which they can provide a 'decent' living which includes two meals, a shelter, clothing, fuel, transportation, education, healthcare, etc. In recent times the ILO provides a subsistence wage-level calling it a 'living wage'. If we consider the definitions of 'living wage' provided by the ILO and several NGOs, a dismal picture will emerge. According to the ILO, a living wage is one that permits "[a] basic, but decent, lifestyle that is considered acceptable by society at its current level of economic development ... [such that] [w]orkers and their families [are] able to live above the poverty level, and ... participate in social and cultural life."[121]

'Worker Rights Consortium' depicts a miserable outline about the wages received by the garment workers which are markedly lower than the 'living wage'. It said: "In none of the 15 countries included in the study did the prevailing monthly straight-time wage provide garment workers with the equivalent of a minimum living wage. On average, the prevailing wage in 2011 for garment workers in each of the countries included in the study provided *little more than a third—36.8 per cent—of the estimated living wage* in the same country." Moreover, 10 years ago, i.e. in 2001, the average wage (as percentage of 'living wage') received is almost the same as 2011: "Prevailing wages for garment workers stood in relation to a living wage in *essentially the same place that they had 10 years earlier,* when the average share of a living wage provided by each country's prevailing wage for garment workers was *35.7 per cent.*"[122] The wages received as percentage of 'living wage' in selected countries are given in the Table 3.

Therefore, the wages in India, though increased by a fragment, is pathetically below the so-called 'living wage'—*almost one-fifth* of that! In Bangladesh—the probable next

Table 3: Monthly Wages in 2001 and 2011 as Percentage of 'Living Wage' (Garment Sector)

Country	*2001*	*2011*
India	20%	23%
Bangladesh	14%	14%
Vietnam	23%	29%
Thailand	46%	43%
China	16%	36%
Cambodia	24%	19%
Indonesia	16%	22%
Philippines	32%	32%

[*Source:* Global Wage Trends for Apparel Workers, 2001-2011, Worker Rights Consortium, July 2013, https://cdn.americanprogress.org/wp-content/uploads/2013/07/RealWageStudy-3.pdf, accessed 24.04.16]

'powerhouse' as garment exporter—the wages are almost *one-seventh* of 'living wage'! According to the same organization, the real wage for the garment workers in India has increased by a *mere 1.3 per cent* on an average between 2001 and 2011.[123]

Interestingly, the former UPA and the present NDA governments are keen in inviting foreign investments in garment (and leather) sector where the wage level is staggeringly below the 'living wage'. Former deputy chairman of the Planning Commission Montek Singh Ahluwalia pitched for foreign investment in these sectors saying India has the "strength of cheap labour" as the labour cost in China is "rising".[124] In the same tune the *Economic Survey 2016-17* under the tenure of the NDA government says that: "India ... has the potential comparative advantage in terms of cheaper and more abundant labour" where the monthly wages in different states of India and Asian countries in US dollar are given in Table 4.

Thus, the ruling classes of India are selling India as the hot spot for investing in labour-intensive sectors like garments and leather goods where the potential for the exploitation of the workers is huge.[125]

Table 4: Monthly Wages for Garment Workers in Selected Indian States and Asian Countries

State/Country	*Year*	*Monthly Wages (US$)*
Andhra Pradesh	2016	81
Bihar	2016	84
Odisha	2016	86
Jharkhand	2016	90
Tamil Nadu	2016	93
Uttar Pradesh	2016	95
Karnataka	2016	105
West Bengal	2016	109
Gujarat	2016	114
Madhya Pradesh	2016	115
Maharashtra	2016	118
Haryana	2016	119
Bangladesh	2013	80-120
Vietnam	2015	180-250
Indonesia	2013	120-150
China	2013	250-300

[*Source: Economic Survey 2016-17*, Government of India]

Leather and Footwear Sector

The leather industry plays an important part in the Indian economy. India produces 2.5 billion square feet of leather, accounting for about 13 per cent of global production.[126] India is the world's second largest producer of leather garments and footwear. In 2015 India produced 9.6 per cent of the world's total footwear production. Overall the leather industry is among the ten foreign exchange earners of the country. The most prominent markets for leather and leather products are the USA, the UK, and the other European countries. The UK is India's biggest market for footwear and with Europe taken as a whole accounts for *90 per cent* of India's footwear exports.

Tamil Nadu (Vaniyambadi-Ambur cluster), West Bengal (Kolkata) and Uttar Pradesh (main production centres in Kanpur and Agra) together account for about 90 per cent of all tanneries in India. Although traditionally this sector characterised by small enterprises, recent developments have also seen the growth of modern, large-scale factories, particularly in Tamil Nadu. The leather products are manufactured in supply chains operated globally in which India is one of the integral parts.

> The stages in the leather production process are preparation of the skin, tanning, finishing and manufacturing. Each of the steps in the production chain from hide to handbag [or footwear] can be done in ways that are either purely manual, or highly mechanized or in between. The operations can be done under one roof, or can be split up between as many units as there are operations. Therefore, the supply chain is often complex and may involve units ranging from state-of-the-art production units to home-workers. Most of the manufacturing process of shoes is being done in factories, only the sewing of the shoe uppers is often outsourced to home-workers. Export firms sometimes subcontract (part of) their production to smaller workshops, since it provides them with flexibility, low prices and makes it easier to cater to fashion-specific seasonal demands. *Through subcontractors, the actual work is done by informal workers at stitching centres, in factories or at home by informal home-workers.* At the bottom of the leather production process the collection and trade in hides is controlled by middlemen and traders, who take advantage of the low social status of the Dalit [and Muslim] leather workers by paying low prices.[127]

The tanning industry is one of the world's worst polluting sectors, mainly because of its intensive use of chrome, zinc, arsenic and cadmium. Work in the leather supply chain is risky and hazardous, as it entails working with these hazardous chemicals. The toxic chemicals have a major negative impact on the health of the people working in the tanneries. Tannery workers often suffer from fever, eye inflammation, skin diseases and lung cancer. Furthermore, the semisolid effluent of leather production diffuses toxic gases. The leather workers often lack sufficient protection against these toxic gases. Generally, workers are not adequately protected and trained to ensure their health and safety. Workers suffer from frequent bouts of fever, severe body, bone, joint and muscle pain, severe headaches, nausea and reproductive health problems.

Dalit and Muslim leather workers engaged in leather industry get low wages compared to other profession which reflects both the low status of work in tanning, manufacture of leather goods as 'dirty', polluting and caste discrimination. In Tamil Nadu, for instance, the statutory minimum wage for leather workers is the *lowest* of all sectors. Early in 2016 the minimum wage for leather workers was Rs. 126.48 a day, which is very low compared with, for example, Rs. 236.34 for electronics and Rs. 282.40 for an apprentice in textiles.[128]

One of the leaders of the Uttar Pradesh Grameen Mazdoor Sangh said:

> The leather exports sector, in the name of flexibility is trying to do everything at the cost of the workers; from hire and fire, casualization to contractualization, low wages to having a control over the working conditions of the workers and finally intimidation on a slight pretext. The employers can do this as they please and experiment with the workers' lives simply because the industry is the only livelihood option for Dalits and minority Muslim workers.[129]

A large proportion of the leather workers in all the clusters is contractual and piece-rate workers. There are several examples of children found at work in Indian tanneries under inhuman conditions, forced to work more than 12 hours a day. In the tanneries in the region around Tamil Nadu boys aged 11 or 12 are employed to clean the tanning tumblers, since they can easily climb inside the chambers. Thirty per cent of the 2.5 million workers in the leather industry in India are women, apart from non-registered home-workers who are more often women.

The systematic exploitation continues down the supply chain, as women home-workers provide even more flexibility and low-cost informal labour than the temporary or contract workers. Home-workers are most often used to stitch the uppers of shoes, as this is one of the most labour-intensive parts of the production process. Hand-stitching of uppers in Portugal or Bulgaria, for example is paid at approximately 40 pence (Rs. 34.8) a pair, while in Ambur the same work is paid *at less than 10 pence (Rs. 8.7) a pair*. This explains why as well as exporting finished shoes, Tamil Nadu is also a source of uppers, which are assembled in India and then joined to the soles in European countries such as the UK, Portugal or Slovakia to make up the finished shoes. Moreover, *these shoes sold in the UK for prices between £40 and £100 and more.*[130]

Home-workers are not directly employed by the factories but get their supply of work from an intermediary, often someone in the same village or area as themselves, who in turn gets the work from a subcontractor of the main factory, sometimes with several layers of subcontracting between the main factory and the home-workers. This allows the factories, the principal employers, to take no responsibility for home-workers, even though they are fulfiling an important part of the production process. The home-workers do not always know where the work is coming from and are dependent for their supply of work on their local intermediary, with little or no bargaining power as they are scattered throughout the area.

In Tamil Nadu, there are thousands of female home-workers stitching shoes at home, mostly found in the footwear production centre Ambur. These women labourers working at home experience extreme insecurity, receive very poor wages and have no health or safety protection. *They can earn Rs. 96 a day assuming an 8-hour day, which is far below the minimum wage set at Rs. 126.48 a day in 2016 in Tamil Nadu.* Some women complete a pair in 20 minutes, while others take one hour for one pair, on average it takes half an hour per pair of shoes. Assuming it takes half an hour to complete one pair, eight hours work would then be paid 96 rupees at 6 rupees a pair, well below the minimum wage. In reality, most women combine the work with household tasks and report that they earn *Rs. 50 or 70 in one day.*[131] There is no job security at all, as they are dependent on 'middlemen' who bring the cut pieces material to their homes and collect the finished work to return to the companies. Whoever demands a higher wage, runs the risk that they will no longer receive the work from these 'middlemen'.

The women combine their paid work with numerous unpaid household tasks. They all work long hours when both 'jobs' are taken into account. But with low piece rates, there is constant pressure to work long hours to cover basic family expenses. At other times, there is an urgent deadline that the intermediary needs to meet. A home-worker says:

> Sometimes (I wake up) at 6 am and sometimes at 7 am. Sometimes they give us the pieces the previous night and say it is urgent. They wake up at 4 am but I wake up only at 6 am. I cannot wake up early so at times I work late at night. But when I do so, I cannot work the next day, my fingers are swollen. *After I complete a pair, it takes about an hour for my hands to return to their normal condition.* So I do not take on any urgent work. I finish work by 11 pm.... No way stitching this upper is a good work at all. We will develop pain in the chest. Our hands will get infected because of the germs in the leather. I also developed fibrosis because of this work. Say, for example, if you give me something to eat while I am working, and then I take it and put it into my mouth, will I not get infected? This is leather, is it not? And it has a lot of chemicals.[132]

Workers in the leather industry are denied to be unionized. In Tamil Nadu across the Vaniyambadi-Ambur area, there is severe restriction of unionization and union activities of workers within the workshop premises. Union activities mostly take place outside the units. In Kolkata in West Bengal leather workers are denied to organize in unions often with open threats. In the Kasba Industrial Estate, the security guards prevent outsiders from entering the main complex and the units. Union leaders cannot enter the factory premises and have to meet workers outside. Workers are afraid of losing their jobs if they protest or join unions. By law workers are free to join any union, but if they engage in union activities at the workplace or voice union demands, it often leads to suspension, dismissal, police cases, and so on.

Working Conditions in Other Sectors

The working conditions in the automobile, garment and leather sectors vividly depict the precarious state of the workers in India in general. But it is in fact the tip of the iceberg. Understandably, in other industries and sectors also, in the same type of sub-human, exhausting and abusive workplaces workers have to do tedious jobs with extreme workload, long work-hours, forced overtime at the single rate, paltry wages, and live in hell-like places and so on. In almost all other industries workers can hardly reproduce their labour-power in these torturous work-conditions and low wages. Extreme dangerous work-conditions are found in mining and quarrying operations and ship-breaking activities in India where severe industrial and occupational hazards are common. In many industries like carpet, jute, tea, construction, manufacture of bricks the workers have to struggle to work and live in a condition reminiscent of the 'industrial age' in England which Engels narrated in his path-breaking book *The Condition of the Working Class in England*. Moreover, thousands of child labourers are engaged in many activities where even five-year-old children are forced to perform dangerous and 'illegal' work. It is to be noted that most of these sectors are though export-driven, all of them are not necessarily integrated with the global supply chain.

Mining and Quarrying

India produces 89 minerals by operating 569 coal mines, 67 oil and gas mines, 1,770 non-coal mines, and several more small mines, running into over a lakh.[133] Overall the mining and quarrying sector contributes 5 per cent of India's GDP. India is rich in coal reserves and according to the government estimate, India is the third largest producer of coal and lignite in the world. Coal is used for generating electricity and heating purposes and coal largely contributes to the 'development' of the Indian economy. But coal mining is one of the most dangerous activities (along with other mining operations) where every ten days a fatal accident occurred in 2015.[134] Moreover, thousands of children are involved in this deadly operation along with other rickety workers where the working conditions are horrible and though reduced to a certain extent compared to earlier decades, major accidents occur at regular intervals.

In the mineral-rich state of Jharkhand, 400,000 children aged between five to fourteen years are engaged in mining activities (mostly in coal mining) and armed with shovels and cane baskets, they tip-toe over the jagged surface, settle down in a corner and start digging a hole through rocks of solid coal. A few back-breaking hours later, their baskets fill up with pieces of coal that had been chipped away, and they hurry to the nearest market to sell their day's treasure. It is dangerous to work in the mines, particularly those that are underground where fatal cave-ins are frequently reported. But the penury of their parents (who are also working in some other mines) leaves the children with few choices.[135]

But the story does not end here. In the coalfields of Meghalaya, a state in the north-eastern part of India, hundreds of boys and men descend 65 metres (213 feet) into the underground coal mines through narrow tunnels dug into the side of the hills and extract coal which is exported to more developed states for use in lighting and heating purposes. These deep box mines and innumerable long tunnels—commonly known as 'rat holes'—are spread across the hilly region near Shillong, a picturesque city of north-east India. Nobody knows how many 'rat holes' are operating in this region; nobody knows how many children crawl every day in these narrow holes. The Meghalaya 'rat holes' are cut from limestone and sandstone, typically plunge 60 to 70 metres (197 to 230 feet) straight down to the coal seams at the black bottom. The hardest path down is to descend, step by step, on the makeshift ladders constructed from tree branches that drop at steep angles along the mine's four walls. During the summer monsoon the ladders get slick with rain and mud. Falls are common.

The children of Meghalaya's coal mines are especially vulnerable. Many are from outside the state, and are here on their own. They come from neighbouring Assam, or illegally over the border from Bangladesh and Nepal, sold—sometimes literally—on promises of good money, and less-than-truthful assurances about the nature of the work. They live in single-room shanties, with no electricity or running water, and little protection from the wind and rain. In winter it is near-freezing in these hills. One of them is Gayasuddin who is now 15, but has been mining since he was 12. "I do not like this work, but I have to do it," he says, breathing heavily with the effort. "If I do not work, how can I put food in my stomach?" Six days a week, for up to eight hours a day, Gayasuddin works crouched or lying flat in the tiny, claustrophobic tunnel, usually little more than half a metre high and up to 200 metres long. He works more than 30 metres underground, under a precarious, unknowably large tonnage of rock. Smaller and more flexible than his older colleagues, his job is to load the coal someone else has mined with a pick into the rickety cart and drag it back into the mine shaft. Two cartloads is a good day. It earns him about 500 rupees ($8.3), but leaves him exhausted.

It is Dickensian work, slow and labour-intensive, but for India, profitable. In spite of numerous laws on India's statute books banning children from working in mines, the industry employs tens of thousands of them in dark, difficult and dangerous conditions. They work without safety gear or supervision, in makeshift, flood-prone mines. If they are injured or killed, they are quickly replaced.[136]

Almost the same story will be found in case of mica mining concentrated in states like Jharkhand, Bihar, Rajasthan, and Andhra Pradesh. Mica is a key ingredient in products such as facepacks, mascara, eyeliner, lipstick, and nail polish. Moreover, mica gives automotive paints their shine, is used in building materials, and as an insulator in electronic chips. It is found in lasers and radar. Thus mica is invaluable in the beauty industry as well as in modern 'civilization'. India officially produces about 19,000 tonnes of crude and scrap mica a year, according to the government's Bureau of Mines. Unofficially India produces more mica coming from 'illegal' mines. India exported over 128,000 tonnes—nearly seven times the official production figure—in 2011-12, more than half of it to China and followed by Japan, the United States, the Netherlands and France. At least 12 MNCs are involved in the massive beauty industry and *at least 20,000 children* in Jharkhand and Bihar are engaged in mica mining adding glitter to natural cosmetics—which is bought by intermediaries and then exported to high-profile international customers such as L'Oreal and Estee Lauder. While the industry is economically unfeasible for advanced/ rich countries due to the need for manual labour, it remains a key earner in India where labour costs are extremely low—particularly when child workers are used.

In vast open-pits in Jharkhand, children as young as six squat among glittering rocks scouring with their bare hands for shiny, brittle mica flakes, while older ones descend rickety ladders into shafts seeking better quality silicate. In Giridih a woman worker sifts through the reddish earth searching for pieces of mica while her 10-year-old son climbs into a rat-hole dug in the side of the hill and descends 3 metres (10 ft) to pound on the wall with a pick-axe. His mother said the skinny boy has been working in the mines *since he was seven* and, with his contribution, the family earns *300 rupees ($4.6) daily*. Another boy fills the cracked plastic tray with mica flakes which can carry a kilogram. *He fills it 10 times a day. Each kilogram earns him five rupees, about 8¢*. Depending on its quality and type, mica on the international market can fetch anywhere from several dollars a kilogram to *more than $1000*.

The work is hard and dangerous. Children working long hours risk snake and scorpion bites, and the hollowed-out caves they mine in often collapse. They suffer cuts and skin infections, as well as respiratory illnesses, such as bronchitis, silicosis and asthma. Those who work at the mine are unaware of where their product ultimately ends up, and those who buy the mica are wilfully blind to where it comes from. It is like a mafia—there is a black market for this, there are subcontractors in each village who rely on these children's labour. But the miners do not know where the mica they mine ends up. They are the third, fourth, fifth layer in the supply chain, and the subcontractors and the suppliers deliberately do not tell them where it goes and how it is used.[137]

Silicosis is the most common disease in these dangerous mining zones. It is also found among the gemstones polishing workers. The National Labour Commission (NLC) published a report titled, "Hearts of Darkness," saying "Workers in India, including children, will die young grinding gemstones for Valentine's Day," explaining that:

- Since record-keeping began in 1988, over 2,000 men, women and children died from silicosis (by breathing silica dust), from polishing gemstones for export to the West.
- All workers inhale it on the job and experience other occupational hazards, including toxic chemicals exposure, ergonomic dangers, and high noise levels.
- Items made include semi-precious gemstone hearts, beads, pendants, earrings, bracelets, ornaments, rosary beads, and the Star of David.
- Workers are paid 17.5-33.5 cents an hour "to do one of the most dangerous jobs in the world," exposing themselves to deadly silica dust.
- They begin as young as 12 or 13 (some younger), paid from 11 to 13.5 cents an hour.
- 30-38 per cent of them die from silicosis.
- Up to 13 per cent of non-working family members and neighbours, living near grinding units, also die from exposure to airborne silica dust; scores of others are reduced to skin and bones, unable to walk and struggling to breathe.

- Workers become "bonded labour" by borrowing money from "traders" who supply raw stones, and arrange for manufacture and export; wives are asked to continue their husbands' work if they die; then their children if they are incapacitated.
- With proper safeguards (including wet grinding and exhaust ventilation), silicosis is up to "100 per cent preventable;" without it, grinding gemstones is a death or disability sentence.
- The Indian government has done nothing to enforce its labour laws, in deference to its monied interests.[138]

Interestingly, these observations are made on Khambat, a gemstone processing centre on the soil of Gujarat—one of the most 'developed' states in India. Throughout the West, gemstones are widely distributed, in over 600 US bead stores alone, much supplied from India, consumers unaware of the human toll for their trinkets.[139]

According to the Indian Council of Medical Research (ICMR), more than three million people, mostly coal, manganese and zinc miners, were found to have silicosis. The disease was also found among workers at quarry sites and slate and glass units. A report by the Ahmedabad-based National Institute of Occupational Health (NIOH), under ICMR, said at least 10 million people in India are at risk from silicosis. Yet, these afflicted workers remain largely invisible in the records of the Labour Ministry.[140]

In the quarrying fields of granite in states like Andhra Pradesh, Telangana, and Karnataka same occupational hazards are common among the workers. India is a top producer and exporter of granite, widely used for wall and floor tiles, tombstones and kitchen tops in Western countries. Western governments are an important end-buyer of granite for buildings, pavements, public squares, etc. Half of the total world exports of raw granite originate from India. But this decorative and highly valued natural stone comes with a high price, mainly 'paid' by the workers. These three states account

Box: Salt Mining Leaves Bitter Taste for Indian Workers

In India's salt-producing area thousands of families—including children as young as 10—toil in the desert using a harvesting technique unchanged in centuries.

India is the world's third biggest producer of salt after China and the US, government figures suggest, and about 70 per cent of the 19 to 20 million tons it produces annually comes from the western state of Gujarat. In Little Rann of Kutch, a barren brown desert and local centre of inland salt production, an estimated 200,000 people work barefoot in extreme hardship, exposed to a relentless sun and serious occupational dangers.

Pola Degama and his wife have been raking salt in Gujarat's desert since they were children, digging wells to draw the briny groundwater to the surface then relying on evaporation to leave the white crystals. Several square salt pans lie next to the shack where his family of six lives.

"Because we work in the saltpans, our feet become septic and they absorb the salt. Nobody lives more than 50 or 60 years," he said. Even after death, he says, saltpan workers suffer an ignoble fate: *their hands and feet are difficult to burn during cremation because of the salt content.*

Wages are low and offer few chances for the children of saltpan workers to escape a cycle of poverty and poor health. Local traders buy low-quality crystals for as little as 50 US cents for 100 kilograms (220 pounds). Higher quality produce can sell for four to six US dollars for the same weight.

"We produce the most important food ingredient, but we are never given importance. Poverty is our fate," complained Daya Ranto, a 48-year-old father of three.

A study conducted by The National Institute of Occupational Hazards in 2000 found that eye problems and blindness were caused by the intense reflection of the sun from the water surface. Exposure to salt also causes skin lesions among the workers. The government provides inexpensive rubber boots and gloves to the salt workers, but they wear out quickly and are seldom replaced.

There is a saying here that if you are a saltpan worker, you have three ways to die: first gangrene, second TB (tuberculosis) or third blindness. In every house, people die this way.

[*Source:* Salt Mining Leaves Bitter Taste for Indian Workers, 24.02.10, http://www.telegraph.co.uk/expat/expatnews/7305988/Salt-mining-leaves-bitter-taste-for-Indian-workers.html, accessed 06.05.16] for 75 per cent of the granite production in India. Almost half the quarries have direct linkages with foreign importers. Other quarries also produce granite for export markets, but this is traded through intermediaries. Major importers of Indian granite are China, the USA and European countries, with Germany, Italy and the United Kingdom as the biggest buyers.

More than 70 per cent of the workforce in granite quarries is casual labourers employed on a daily wage or piece rate basis. With wage advances equivalent to a wage of one to three months, and high interest loans, the quarry owners have found a method to tie the workers to the job. Nearly 25 per cent of the workers, mostly in Telangana and Karnataka, are recruited by providing loans, with *annual interest rates of 24 per cent to 36 per cent*. In Telangana 42 per cent of the local workers and 58 per cent of the migrant workers report that they owe large sums of money varying from Rs. 10,000 to Rs. 20,000 to quarry owners or contractors. Substantial advances create debt bondage, as workers must clear the owed amount before they can change to another employer.[141]

In the quarrying of granites these casual labourers are mostly migrant workers. Seventy Five per cent of the migrant workers migrate from other states like Odisha, Rajasthan and Chhattisgarh, leaving behind their families. Migrants constitute 70 per cent of the total workforce in granite quarries in Andhra Pradesh and Telangana. Migrant workers are preferred over local workers as they are likely to be more *obedient, work longer hours and are more flexible* as they often have fewer social or family commitments. Migrants do not switch employers frequently and are *less likely to strike*. Workers, including migrants, mostly come from so-called 'lowest caste' of Dalits or Adivasis. They are extra vulnerable due to their low social status in the Indian society.[142]

Ship-Breaking Workers

One of the most deadly jobs is found on the coastline of Gujarat where thousands of workers break old ships imported from the advanced countries. Ship-breaking yards in Europe and elsewhere in the West have largely closed due to the high cost of health and safety measures and insurance for the workers. Most ship-breaking—nearly 90 per cent—is now done in Asian yards, including India, Pakistan and Bangladesh, *to take advantage of very low pay, poor conditions and the lack of safety regulations*. India's ship-breaking industry has had an annual turnover of 25 billion rupees, but competition is fierce.

Gujarat's Alang (known as 'Asia's ship graveyards') is the world's largest ship-breaking yard and employed up to 160,000 workers directly or indirectly in 183 different units. Besides the ship demolition there were many related businesses, including oil re-processing units, steel re-rolling mills, oxygen plants, transportation companies and a local scrap goods store. Unlike in Europe and the United States, where machines do most of the 'dirty' work, Asian shipyards often lack power tools. Workers there generally use little more than blow torches and hammers to scrap a ship. That is the reason why accidents are common at Alang. Pointing towards "inadequate protective measures", Deutsche Welle (DW), Germany's international broadcaster says, "No safety goggles, no steel-toed boots—scrapyard workers in Asia put their health at risk every day." How poorly does the workers' health safety system operates is clear from the fact that, says DW, "The nearest hospital in Alang, India, is 50 kilometres away. A modest first-aid station from the Red Cross can only provide sparse medical care."

The ships being broken up contain various toxic substances including asbestos, polychlorinated biphenyls (PCBs), lead, chromates and mercury, despite international treaties banning the export and transport of some of these substances. Alang's workers are not equipped or trained to deal with toxic chemicals. They are not informed of the dangers and possible long-term side effects and work without basic safety equipment, such as helmets, gloves, masks and boots. Most of them work with their bare hands and wear old slippers.

Most ship-breaking workers are immigrants from other Indian states including Odisha, Uttar Pradesh and Bihar and are on daily or monthly contracts. The workers are mostly employed by subcontractors known as 'muqadam'. The workers have no right to see the ship owner or government officials. Any infraction—including attempting to speak to a journalist or to form a trade union—can result in *dismissal*. Working hours are not fixed and regulated. Nominally the working day starts at 8 am and finishes at 7 pm but overtime is often required. *There is no extra pay for overtime or weekend work*. No canteen is provided. The subcontractors fix wages and hire and fire workers according to their needs. There is no paid leave and no guaranteed compensation in the event of an accident. Unskilled workers start on less than $US1 a day and skilled workers are paid a maximum of $US1.85 a day in the year 2006. Those who risk their lives undertaking the most dangerous work can get higher wages. Most employees live in rented shanties or small shacks built of scrap near the yard so they breathe in fumes day and night. There are no toilets or showers and no clean drinking water.[143]

Brick-Kiln Workers

The present Government of India is ushering in a new era where 40 new 'smart' cities will be developed. As the country runs along the so-called developmental track, more call centres, shopping malls, sky-kissing building projects, mammoth construction works, making of industrial corridors are in progress with break-neck speed. But this 'miraculous' boom comes at a price of the hapless brick-kiln workers.

India is the second-largest brick producer in the world, producing 200 billion bricks every year that comprises 13 per cent of global production. Despite its gargantuan size, the brick kiln sector of India remains largely unorganized. The brick industry is considered the industry of the poor, employing around ten million people directly and indirectly.[144]

A website reports:

> On the outskirts of Hyderabad, the sprawling capital of the southern Indian state of Andhra Pradesh, thick clouds of smoke hang above a primal scene of bare-footed workers

> clambering atop kilns, hacking at mounds of clay and hauling heavy loads. This is just one of over 150,000 brick production units in the country, which together employ an estimated 10 million workers, churning out the building blocks of the new offices and apartments, factories and shopping malls. All told, India's brick industry—the second largest in the world after China—contributes around £3bn to the country's economy every year. Not that the workers see much of that.
>
> "It is modern-day slavery," says Andrew Brady, of Union Solidarity International (USI), a UK-based NGO.... "Entire families of men, women and children are working for a pittance, up to 16 hours a day, in terrible conditions. There are horrific abuses of minimum wage rates and health and safety regulations, and it is often bonded labour, so they cannot escape."
>
> The six-month production season is now beginning, when tens of thousands of families flock to work in the brick kilns of Andhra Pradesh, mostly travelling from the state of Orissa. A report by the BBC this week discovered children *as young as four* smashing coal to fuel the kilns, and stories of labourers having their *hands cut off* when they tried to leave their jobs. The report found workers forced to produce over 1,500 bricks every day, paid in advance and only able to leave after six months, along with children suffering from severe respiratory problems.[145]

Usually, an entire family is involved in brick production and they get Rs. 400-500 for 1,000 bricks. Although the industry provides employment to a large number of people, it violates their rights as the labourers are underpaid and super-exploited. "The labourers become bonded after they take advance. They are physically tortured by the contractor if they wish to leave their job. Even their payments are stopped, making it hard for an entire family to survive," Sudhir Kumar Katiyar, project coordinator of the Udaipur-based non-profit, Prayas Centre for Labour Research and Action, said at the dialogue.[146]

A recent study by the watchdog 'Anti-Slavery' reports the following precarious conditions in the brick-kiln industry:

Children:

- Children make a third of the total population in the brick kilns.
- 65 to 80 per cent of children between the ages of five to fourteen reported working in the brick kilns. They work an average of nine hours a day in the summer months and seven hours a day in winter.
- 100 per cent of older children interviewed (over the age of fourteen) reported working at the kiln. Children in this age group work on average 12 hours a day in summer months and 10 hours a day during the winter months.

Adults:

- 84 per cent of workers were paid a different rate to what had been agreed/promised at the beginning of the season.
- Workers reported on average fourteen hours a day in the summer months and 11 hours a day in the winter months.
- 100 per cent of brick moulders were from traditionally marginalized classes and castes.
- None of the women workers receive wages. Wages are paid to the male head of the household for the whole family. Women are not formally registered as workers and cannot access related employment benefits.
- 33 per cent of workers reported being paid less than the minimum wage for 1000 bricks. From those workers who thought they have been paid a minimum wage, vast majority did not know what the minimum wage rate is.
- The workers are never paid overtime, despite routinely working 5 hours over the daily legal limit.

Harmful Environment:

- 87.72 per cent of the kilns surveyed have access only to untreated ground water as drinking water, much of it polluted and sometimes not safe for drinking.

- 75.8 per cent of all toilet facilities had no water provided to them at all.
- Worksites have a large amount of dust and other chemicals present.
- Living conditions can be cramped, with average housing dimensions for entire families being 7.6 square metres. By law, it is required to be a minimum of 10 square metres.[147]

Lives in the Biggest Slum

At the edge of India's greatest slum, [in] Shaikh Mobin's decrepit shanty.... carpenters are assembling furniture on the ground floor. One floor up, men are busy cutting and stitching blue jeans. Upstairs from them, workers are crouched over sewing machines, making blouses. And at the top, still more workers are fashioning men's suits and wedding apparel. One crumbling shanty. Four businesses.

In the labyrinthine slum known as Dharavi are 60,000 structures, many of them shanties, and as many as 1 million people living and working on a triangle of land barely two-thirds the size of Central Park in Manhattan. Dharavi is one of the world's most infamous slums, a cliche of Indian misery. It is also a churning hive of workshops with an annual economic output estimated to be $600 million to more than $1 billion.

India is a rising economic power, even as huge portions of its economy operate in the shadows. Its 'formal' economy consists of businesses that pay taxes, adhere to labour regulations [sic!] and burnish the country's global image. India's 'informal' economy is everything else: the hundreds of millions of shopkeepers, farmers, construction workers, taxi drivers, street vendors, rag pickers, tailors, repairmen, middlemen, black marketeers and more. This divide exists in other developing countries but it is a chasm in India: Experts estimate that the informal sector is responsible for the overwhelming majority of India's annual economic growth.

For years, India's government has tried with mixed success to increase industrial output by developing special economic zones to lure major manufacturers. Dharavi, by contrast, could be called a self-created special economic zone for the poor. It is a visual eyesore, a symbol of raw inequality that epitomises the failure of policy makers to accommodate the millions of rural migrants searching for opportunities in Indian cities. It also underscores the determination of those migrants to come anyway.

The streets smell of sewage and sweets. There are not enough toilets. There is not enough water. There is not enough space. Labourers sleep in sheds known as pongal houses, six men, may be eight, packed into a single, tiny room—multiplied by many tiny rooms. Hygiene is terrible. Diarrhoea and malaria are common. Tuberculosis floats in the air, spread by coughing or spitting. Dharavi, like the epic slums of Karachi, Pakistan, or Rio de Janeiro, is often categorised as a problem still unsolved, an emblem of inequity pressing against Mumbai, India's richest and most glamorous city. A walk through Dharavi is a journey through a dank maze of ever-narrowing passages until the shanties press together so tightly that daylight barely reaches the footpaths below, as if the slum were a great urban rain forest, covered by a canopy of smoke and sheet metal.

Traffic bleats. Flies and mosquitoes settle on roadside carts of fruit and atop the hides of wandering goats. Ten families share a single water tap, with water flowing through the pipes for less than three hours every day, enough time for everyone to fill a cistern or two. Toilets are communal, with a charge of two rupees to defecate. Sewage flows through narrow, open channels, slow-moving streams of green water and garbage.

At the slum's periphery, Sion Hospital treats 3,000 patients every day, many from Dharavi, often children who are malnourished or have asthma or diarrhoea. Premature tooth decay is so widespread in children that doctors call them dental cripples. "People who come to Dharavi or other slum areas—their priority is not health," said Dr. Pallavi Shelke, who works in Dharavi. "Their priority is earning."

The order was for 2,700 briefcases, custom-made gifts for a large bank to distribute during Diwali. The bank contacted a supplier, who contacted a leather-goods store, who sent the order to a manufacturer. Had the order been placed in China, it probably would have landed in one of the huge coastal factories that employ thousands of rural migrants and have made China a manufacturing powerhouse.

In India, the order landed in the Dharavi workshop of Mohammed Asif. Asif's workforce consists of 22 men, who sit cross-legged beside mounds of soft, black leather, an informal assembly line, except that the factory floor is a cramped room doubling as a dormitory: The workers sleep above, in a loft. The briefcases were due in two weeks. "They work hard," Asif said. "They work from 8 in the morning until 11 at night because the more they do, the more they will earn to send back to their families. They come here to earn."

Today, more than 8 million people live in Mumbai's slums, according to some estimates, a huge figure that accounts for more than half the city's population. Many people live in slums because they cannot afford to live anywhere else, and government's efforts to build affordable housing have been woefully inadequate.

[*Source:* Dharavi: Self-Created Special Economic Zone for the Poor, http://www.deccanherald.com/content/216254/dharavi-self-created-special-economic.html, accessed 19.08.14]

Carpet Industry

India is the world's largest producer and exporter of handmade carpets in terms of value and volume. Around 75-85 per cent of carpets manufactured in India are exported. India is responsible for around 40 per cent of worldwide export of handmade carpets. Indian handmade carpets are exported to 73 countries in the world, the US being the largest importer.[148] The carpets are sold in the USA and all over the world in major retail chains like Macy's, Neiman Marcus, Bloomingdale's, Target, Sears, Crate & Barrel, Williams-Sonoma, and so on. Forty six per cent of total hand-made carpets were imported by the United States from India in 2012 which amounts to a retail value between $1.8 and $3.1 billion. From 1991 to 2012, imports of carpets from India to the US grew 136 per cent.[149]

Nearly 2 million workers are engaged in the carpet sector of India; out of which approximately 900,000 are *forced labour* and approximately 400,000 are *child labour* and most of them are either of minority communities or lower castes. The industry is mainly concentrated in Uttar Pradesh and Madhya Pradesh where the workers toiled in sub-human conditions. One investigation observes:

- Factories and shacks were cramped, filthy, unbearably hot and humid, imperilled with stray electrical wires and rusty nails, filled with stagnant and dust-filled air, and contaminated with grime and mould. Some sites were so filthy, pungent, and dangerous that the researchers were afraid to enter owing to the risk to their safety.... Physical and verbal violence against the workers was all too common.
- Carpet weavers, especially children, face numerous health ailments as a result of hazardous working conditions, particularly in situations of severe labour exploitation. Forced labourers and those in similar conditions are often coerced to work twelve or more hours a day, allowed to eat only two meals a day, live and sleep in the same place as they work, suffer beatings and abuse, and are frequently injured with the sharp claw tool or scissors used in the weaving process.... Even in supposedly lawful looms that pay a reasonable wage and do not coerce adults or children, the conditions in the workplace are exceedingly dangerous, filthy, and pose serious health risks to the carpet weavers and their families. Infants are often present, inhaling thread-dust all day, and children of adult workers may play in the looms amid stray electrical wires, rusty tools, and exposed nails. In several cases, researchers saw young women weaving while babies slept in their laps, exposing the infants at a minimum to substantial risks of pulmonary ailments.
- Earning between $0.37 and $0.50 per hour for exceedingly painstaking, tedious, harmful work such as carpet weaving is not only far too little given the nature of the work, it is also completely inadequate to meet the basic needs of even the most modest rural worker. Individuals who receive full wages report still having insufficient income for basic food, fuel, and shelter, leave alone savings for life rituals or emergencies. Underpayment of wages revealed significant divisions between wages paid to males and females, as well as adults and minors. Adult

males were paid on average $1.92 for an eight-hour day ($0.24 per hour) and adult females were paid an average of $1.69 for an eight-hour day ($0.21 per hour). Minors were of course paid less, with minor females being paid an average of $1.46 per eight-hour day ($0.18 per hour) and minor males being paid an average of $1.31 per eight-hour day ($0.16 per hour).

- The brutish, hazardous, and deeply exploitative conditions are a direct result of poverty, corruption, intransigence, and a wilful disregard for the humanity of minority and low caste workers at the bottom of the supply chain. Indeed, the conditions faced by the workers in India's hand-made carpet sector offer a glimpse into the conditions of extreme distress, disenfranchisement, and exploitation faced by all of India's marginalized and vulnerable populations.[150]

Tea Industry

India is the second largest tea producer after China in the world, with the production of 1.2 million metric tons in 2014. It was ranked fourth in terms of tea exports in 2014-15, with a value of US$ 619.96 million. At the same time, India is also the world's largest consumer of black tea, with a domestic market consumption of 911 million kilograms of tea in 2013-14. Tea production in 2013-14 was led by Assam (304.40 thousand hectares), followed by West Bengal (140.44 thousand hectares), Tamil Nadu (69.62 thousand hectares) and Kerala (35.01 thousand hectares). The supply chain of tea from production to consumption is long and complex and involves several controlling intermediaries who add value along the line. Around *85 per cent of world tea production is sold by a few multinational corporations* which have enormous marketing skill and influence. At present, global tea trade is dominated by the following four corporations: Unilever (which produces Lipton and PG Tips), Tata Tea (which produces Tetley), Van Rees (a tea trading company) and James Finlay (a tea packing company).

The industry employs over 3.5 million people across some 1,686 estates and 157,504 smallholdings. In Assam and West Bengal, the two main tea growing regions of India, tea plantation workers are mostly Adivasis. The current average daily wage is *Rs. 115 in Assam and Rs. 122 in West Bengal*. By comparison, the minimum wage for an unskilled agricultural worker in India is Rs. 222, almost twice as much as what female tea workers are paid (though the minimum wage fixed by the government is also abysmally low). Furthermore, on an average, a tea plantation has around 30 to 40 per cent of permanent workers, and the rest are *casual* workers—which are also made up of a higher proportion of *women*—who receive daily wages but little or almost no benefits. There is also *child labour*. These tea plantation workers exclusively depend on wage payment (cash and food rations) and welfare schemes (such as housing, medical facilities, schools, etc.), which are provided by plantation owners, in order to sustain their livelihoods and ensure their limited access to food and nutrition. Despite generations having lived in the same estate and same house during a span of 200 years, tea workers have still not been given any right to their homestead. They can be evicted at any moment by the management from their houses if they protest about their conditions of work or if they refuse to work for the pittance wages that the employer pays. Thus, while men may migrate to better paid jobs, one or more of the women in a family will continue to work on the estate, just to retain possession of the house. This means that the workers are actually working as *bonded labourers*. The lack of alternative employment near the estate makes the bondage situation even worse.[151]

Workers commenting on the lack of flexibility in their working hours said that since 2012 or 2013, the working hours have been set from 8 am to 4 pm. This time excludes commuting time and time spent weighing leaves, for which workers are not paid. Workers said that the time spent travelling to and from work as well as time spent queuing to weigh the leaves that were picked during the lunchtime hour is a significant amount of time that takes up the space of other activities and should be counted as working hours. In line with this, workers observed that there is never any time to rest during the day, primarily because the weighing of tea leaves takes place either during lunch or after working hours. Before the wage increase, the task entailed picking 21 kgs of tea leaves; however, under the new wage, they are required to pick 24 kgs in the same amount of time. If the amount picked is less, their wage is deducted by Rs. 1 for each kg picked.

The percentage of profit made from the tea industry, particularly by the big multinational traders is massive. Out of the profits gained, the retailer (e.g. supermarkets) grabs 53 per cent, blender (e.g. Typhoo, Tetley) 33 per cent, factory 7 per cent, trader/buying agent 6 per cent, tea auction/brokers 1 per cent and the tea pickers get *only 0.16 per cent*.[152]

Most of the tea workers and their families live in a situation very similar to bonded labour, in precarious housing, many times exposed to extreme weather conditions, and to contaminated water, in different degrees of food and nutritional insecurity. Both tea garden and domestic work are hard, extensive and unsafe, in particular for pregnant and lactating women. All these conditions increase the vulnerability to diseases, which in turn place an added nutritional burden and lead to further loss of working days and income. In breach of Indian law, medical facilities are either not available within the plantation or inadequate. Plantation hospitals and dispensaries are understaffed, run-down, and do not provide proper treatment. Free medication is not provided to all the workers, and especially casual workers are discriminated against in accessing medical facilities. Due to the non-availability of medical facilities within the plantation (or within the vicinity), workers are forced to visit state-owned hospitals which are usually at a distance, thus paying extra money for the journey and medication and further exhausting their subsistence. These situations further affect the ability of the workers to feed themselves, and therefore lead to further aggravation of health status. Very often, there is either a lack of adequate potable water (both in quality and quantity) or a total lack of potable water at the labour lines as well as at the plantations. The management often fails to provide toilet/latrines at the labour lines and at work. Mixing of chemicals is done near the tube well/water pumps, thus eventually contaminating the sources of drinking water.[153]

A joint investigation by Radio 4's File on Four and BBC News in Assam observes that tea workers live in broken houses with terrible sanitation. Many families have no toilets and say they have no choice but to defecate amongst the tea bushes. They observe:

> Living and working conditions are so bad, and wages so low, that tea workers and their families are left malnourished and vulnerable to fatal illnesses. Homes on the tea estates were in terrible disrepair, with leaking roofs and damp and cracked walls. Many toilets are blocked or broken. Workers said their homes were not repaired despite repeated requests to management, often over many years. The drains are open and unlined and many clogged with effluents. In some cases, cesspits overflow into the living areas of people's homes. Many homes have no electricity, and on one estate workers had to drink rainwater piped from a stream.
>
> Many Indians live in dismal housing, but Indian law says decent housing and sanitation are part of a tea worker's pay. This is the justification plantation owners give for the extremely low wages in the industry. Tea workers in Assam earn 115 rupees a day, just over £1 ($1.8), significantly below the minimum wage (177 rupees in Assam). This combination of appalling conditions and low pay on tea plantations is deadly. Studies have confirmed levels of malnutrition on tea estates are very high, even by India's woeful standards. Nine out of 10 patients from tea plantations are malnourished, according to the medical director of Assam Medical College, one of the main general hospitals serving the tea region.
>
> Professor A.K. Das says malnutrition makes tea workers and their families vulnerable to diseases caused by their unhygienic living conditions. "Diseases of poverty" are common, he says, with many patients coming in with diarrhoea, respiratory tract infections, skin lesions and serious infections like TB and meningitis. He describes a

> tragic cycle: children come in so weak from malnutrition they struggle to recover from curable illnesses, and then quickly relapse after they are released from hospital. As a result, Prof. Das says, tea workers' children—and their parents—are significantly more likely to die of their illnesses than other patients at the hospital.[154]

Such precarious working conditions are prevalent in other industries and sectors as well. Even in heavy and big industries, where automation does a large part of the work apart from manual labour of the workers, the tremendous work-speed and work-load, long work-hours, use of hazardous chemicals, etc. make the working conditions appalling. Whether the sectors are integrated with Global Supply Chains or not—it is iterated in many cases—a Dickensian age of industrial England still prevails largely in the industrial zones and clusters all over India. It is not surprising that the fruits of these precarious, tedious, inhuman jobs are expropriated by the MNCs and domestic corporate houses.

Notes

1. Statistics, *Economic and Political Weekly* (EPW), 18.04.15.
2. The Problem of Jobless Growth, 24.05.16, http://www.livemint.com/Politics/KB4m2LtxaZEpTrSo1yXJLI/The-problem-of-jobless-growth.html, accessed 22.06.16.
3. Modi's Mega 'Make in India' will bring in a lot of money but not enough jobs, 17.02.16, http://qz.com/620145/modis-mega-make-in-india-will-brings-in-lots-of-money-but-not-enough-jobs/, accessed 22.06.16.
4. India's jobless growth is undermining its ability to reap the demographic dividend, 29.04.16, http://indianexpress.com/article/opinion/columns/economic-survey-india-unemployment-2775236/, accessed 22.06.16.
5. India's job growth lowest since 2009: Where are the jobs PM Modi? 15.04.16, http://www.firstpost.com/business/where-are-the-jobs-mr-modi-2731002.html, accessed 22.06.16.
6. http://www.hindustantimes.com/india-news/three-years-of-modi-govt-job-creation-promise-falls-short-as-unemployment-rate-up/story-NiJ519kWe56MjNCfMtgEeO.html, accessed 04.07.17.
7. Centre for Monitoring Indian Economy (CMIE), https://www.cmie.com/kommon/bin/sr.php?kall=warticle&dt=2017-07-11%2011:07:31&msec=463, accessed 05.11.17.

8. By Vinoj Abraham, *EPW*, Vol. 52, Issue No. 38, September 23, 2017, http://www.epw.in/journal/2017/38/commentary/stagnant-employment-growth.html, accessed 23.09.17.
9. Joblessness in India at 5-year high, reveals survey, 01.10.16, http://economictimes.indiatimes.com/jobs/joblessness-in-india-at-5-year-high-reveals-survey/articleshow/54622907.cms, accessed 06.10.16.
10. Growth and Prospects of Non-farm Employment in India: Reflections from NSS Data, Jajati Keshori Parida, *The Journal of Industrial Statistics*, 2015, http://mospiold.nic.in/Mospi_New/upload/JIS_2012/2_jisvl4_2_sept2015.pdf, accessed 21.03.17.
11. Over 8 million internal migrants, economic slowdown hits their flow, 01.02.17, http://indianexpress.com/article/business/economy/over-8-million-internal-migrants-slowdown-hits-their-flow-4501586/, accessed 03.02.17.
12. Report of the National Commission for Enterprises in the Unorganized Sector (NCEUS), Government of India, 2009.
13. An Analysis of the Informal Labour Market in India, A. Srija and Shrinivas V. Shirke, Confederation of Indian Industries (CII), www.ies.gov.in/pdfs/CII%20EM-october-2014.pdf, accessed 07.02.17.
14. Report of the Sub Committee of a NCEUS Task Force, National Commission for Enterprises in the Unorganized Sector, June 2008, GoI.
15. *Economic Survey, 2015-16*, Government of India.
16. What the economic census really tells us, 14.08.14, http://www.livemint.com/Opinion/VrXt0XflHkdtKiZKOcQa1J/What-the-economic-census-really-tells-us.html, accessed 12.03.17.
17. See Note 13.
18. Rise of contract workers in manufacturing, C.P. Chandrasekhar and Jayati Ghosh, 28.04.14, http://www.thehindubusinessline.com/opinion/columns/c-p-chandrasekhar/rise-of-contract-workers-in-manufacturing/article5956895.ece, accessed 29.04.16.
19. The Informality and Precarious Work in Production Chain Capitalism, Surendra Pratap and Annavajhula J.C. Bose, *Asian Labour Review*, Vol. 1, 2015, www.asianlabourreview.org, accessed 25.05.16.
20. 39 per cent rise in number of contract workers last year: Assocham, 05.02.14, http://www.thehindubusinessline.com/economy/39-rise-in-number-of-contract-workers-last-year-assocham/article5656643.ece?ref=relatedNews, accessed 29.04.16.
21. Ibid.
22. 21.01.15, http://scroll.in/a/736208, accessed 31.01.17.
23. With workforce in agriculture shifting to industry, contractualization of labour becomes a major factor both in Gujarat and across India, 28.03.14, https://counterview.org/2014/03/28/with-workforce-in-agriculture-shifting-to-industry-contractualization-of-labour-becomes-a-major-factor-both-in-gujarat-and-across-india/, accessed 31.01.17.
24. The casualization of organized labour, 10.11.17, http://www.livemint.com/

Money/WMJmHeto3P0ZgoPk7CjydI/The-casualization-of-organized-labour.html, accessed 10.11.17.

25. Move over India Inc, govt. relying on contract labour now, 21.08.14, http://www.financialexpress.com/news/move-over-india-inc-govt-relying-on-contract-labour-now/1281049/0, accessed 21.08.14.
26. Contract Workers in India's Organized Manufacturing Sector, A.K. Panigrahi, CSO, *The Journal of Indian Statistics*, 2016, http://mospiold.nic.in/Mospi_New/upload/JIS_2012/3ContractWorkers-in-India_Organized_Manufacturing_Sector.pdf, accessed 12.01.17.
27. Report of the 5th Employment-Unemployment Survey 2015-16, Vol. 1, Ministry of Labour and Employment, Government of India, http://labourbureaunew.gov.in/UserContent/EUS_5th_1.pdf, accessed on 12.01.17.
28. *Capital*, Vol 1, Karl Marx, p. 168.
29. *Imperialism in the Twenty-First Century*, John Smith, Dev Publishers and Distributors, New Delhi, pp. 197-98.
30. 'The Endless Crisis: How Monopoly Finance Capital Produces Stagnation and Upheaval from the USA to China', John Bellamy Foster and Robert McChesney, 2012, *Monthly Review Press*, New York, pp. 138-39.
31. Higher productivity equals higher wages? Not for the Indian industrial worker, 22.01.15, http://www.livemint.com/Opinion/Vxmd5HHO8qeLuqYUiobbpM/Higher-productivity-equals-higher-wages-Not-for-the-Indian.html, accessed 31.01.17.
32. See Note 26.
33. *The Challenge of Employment in India, An Informal Economy Perspective*, Vol. I, NCEUS, April, 2009, http://dcmsme.gov.in/The_Challenge_of_Employment_in_India.pdf, accessed 12.09.11.
34. See Note 27. It is noticed further that wage payments, as a percentage of the net value created by firms, have dropped from 30.3 per cent to 11.6 per cent over 30 years, as profits have increased from 23.4 per cent of the net value to 56.2 per cent, suggesting that firms have become more efficient, but wages have not risen in proportion with profits. [Down and out on India's shop floor, 29.07.12, http://www.thehindu.com/business/Industry/down-and-out-on-indias-shop-floor/article3697113.ece, accessed 28.01.17]
35. It is also reported that "For nearly 75 per cent of the 17.9 crore (nearly 180 million) households in rural India, the monthly income of a highest-earning member is less than Rs. 5,000, even as 40 per cent are landless, toiling as manual casual labourers, as per latest official data… Only 8.29 per cent of the rural households reported a member who was drawing more than Rs. 10,000 per month, while for 17.18 per cent others the monthly earning was between Rs. 5,000 and Rs. 10,000 per month." [In bulk of rural India, Rs. 5,000 is highest monthly wage, 04.07.15, http://www.news18.com/news/india/in-bulk-of-rural-india-rs-5000-is-highest-monthly-wage-1015585.html, accessed 05.05.16]

36. Workers grapple with low wages amid rising prices, 03.05.14, http://timesofindia.indiatimes.com/business/india-business/Workers-grapple-with-low-wages-amid-rising-prices/articleshow/34560075.cms, accessed 21.03.17.
37. In comparison, the capitalist class and the upper echelons of the society grab enormous wealth during the last three decades. A recent study shows that the top 1 per cent of earners captured only 6 per cent in the early 1980s which is risen to 22 per cent today. Over the 1980-2014 period, the top 0.1 per cent of earners captured a higher share of total growth than the bottom 50 per cent (12 per cent versus 11 per cent), while the top 1 per cent received a higher share of total growth than the middle 40 per cent (29 per cent vs. 23 per cent). [Income inequality in India at its highest level since 1922, says Lucas Chancel, 08.09.17, http://www.thehindu.com/opinion/interview/income-inequality-in-india-at-its-highest-level-since-1922/article19645881.ece, accessed 08.11.17]
    Oxfam Report finds in 2017 that 57 billionaires in India own as much as the bottom 70 per cent of the population and, more broadly, the richest one per cent holds 58 per cent of the country's total wealth—higher than the global average of 50 per cent. [Startling figures of inequality in India offer an incomplete picture, 08.08.17, https://economictimes.indiatimes.com/news/economy/policy/startling-figures-of-inequality-in-india-offer-an-incomplete-picture/articleshow/59968236.cms, accessed 08.11.17]
    And finally, the latest Oxfam report on inequality says that "India's richest 1 per cent garnered as much as 73 per cent of the total wealth generated in the country in 2017". On the contrary, "67 crore Indians, comprising the population's poorest half, saw their wealth rise by just 1 per cent in 2017." It has noted further that "the wealth of India's richest 1 per cent increased by over Rs. 20.9 lakh crore during 2017—an amount equivalent to total budget of the central government in 2017-18.... In India, it will take 941 years for a minimum wage worker in rural India to earn what the top paid executive at a leading Indian garment firm earns in a year, the study found." [Richest 1 per cent Cornered 73 per cent of Wealth Generated in India in 2017: Oxfam Survey, 22.01.18, https://thewire.in/216160/richest-1-cornered-73-wealth-generated-india-2017-oxfam-survey/, accessed 23.01.18]
38. President okays Rajasthan labour reforms: Firms with 300 workers need no govt. nod to sack, 08.11.14, http://www.business-standard.com/article/economy-policy/president-okays-rajasthan-labour-reforms-firms-with-300-workers-need-no-govt-nod-to-sack-114110801356_1.html, accessed 10.11.14.
39. Proposed Labour Law Reforms: Should we sacrifice democracy and well-being of people for FDI and high growth rate? 27.07.14, Surendra Pratap, http://sanhati.com/excerpted/10936/, accessed 18.11.14.
40. Hire and fire: Maharashtra factory owners with 300 employees can soon sack them without government nod, 10.11.17, http://www.

hindustantimes.com/mumbai-news/hire-and-fire-maharashtra-factory-owners-with-300-employees-can-soon-sack-them-without-govt-nod/story-kLl4tvPm4S4Y8G7aKcht5J.html, accessed 10.11.17.

41. Narendra Modi govt. set to unleash major labour reforms push, 07.03.17, http://www.financialexpress.com/economy/narendra-modi-govt-set-to-unleash-major-labour-reforms-push/577741/, accessed 05.05.17. (The proposed draft code is so much complex and elaborate that discussion on this subject becomes out of purview of this book.)
    Moreover, "The Labour Ministry introduced the Code on Wages Bill 2017 in the Lok Sabha on August 10.... The Code seeks to replace the four existing laws relating to wages—the Payment of Wages Act, 1936; the Minimum Wages Act, 1948; the Payment of Bonus Act, 1965; and the Equal Remuneration Act, 1976.... The first obvious problem is that the Bill makes a mockery of the idea of a 'national minimum wage' by providing for different national minimum wages to be fixed for different states—instead of providing for a uniform national minimum wage for the entire country.... Hence, the 'national minimum wage'—even as the phrase is repeatedly used—is reduced to a 'state-level minimum wage'." [Trade Unions Reject the Wage Code Bill 2017, 15.09.17, https://newsclick.in/trade-unions-reject-wage-code-bill-2017, accessed 02.11.17]
42. Changes in labour law will affect half of all factories, 14.08.14, http://indianexpress.com/article/india/india-others/changes-in-labour-law-will-affect-half-of-all-factories/, accessed 19.08.14.
43. Ibid.
44. Ad hocism in the Decisions to Modify Labour Laws, K. Chandru, *EPW*, Vol. XLIX, No. 30, July 26, 2014.
45. Labour Law Amendments: An Onslaught on Workers' Rights and Livelihood, 17.08.14, http://peoplesdemocracy.in/2014/0817_pd/labour-law-amendments-onslaught-workers%E2%80%99-rights-livelihood, accessed 18.11.14.
46. See Note 44.
47. LS passes Factories Amendment Bill to increase overtime hours for workers, 10.08.16, http://www.thehindu.com/news/national/LS-passes-Factories-Amendment-Bill-to-increase-overtime-hours-for-workers/article14562210.ece, accessed 22.12.16.
48. The Political Economy of Labour Law Reforms in India, Surendra Pratap, https://workerscentre.wordpress.com/2015/05/25/the-political-economy-of-labour-law-reforms-in-india-part-iii-2/, accessed 12.01.17.
49. *Imperialism in the Twenty-First Century*, John Smith, Dev Publishers and Distributors, New Delhi, p. 54.
50. Economic development and working conditions in export processing zones, ILO, 2008, http://citeseerx.ist.psu.edu/viewdoc/download?doi=10.1.1.490.1514&rep=rep1&type=pdf, accessed 02.11.17.
51. Trade Unions and Special Economic Zones in India, ILO, March 2012, http://www.ilo.org/wcmsp5/groups/public/---ed_dialogue/---actrav/documents/publication/wcms_221002.pdf, accessed 12.01.17.

52. *Economic Survey 2016-17*, Government of India.
53. SEZs: The New War Zones of Working Class in India, Surendra Pratap, Centre for Workers Education, 2010, https://workerscentre.files.wordpress.com/2011/07/sezs-the-new-war-zones-of-working-class-in-india.pdf, accessed 12.01.17.
54. Ibid.
55. See Note 51.
56. See Note 53.
57. Ibid.
58. See Note 51.
59. Exports need to grow at 26.5 per cent annually for India to grab 5% share of the world trade, 12.08.17, http://www.thehindubusinessline.com/economy/policy/exports-need-to-grow-at-265-annually-for-india-to-grab-5-share-of-the-world-trade/article9814384.ece, accessed 24.11.17.
60. China's proportion of global exports rose to 13.8 per cent last year from 12.3 per cent in 2014, data from the United Nations Conference on Trade and Employment shows, the highest share any country has enjoyed since the United States in 1968. [China seizes biggest share of global exports in almost 50 years, 22.04.16, https://www.reuters.com/article/us-china-exports/china-seizes-biggest-share-of-global-exports-in-almost-50-years-idUSKCN0XJ097, accessed 24.11.17] It is to be noted also that IT and IT enabled services, not the manufacturing sector, occupy a major part of the India's export basket. Interestingly, the IT and IT enabled services exports are decreasing in the recent years. According to Reserve Bank of India data the rate of growth of the combined exports of software and IT-enabled services has fallen from 20.8 per cent in 2012-13 to 14.9 per cent in 2014-15 and to a low of 7.3 per cent in 2015-16. [The imbalance that underlies India's software success, 13.04.17, http://www.thehindubusinessline.com/opinion/columns/c-p-chandrasekhar/indias-software-exports-and-rising-hardware-imports/article9582278.ece#, accessed 24.11.17]
61. According to the World Bank, India's manufacturing sector has grown only steadily in recent years, with the GDP share of the manufacturing sector rising from 15 per cent in 2000 to 17 per cent in 2015. According to WTO figures, India's exports totalled US$322 billion in 2014, only 1.7 per cent of the world's total exports. This was dwarfed by China's exports of US$2.4 trillion, which accounted for 12.7 per cent of total world exports. In 2014 India's exports comprised many traditional light manufactures, like jewellery and garments, though high-tech manufactures, including engineering goods, were also increasing. [20.06.16, http://economists-pick-research.hktdc.com/business-news/article/Research-Articles/Make-in-India-An-Alternative-Production-Base-with-a-Huge-Local-Market/rp/en/1/1X000000/1X0A50ME.htm, accessed 20.03.17]
62. 25.10.11, http://pib.nic.in/newsite/PrintRelease.aspx?relid=76843, accessed 26.11.17.

63. Make in India: Government gives shape to five industrial corridors, 11.05.15, http://economictimes.indiatimes.com/news/economy/policy/make-in-india-government-gives-shape-to-five-industrial-corridors/articleshow/47173937.cms, accessed 29.12.16.
64. Post-Fordism, Global Production Networks and Implications for Labour: Some Case Studies from National Capital Region, India, November 2014, Praveen Jha and Amit Chakraborty, Institute for Studies in Industrial Development, http://isid.org.in/pdf/WP172.pdf, accessed 12.01.17.
65. http://www.indianeconomy.net/splclassroom/210/the-delhimumbai-industrial-corridor-dmic-project/, accessed 30.12.16.
66. 02.04.16, http://www.dmicdc.com/newsdetail.aspx?mpgid=40&pgidtrail=41&Eventsid=28, accessed 30.12.16.
67. A website writes: Prime Minister Narendra Modi has claimed the bullet train offered to India by Japan is virtually free of cost. A 50-year yen loan amounting to Rs. 88,000 crore at 0.1 per cent interest is being described by the Prime Minister as free of cost. This is patently absurd.... For one, India may have to repay much more than Rs. 88,000 crore over a 50-year period because the rupee will most likely depreciate against the Japanese yen over a long period.

    Why is this? Simply put, it is because the exchange rate between the currencies of two countries is determined by their inflation differential. If India's inflation rate is average 3 per cent over the next two decades and Japan's inflation rate is zero, as is widely anticipated, then it stands to reason that the rupee must depreciate 3 per cent every year because the rupee's value is eroding by 3 per cent as against no erosion in the yen. So, the rupee is bound to weaken by over 60 per cent in two decades. This means that on a loan of Rs. 88,000 crore, the repayment, in rupee terms, goes up to more than Rs. 1,50,000 crore at the end of 20 years.

    As is being anticipated, if the Japanese build three more such projects connecting other cities in the south, north or east, one can well imagine the total foreign debt burden that will arise. After all, the loans will have to be paid back with the exchange risk built into it. The yen is considered the most volatile currency among all the hard currencies today.

    Another factor to be considered is that while an interest rate of 0.1 per cent may appear free from an Indian perspective, it is not so in Japan. Japanese short-term interest rate (Tokyo Inter Bank Offer Rate) is 0.06 per cent. The interest rate offered by ten-year Japanese government bonds is 0.04 per cent. India's ten-year government bond offers 6.5 per cent. The gap between Japan's 0.04 per cent and India's 6.5 per cent is explained by the inflation expectations in the two countries. This perspective cannot be lost sight of. So what you pay back to Japan in rupee terms will be way higher than what you borrow. [15.09.17, M.K. Venu, https://thewire.in/177815/mumbai-ahmedabad-bullet-train-many-things-not-free/, accessed 02.11.17]

68. See Note 64.
69. The Informality and Precarious Work in Production Chain Capitalism, A Case Study of Automobile Industry in India, Surendra Pratap and Annavajhula J.C. Bose, *Asian Labour Review*, Vol. 1, 2015, https://asianlabourreviewdotorg.files.wordpress.com/2016/02/03-alr-v1_patrap.pdf, accessed 24.04.16.
70. SMEs in Auto Component Industry, http://test.dnb.co.in/SMEs/smes.asp, accessed 12.01.17.
71. 07.07.15, http://www.autocarpro.in/analysis-reports/india-auto-industry-million-skilled-workers-2022-8811, accessed 11.04.16.
72. See Note 69.
73. http://www.makeinindia.com/sector/automobiles, accessed 28.11.17.
74. http://www.ey.com/Publication/vwLUAssets/EY-making-india-a-world-class-automotive-manufacturing-hub-1/$FILE/EY-making-india-a-world-class-automotive-manufacturing-hub.pdf, accessed 28.11.17.
75. November 2017, https://www.ibef.org/industry/india-automobiles.aspx, accessed 28.11.17.
76. https://openknowledge.worldbank.org/bitstream/handle/10986/25119/108826revdOctober2016.pdf?sequence=5&isAllowed=y, accessed 28.11.17.
77. See Note 71.
78. 17.08.16, http://www.livemint.com/Companies/E1c3nEBpJkD8I4YFl1RrPN/Maruti-Suzuki-steps-up-hiring-of-contract-workers.html, accessed 28.11.17.
79. 07.03.17, https://auto.economictimes.indiatimes.com/news/passenger-vehicle/cars/maruti-suzuki-set-to-cross-15-lakh-production-milestone-this-fiscal/57751171, accessed 28.11.17.
80. 16.10.12, http://profit.ndtv.com/news/auto/article-marutis-manesar-plant-to-produce-2-000-cars-per-day-by-november-end-312115, accessed 28.11.17.
81. http://www.marutisuzuki.com/manufacturingfacilities.aspx, accessed 31.01.17.
82. Driving Force: Labour Struggles and Violation of Rights in Maruti Suzuki India Limited, PUDR, May 2013, http://pudr.org/content/driving-force-labour-struggles-and-violation-rights-maruti-suzuki-india-limited, accessed 14.10.16.
83. Chronicle of a Disaster Foretold? Rahul Varman, Infochange News & Features, August 2012, http://infochangeindia.org/corporate-responsibility/analysis/chronicle-of-a-disaster-foretold.html, retrieved from http://doccentre.net/cc/cc_labour_strikes.pdf on 14.10.16.
84. Speed and Control at Manesar: Why is the Maruti-Suzuki Management Keeping Workers Out of Its Factory?, 06.09.11, Shuddhabrata Sengupta, http://kafila.org/2011/09/06/speed-and-control-at-manesar-why-is-the-maruti-suzuki-management-keeping-workers-out-of-its-factory/, accessed 14.10.16.
85. See Note 82.
86. Workers' problems: The more things change at Maruti's Manesar plant, the more they stay the same, 14.12.15, https://scroll.in/article/773241/

workers-problems-the-more-things-change-at-marutis-manesar-plant-the-more-they-stay-the-same, accessed 28.11.17.

87. http://www.moneycontrol.com/financials/marutisuzukiindia/profit-loss/MS24, accessed 28.11.17.
During turbulent years of the first decade when labour discontent is brewing in the Maruti-Suzuki Company, MSIL's annual sales have rocketed from around Rs. 900 crore in 2001-02 to over Rs. 36,000 crore in 2010-11, i.e. an increase of *400 per cent*. Profit after tax has increased from Rs. 105 crore in 2001-02 to Rs. 2,289 crore in 2010-11, i.e. an increase of almost *2200 per cent*! The annual remuneration of MSIL's CEO has increased from Rs. 47.3 lakh in 2007-08 to Rs. 2.45 crore in 2010-11. The annual remuneration of the Chairman of MSIL has also increased by 91.4 per cent during this period. [Workers' struggle in Maruti-Suzuki, Prasenjit Bose and Sourindra, 26.07.12, http://www.thehindu.com/opinion/op-ed/article2490903.ece, retrieved from http://doccentre.net/cc/cc_labour_strikes.pdf on 14.10.16]
88. The Strife Within, 17.07.16, http://www.businesstoday.in/magazine/features/labour-trouble-continues-to-torment-automobile-companies/story/234237.html, accessed 28.11.17.
In Bajaj Auto's Chakan plant in Pune, 900-odd permanent workers, tired of excessive workloads, arbitrary changes to their shift timings and constant bargaining over low yearly increments, decided to form a union. The labour cost of a Bajaj motorcycle that costs, say, Rs. 70,000, is barely Rs. 300, according to the union's calculations. The management itself says their employee costs constitute only 3 per cent of sales. [06.08.13, http://mumbaimirror.indiatimes.com/mumbai/other/union-jacked/articleshow/21636998.cms?, accessed 28.01.17]
89. Workers exposed to accidents in tier III auto component industry, 06.10.15, http://www.business-standard.com/article/companies/workers-exposed-to-accidents-in-tier-iii-auto-component-industry-115100600954_1.html, accessed 07.09.16.
90. How India's cars have been built on an assembly line of broken fingers, 02.12.14, http://qz.com/304784/how-indias-cars-have-been-built-on-an-assembly-line-of-broken-fingers/, accessed 07.09.16.
91. See Note 64.
Aliyar in Manesar, once a village of around 500 peasant families, is now an ad hoc workers' colony. Several villagers have converted their homes into multi-storeyed buildings, with eight to ten small rooms on each floor that they rent out. Several accommodations lack windows. Each toilet is usually shared between 20 to 25 residents. A few spacious, well-lit rooms are available but only the better-paid, permanent workers can afford them. At his home near the entrance of the village, Ishwar Chand, the sarpanch of Aliyar, said he supported the management in any conflict with workers because the villagers were financially dependent on the company. Chand owns a building with 50 small rooms, which he leases to workers at a monthly rent of Rs. 2,000. Along

with his two sons, he owns 40 commercial vehicles that ferry material to the company; they also operate six *theka*, or alcohol stores, in Aliyar, Dhana and Baskuda villages at the periphery of the workers' colonies. [14.12.15, https://scroll.in/article/827506/donald-trump-as-president-does-it-mark-a-rise-of-illiberal-globalism, accessed 26.01.17]

92. See Note 64.

    Hero Honda management chooses the 'right' candidate in the following manner who can be fit for work in the factory:

    "The Gurgaon plant has taken considerable trouble to recruit the right kind of individuals at the shop floor level. The personnel manager at the Gurgaon plant told the researcher that apart from technical knowledge he looked for honesty and earnestness in the candidates. Moreover the integrity of the candidate, past record of alcoholism, vandalism and involvement in union activity is given due consideration. The department has therefore ventured into a time consuming policy of background checks. A candidate's background is given a thorough checking by contacting his previous employer. Moreover, someone from the plant goes and meets the employees in his previous company, as well as gathers information about him from nearby shops and tea stalls. Hero Honda management supports this sentiment and even rejects a candidate with very good qualifications, if he is found to have some past history of unionism." [Gurgaon Workers' News, Newsletter 4, June 2007, https://gurgaonworkersnews.wordpress.com/, accessed 10.10.07]
93. See Note 82.
94. Quoted in *Southern Insurgency: The Coming of the Global Working Class*, Immanuel Ness, Pluto Press, 2016, p. 87.
95. Why Are India's Automobile Workers in Jail? 01.04.17, http://cpiml.org/commentary/why-are-indias-automobile-workers-in-jail/, accessed 28.11.17.
96. In one of the tier II company in the automobile global value chain a permanent worker of Rico Auto Industries located in Gurgaon narrates the following story:

    "It is a big factory. After casting in iron and aluminium through machining, various parts of vehicles are made. The company has factories in Ludhiana, Dharuheda, Manesar. Rico Auto, Continental Rico, Magna Rico, FCC Rico…In these factories, work of Hero Honda, Maruti-Suzuki, Honda, Ford, General Motors, etc. is done. Work has to be performed standing and after 8½ hours duty, they force you to keep working. Even on the weekly rest day, shift workers have compulsory duty. Payment of overtime is at single rate. They keep increasing the production target and for not completing the production target, they harass us. Wages are said to be 5,500 but really 4,200 are given. Basic wages are low and there are various allowances. Leave Travel Allowance (LAA) money is cut from the wages each month and given at the end of the year when LAA is supposed to be provided by the company. In the canteen, bad food for more money. No arrangement for transport.

Despite many efforts, workers get tired of asking but many of the permanent workers also are not given the ESI card."

In the Neolite factory located in Gurgaon the workers' experiences are as follows:

"We work from 9 am till 9 pm, manufacturing light-systems for Maruti Suzuki, Eicher and Tata vehicles. We used to be paid Rs. 16 per hour, since July 2009 this has been reduced to Rs. 15.40. Over-time is also paid at this rate. We have to work on Sundays, too. If you take a day off, they kick you out. When they hire you, you have to work a day without being paid. If you are five minutes late they cut one hour of your wages. On one line 40 workers are employed, but there is only one fan. The heat causes a lot of distress. There is a cooler, but it does not work. If you tell them they say that the cooler stirs up dust which would damage the parts."

Workers of these tiers of industries face punishment for their fault in the assembly line in another factory of Napino Auto and Electronics Ltd located near Gurgaon:

"The worker was asked to get on a table, hold his ears, squat, and then stand up again-a form of discipline across northern India and known as the "murga" (rooster) employed mostly on errant schoolchildren by teachers and by policemen on small-time criminals." [Gurgaon Workers' News, No. 22, January 2010, https://gurgaonworkersnews.wordpress.com/, accessed 11.08.10]

97. See Note 69.
98. Ibid.
99. Developing Asia's garment and footwear industry: Recent employment and wage trends, October 2017, http://www.ilo.org/wcmsp5/groups/public/---asia/---ro-bangkok/documents/publication/wcms_581466.pdf, accessed 08.12.17.
100. November 2017, https://www.ibef.org/industry/textiles.aspx, accessed 08.12.17.
101. http://www.businesswire.com/news/home/20170926006822/en/BizVibe-News-Readymade-Garment-Industry-India-Enjoying, accessed 08.12.17.
102. See Note 100.
103. See Note 101.
104. Wages in Context in the Garment Industry in Asia: The Case of India, https://wageindicator.org/documents/publicationslist/publications-2016/wages-in-context-in-the-garment-industry-in-asia-the-case-of-india, accessed 08.12.17.
105. The Global Apparel Value Chain: What Prospects for Upgrading by Developing Countries? https://www.researchgate.net/publication/228150738_The_Global_Apparel_Value_Chain_What_Prospects_for_Upgrading_by_Developing_Countries, accessed 12.01.17.
106. Richer Bosses, Poorer Workers: Bangalore's Garment Industry, CIVIDEP, July 2009, www.indianet.nl/pdf/RicherBosses.pdf, accessed 01.05.16.

107. Maid in India: Young Dalit Women Continue to Suffer Exploitative Conditions in India's Garment Industry, SOMO & ICN, April 2012, https://www.somo.nl/wp-content/uploads/2012/04/Maid-in-India.pdf, accessed 01.05.16.
108. A huge underclass of ghost workers are making your shirts in their homes, 17.12.15, http://qz.com/494818/in-much-of-the-world-the-sweatshop-isnt-a-factory-its-someones-kitchen-floor/, accessed 01.05.16.
109. See Note 107.
110. Ibid. According to 'Committee of Concerned Citizen-Students and Youth' which conducted a fact-finding investigation in Tirupur in 2011, found that: "More than 800 workers have committed suicide in the last two years and the new district of Tirupur witnesses 20 suicide attempts every day! The workers of the textiles units of Tirupur were committing suicides and such a mass phenomenon could not but be the result of the conditions under which the working class of Tirupur worked and lived." [20 Suicide Attempts a Day—Tirupur, Tamil Nadu: Textile Workers in a Globalized Workplace, June 18, 2011, www.sanhati.com, accessed 26.06.11]
111. I Tried to See Where My T-Shirt Was Made, and the Factory Sent Thugs After Me, by Dana Liebelson, 29.11.13, http://www.motherjones.com/politics/2013/11/india-garment-factories-sumangali, accessed 02.05.16.
112. Ibid.
113. India's clothing workers: 'They slap us and call us dogs and donkeys', by Gethin Chamberlain, 25.11.12, http://www.theguardian.com/world/2012/nov/25/india-clothing-workers-slave-wages, accessed 18.08.14.
114. "We cannot talk about it": Factory workers for major fashion labels live confined by guards, 29.01.16, http://qz.com/605914/we-cannot-talk-about-it-factory-workers-for-hm-and-others-live-confined-by-guards/, accessed 02.05.16.
115. Fashionable and famous—at the garment worker's cost! By Suhasini Singh, April 2009, http://infochangeindia.org/agenda/occupational-safety-and-health/fashionable-and-famous-at-the-garment-workers-cost.html, accessed 19.08.14.
116. See Note 64.
117. Gurgaon Workers Newsletter 4, June 2007, https://gurgaonworkersnews.wordpress.com/, accessed 11.08.10.
118. Gurgaon Workers Newsletter, November 2009, https://gurgaonworkersnews.wordpress.com/, accessed 11.08.10.
119. Gurgaon Workers Newsletter 29, August 2010, https://gurgaonworkersnews.wordpress.com/, accessed 01.12.10.
120. Brief Guide to Garment Manufacturing and Child Labour in Garment Sector in India, http://globalmarch.org/sites/default/files/pub/Brief%20Guide-GarmentManufacturing&ChildLabour%20in%20GarmentSector%20in%20India.pdf, accessed 04.05.16.
121. Global Wage Trends for Apparel Workers, 2001-2011, Worker Rights

Consortium, July 2013, https://cdn.americanprogress.org/wp-content/uploads/2013/07/RealWageStudy-3.pdf, accessed 24.04.16.

122. Ibid.
123. Ibid.
124. 20 Suicide Attempts a Day–Tirupur, Tamil Nadu: Textile Workers in a Globalized Workplace, 18.06.11, www.sanhati.com, accessed 26.06.11.
125. Suppose the Government of India while giving the estimates of monthly wages means the official minimum wages in the states mentioned here. Interestingly these minimum wages fixed by Indian states (or the Government of India) and other Asian countries are in majority cases below the internationally recognized poverty level wage (i.e. poverty line). In countries like India, Sri Lanka, Vietnam, Pakistan and Cambodia, the minimum wage is below or around the UN-defined poverty line of US$2 a day. In China, Indonesia, and Thailand wages are marginally higher—US$2-4 a day—but the cost of living in these countries is higher. [Stitching a Decent Wage Across Borders, 2009, https://cleanclothes.org/resources/publications/afw.pdf, accessed 12.01.17]
126. http://www.makeinindia.com/sector/leather, accessed 28.11.17.
127. Do Leather Workers Matter? March 2017, ICN, http://www.indianet.nl/pdf/DoLeatherWorkersMatter.pdf, accessed 28.11.17.
128. Ibid.
129. Ibid.
130. Stitching Our Shoes: Home-Workers in South India, Homeworkers Worldwide, Labour Behind the Label and Cividep, March 2016, http://labourbehindthelabel.net/wp-content/uploads/2016/03/Homeworkers-Document-WEB.pdf, accessed 28.11.17.
131. In fact, the workers' wages make up *only 2 per cent* of the final price of the shoe, while the brands keep a quarter of the price and one third goes to the retailers. Moreover, the types of shoes made in India are generally sold in the UK market for between £50 and £100 if not more. [Do Leather Workers Matter? March 2017, ICN, http://www.indianet.nl/pdf/DoLeatherWorkersMatter.pdf, accessed 28.11.17]
132. See Note 130.
133. Safety concerns: Inside India's mines, a worker dies every 10 days, 01.06.16, http://indianexpress.com/article/business/business-others/safety-concerns-inside-indias-mines-a-worker-dies-every-10-days-2828182/, accessed 08.12.17.
134. Ibid.
135. Child miners: India's crying shame, 07.05.13, http://www.aljazeera.com/indepth/features/2013/05/20135582251240200.html, accessed 04.05.16.
136. Blighted lives of India's child coalminers, 19.04.13, http://www.smh.com.au/world/blighted-lives-of-indias-child-coalminers-20130419-2i4xt.html, accessed 04.05.16.

According to the 2001 census, there were 12.6 million child workers between the ages of five and 14 in India. In 2011, this number fell to 4.35 million. The National Sample Survey Office's survey of 2009-10 put the number at 4.98 million. Despite the fall, India has the highest incidence of adolescents in hazardous work in the world. [No country for a child, http://www.thehindubusinessline.com/specials/india-file/no-country-for-a-child/article9150522.ece, accessed 08.12.17]

Interestingly, the Child Labour (Prohibition and Regulation) Amendment Act, 2016, defines a 'child' as a person who has not completed 14 years of age, and an 'adolescent' as a person who is older than 14 but has not reached 18 yet. The Act prohibits the employment of children in any occupation and that of adolescents in hazardous occupations. The Act also calls for the imposition of fines on those who employ children. However, on closer reading, it would seem that the Act has not been … progressive. It has reduced the number of 'hazardous occupations' from 83 to just mining, explosives and the ones mentioned in the Factories Act, 1948. It also permits child labour in 'family-based enterprises' and allows a child to be 'an artist in an audio-visual entertainment industry'. It also does not define working hours but states that a child can work after school or during vacations. Despite constitutional provisions like Article 24 (which calls for the prohibition of employment of children below 14 years in hazardous occupations) or Article 21A and Article 45 (both of which call for compulsory education of children between the age of six and 14), the problems still persist. [Why Over 10 Million Children in India Are Working As Labour Despite 'Progressive' Laws, 09.08.17, https://www.youthkiawaaz.com/2017/08/child-labour-2/, accessed 08.12.17]

137. India's mica mines: The shameful truth behind mineral make-up's shimmer, 19.01.14, http://www.smh.com.au/national/indias-mica-mines-the-shameful-truth-behind-mineral-makeups-shimmer-20140118-311wk.html, accessed 04.05.16; Blood Mica: Deaths of child workers in India's mica 'ghost' mines covered up to keep industry alive, 08.08.16, http://in.reuters.com/article/india-mica-children-idINKCN10E0CV, accessed 25.08.16.
138. India's 'Hearts of Darkness'—Horrific Sweat Shops, 07.11.10, http://rense.com/general91/hor.htm, accessed 08.04.16.
139. Ibid.
140. Silicosis, the curse of Khambhat, 07.10.09, http://www.livemint.com/Home-Page/5fGuJN7WRSWrjRSnflbW3J/Silicosis-the-curse-of-Khambhat.html, accessed 15.08.12.

'Down to Earth' observes that: "One of the worst health hazards that miners engaged in stone quarrying, crushing, quartz mining, glass and ceramic manufacturing face is dust pollution. The deadly disease silicosis continues to silently kill hundreds of workers. Thousands of mine workers die before reaching the age of 40. It is also reported that 50 per cent of miners are found to be suffering from silicosis in any given age group.... A recent report on stone quarrying in Rajasthan (*The Times of India*, June 29, 2016) states that official figures for workers suffering from silicosis stand at 5,307 till April 2016 and 248 people have died between 2013 and 2016." [How many people die of silicosis in Indian mines? 13.07.16, http://www.downtoearth.org.in/blog/how-many-people-die-of-silicosis-in-indian-mines--54863, accessed 08.12.17]

141. A website observes: "India banned the practice of bonded labour in 1976, but the country is still home to 11.7 million bonded labourers, according to the ILO. The labourers may be working to pay off a loan from their employer, or a debt inherited from a relative." [India's children of bonded labourers use memories to rescue others, 24.10.16, http://www.livemint.com/Politics/iGcs6yH2uTuYrjPBaidFWI/Indias-children-of-bonded-labourers-use-memories-to-rescue.html, accessed 08.12.17]
142. The Dark Side of Granite, August 2017, http://www.indianet.nl/pdf/TheDarkSitesOfGranite-abstract.pdf, accessed 08.12.17.
143. Terrible conditions facing workers in Asian ship-breaking yards, 27.03.06, https://www.wsws.org/en/articles/2006/03/alan-m27.html, accessed 20.03.10.
144. Controversy over How Indian Brick Kilns Clean up Their Act, 22.06.16, https://thewire.in/44503/controversy-over-how-indian-brick-kilns-clean-up-their-act/, accessed 08.12.17.
145. Blood bricks: How India's urban boom is built on slave labour, 08.01.14, http://www.theguardian.com/artanddesign/architecture-design-blog/2014/jan/08/blood-bricks-india-urbanization-human-rights-slave-labour, accessed 02.05.16.
146. 'Brick kiln workers in India underpaid and exploited', 12.03.16, http://www.downtoearth.org.in/news/brick-kiln-workers-in-india-underpaid-and-exploited-48958, 08.12.17.
147. Appalling levels of slavery in India's brick kilns, September 2017, https://www.antislavery.org/report-slavery-india-brick-kilns/, accessed 08.12.17.
148. October 2017, https://www.ibef.org/exports/carpet-industry-in-india.aspx, accessed 08.12.17.
149. Tainted Carpets: Slavery and Child Labour in India's Hand-Made Carpet Sector, 2014, https://cdn2.sph.harvard.edu/.../Tainted-Carpets-Released-01-28-14.pdf, accessed 02.05.16.
150. Ibid.
151. A life without dignity—the price of your cup of tea, May 2016, www.fian.org/en/library/publication/a_life_without_dignity_the_price_of_your_cup_of_tea/, accessed 28.11.17.
152. Ibid.
153. Ibid. A study, while commenting on the tea workers of Darjeeling, shows that: "In the last decade more than 1,400 tea workers have died due to acute malnutrition and starvation. As recent as January 2013, 95 workers of the locked out Dheklapara Tea Estate in Dooars sent a letter to the Chief Minister of West Bengal seeking her "order" to kill themselves because they were suffering from acute starvation. The tea workers therefore are forced to languish till they die of hunger and malnutrition. Studies show that 70 per cent of the people of the closed tea gardens suffer from chronic energy deficiency III stage. In the gardens

affected by starvation death, it was found that workers and their families have Body Mass Index (BMI) identical to those populations affected by severe famine." [Behind the Beautiful Tea Gardens of India Lies This Invisible, Ugly Truth, 28.12.15, http://www.youthkiawaaz.com/2015/12/tea-plantation-workers-in-west-bengal/, accessed 02.05.16]

154. The bitter story behind the UK's national drink, 08.09.15, http://www.bbc.com/news/world-asia-india-34173532, accessed 08.04.16.

3
Workers in China: 'Global Assembly Hub'

> I feel like I am serving a prison sentence. The factory is forever pressing down on our heads and will not tolerate even the tiniest mistake. When working, we work continuously. When we eat, we have to eat with lightning speed. When I need to go to the bathroom, I have to try my hardest to control myself, to hold it in and not go. The security guards are like policemen watching over prisoners. We are really livestock and should not be called workers.
>
> —A worker in Dongguan Meitai,
> Keyboard Producing Factory, China

> But if a surplus labouring population is a necessary product of accumulation or of the development of wealth on a capitalist basis, this surplus-population becomes, conversely, the lever of capitalistic accumulation, nay, a condition of existence of the capitalist mode of production. It forms a disposable industrial reserve army, that belongs to capital quite as absolutely as if the latter had bred it at own costs.
>
> —Karl Marx, *Capital*

Two years after the death of Mao Zedong in 1978, the Chinese Communist Party (CCP) decided to integrate the Chinese economy with global capitalist market forces under the leadership of Deng. At first, they decollectivized the agricultural production and dismantled the commune-based system in a gradual manner transferring the land to the households. The abolition of the communes and instigation of the household responsibility system allowed some farmers to prosper in the richest zones, but it has left marginal producers increasingly exposed to low prices, poor soils, small plots, lack of inputs, and the corruption of party cadres. Due to this step taken a vast amount of cheap surplus labour was created which was going to be absorbed in the urban areas.

A second route of the formation of new wage-labour class is out of state-owned enterprises (SOEs). These were the centrepiece of industrialization in the pre-Deng period, accounting for nearly four-fifths of non-agricultural production. Most are in the cities, where they employed 70 million people in the 1980s. This form of employment had been steadily dismantled, starting with a law that allowed temporary hire without social protection and a 1988 bankruptcy law terminating workers' guarantee of lifelong employment. Most decisive was the massive layoffs at the end of the 1990s. By the early 2000s employment in state-owned enterprises was halved, from 70 to 33 per cent of the urban workforce, with some 30 to 40 million workers terminated.

Finally, a transition to wage-labour followed from the collapse of rural township and village enterprises (TVEs). These flourished in the wake of the dissolution of the communes, with the first phase of liberalization in the early 1980s, especially in Guangdong, Fujian, and around Tianjin and Shanghai.[1] As a result of the decline of the TVEs more and more workers, amounting to well over 100 million in the first half of the 2010s migrated to the cities in search of employment. These measures made up a large pool of cheap labour power to be exploited in the burgeoning industrial zones and who are also used to discipline the urban labour force in the private sector.[2]

According to one estimate, nearly 274 million internal migrants were drawn into non-farm works in booming towns and cities in 2014, an increase of 48.5 million from 2008.[3] Approximately 80 per cent of manufacturing workers in China are internal migrants. Over the last twenty-five years, some

150-200 million Chinese have moved from the countryside in search of employment. Although the great majority moved legally, they remain classified as rural residents under the Chinese registration system and thus suffered enormous discrimination. For example, despite paying fees to register as temporary urban residents, they are denied access to the public services (including free or subsidized education, health care, housing, and pensions). The same is true for their children, even if they are born in an urban area.

Therefore, with the 'redundant' workforce of the SOEs and with the vast sea of migrant workforce, China has presented before the MNCs a massive amount of super-exploitable reserve army of labour unprecedented in its history.

During the last three decades, Chinese economy shows 'spectacular' growth which is also unprecedented in its history. Annual growth rate of GDP in China averaged 9.69 per cent from 1989 until 2017, reaching an all time high of 15.40 per cent in the first quarter of 1993 and maintained double digit growth rate for several years. Though sliding in recent times due to the recession in the advanced countries, it still shows strong growth rate of 6.9 per cent in the third quarter of 2017 which is not only more than the other countries in developing Asia, but also far ahead than the growth rate of developed countries.[4]

Though China is projected by many pandits as becoming an economic superpower in the coming years with this 'spectacular' growth rate, Chinese production structure reveals a rather more fragile picture of Chinese economic growth. It is largely in low-value, labour-intensive, export-oriented sectors that China has played a major role in out-competing other developing countries. In fact, China has become the major regional assembly platform on a global scale. A large part of regional trade is the trade in parts and components especially in ICT (Information and Communications Technology) products and electrical goods in the direction of China, where they are assembled on the basis of cheap labour.[5]

In fact, the Chinese growth momentum is increasingly dependent upon exports produced and controlled by multinational corporations. The country's export-to-GDP ratio rose dramatically from 8 per cent in the early 1980s to 18 per cent in the early 1990s, 28 per cent in the early 2000s and 36 per cent in 2007.[6] The exports are mainly destined for the markets in North America and Europe integrating China tightly with the global economy, but also making it dependent on continuing demand in the Global North. Roughly 30 per cent of all exports from China in 1996-2005 ended up in the United States; about 26 per cent in Japan; and around 16 per cent in the European Union. Others, in determining the effects of re-exports, have estimated the US share of China's exports even higher, at 50 per cent.[7]

China's growth has become thus increasingly dependent on exports produced by multinational corporations. John Bellamy Foster and Robert W McChesney write:

> In the complex global supply lines of multinational corporations, China primarily occupies the role of final assembler of manufactured goods to be sold in the rich economies. Export manufacturing is directed not at the actual production of goods, but at commodity assembly using parts and components produced elsewhere and then imported to China. The final commodity is then shipped from China to the developed economies. China is the world's biggest supplier of final information, communications, and technology goods, and multinational corporations accounted for about 87 per cent of China's high-tech exports at the beginning of 2006. The parts and components for these high-tech goods are almost all imported to China by multinationals for assembly prior to their export via multinationals to the markets within the Triads [US, EU, and Japan].
>
> Within the East Asia region as a whole, China's is the final production platform, with other East Asian nations, like Japan, South Korea, and Singapore producing the parts and components. China's imports of parts and components increased almost twenty-four times in 1992-2008, while its final goods trade increased only around twelve times in the same period. In 2009, 17 per cent of its parts and components imports came from Japan, 17 per cent from South Korea, 15

> per cent from the ASEAN6 (Brunei, Indonesia, Malaysia, Philippines, Singapore, and Thailand), 10 per cent from Europe, and 7 per cent from North America.... [Hence] in this global supply-chain system, *China is more the world-assembly hub than the world factory.*[8]

So, the 'roaring' Chinese economy is largely dependent on the export orders from the developed countries and it is nothing more than a biggest export-led 'assembly hub' where the multinational capital is deeply involved. These multinational corporations have turned China into a major exporter of high-tech goods. In 1995, China's high-tech exports amounted to $10.1 billion, only 6.8 per cent of the total exports. The country's world market share was only 2.1 per cent. From 1995 and 2009, high-tech exports grew *30 per cent annually*, considerably faster than the growth in overall exports. In 2009, China's high-tech exports reached $376.9 billion, equal to 31.4 per cent of total exports.[9] Moreover, the share of China's high-tech exports produced by wholly owned MNCs continues to grow, from 55 per cent in 2002 to 68 per cent in 2009, suggesting the tightening grip of foreign control on its economy.[10]

In sum, China's rise as a final assembler platform/hub is noted by *Businessweek* as: "experts familiar with highly touted Chinese achievements such as commercial jets and high-speed trains say the technologies that underpin them were largely developed elsewhere." China may be the world's leading high-tech products, "but subtract the mainland operations of Taiwanese contract manufacturers and the likes of Nokia, Samsung and Hewlett-Packard, and China is an electronics lightweight."[11] In short, China's production is mainly based on cheap labour, low value-added activities, high-tech assembly lines dominated by foreign MNCs and highly dependent on access to markets in the developed countries. If this market falls or dips into recession, the burden of that crisis naturally falls on the workers of China that happened in the 2008-09 global financial crisis.

But, China's rapid export-led growth does develop neither ample opportunities, nor any better-paid, better-treated employment for the Chinese labour. The US Bureau of Labour Statistics notes that total manufacturing employment in China actually fell by almost 7 million during the period 1994-2006, from 119.26 million to 112.63 million. Total urban manufacturing employment, which includes most foreign operations, declined sharply from 54.92 million to 33.52 million.[12] According to an ILO survey, though total urban employment (including construction, services and manufacturing, etc) increased slightly over the period 1990 and 2002, almost all the growth was in irregular employment, meaning *casual-wage or self-employment*—typically in construction, cleaning and maintenance of premises, retail trade, street vending, repair services or domestic services. More specifically, while total urban employment over this thirteen-year period grew by 81.7 million, 80 million of that growth was in irregular employment.[13] This incidence of informalization of the workforce in China shows a similar pattern visible all over Asia—what we have seen in the case of India as well.

The conditions of the workers in China are closely linked with the opening of large numbers of special economic zones, economic and technological development zones, high-technology industrial development zones, export processing zones and so on. Since the late 1970s and in the 1980-90s China set up many of these zones in coastal cities to attract foreign investment. Hong Kong and Taiwanese entrepreneurs, ranging from low-end component processing to sophisticated microchip assembly, invested in the Pearl River Delta and the Greater Shanghai region. Over two decades China's national economy underwent a transformation from one based on heavy industry, with guaranteed lifetime employment and generous welfare for urban state sector workers, to one that mainly relies on foreign and private investments and massive use of *rural migrant labour* in export-led light industries. The surge in foreign investment gets momentum as the Chinese government has offered lucrative tax-breaks, cheap infrastructure, land, several investment benefits, and overall one of the cheapest sources of labour in the world. In recent times, China has pushed reforms to its west and central zones where provincial governments have opened up for investments offering incentives as the flow of migrant labour to the south-eastern (coastal) regions slows down markedly. In 2009, more than 90 million migrants worked in the eastern region, around 24 million in the central region, and nearly 30 million in the western region. Whatever may be the case, the exploitation of the migrant workers in the subcontracting firms located in these zones are maximum in many respects. For an example, throughout the decade of rapid light industrialization, the manufacturing wages of the so-called Asian Tigers rose from approximately 8 per cent of US wages in 1975 to 30 per cent in the 1990s through 2005; by contrast China's manufacturing wages over the years from 1980 to 2005 remained fairly low, at approximately *2-3 per cent of US wages*.[14]

To examine the state of the workers in this economy of China—which have shown 'spectacular' growth in the last three decades—let us first take the example of high tech assembly line production in China—the mainstay of the global supply chain.

Workers in the High Tech Assembly Line

> We are working to eradicate unethical hiring and exploitation of workers—even when local laws permit such practices. We are continuing our efforts to end excessive work hours.
>
> —Apple's Labor and Human Rights webpage

> I think it is fair to say that personal computers have become the empowering tools we have ever created. They are tools of communication, they are tools for creativity, and they can be shaped by their user. —Bill Gates

> Work harder than a donkey; eat food worse than pig's feed; wake up earlier than a rooster; finish work later than a prostitute; behave like a good grandchild; try to look better than anyone else; age five years faster than anyone else.
>
> —Blog message posted by an anonymous Foxconn worker in Shenzhen, China, June 15, 2006

Among the most prominent firms in the global supply chain that operates in China is Foxconn, the Taiwanese-owned multinational electronics contract supplier. Foxconn is the trade name of Hon Hai Precision Industry Company and is currently the world's largest contract electronics manufacturer MNC, meaning that it makes most of its money as a made-to-order manufacturer, not by selling its own brand products. The company was poised to take in over 50 per cent of global electronics manufacturing service industry revenue by 2011. Under the leadership of founder and CEO Terry Gou (who was acclaimed as the "king of outsourcing" by *Businessweek* as early in 2002) Foxconn declares itself "the most trusted and preferred partner in all aspects of global electronics outsourcing to help customers de-risk their business."[15]

Foxconn—the name alludes to the corporation's ability to produce electronic connectors at nimble 'fox-like' speed—supplies components and finished products not only for Apple, but also for IBM, Microsoft, Google, Intel, Cisco, GE, Amazon, HP, Dell, Motorola, Nokia, Panasonic, Sony, Toshiba, Fujitsu, Nintendo, Samsung, LG, Sony Ericsson, Acer, Huawei and Lenovo, a Who's Who of global electronic producers including two of China's own leading tech companies. Indisputably, Apple is the most valued and important customer of Foxconn from which millions of iPads and iPhones are produced each year. In July 2013, *Fortune* Global 500 ranked Foxconn 30th on the list, up 13 places from the previous year, with *annual revenues of US$132 billion*, far higher than most of its corporate customers, with the notable exception of Apple (which had US$156.5 billion in sales). Their products are computers (desktops, laptops and tablets), communications equipment (mobile phones and smartphones), consumer digital (music players, cameras, game consoles and TVs), cars (automotive electronics), content (e-book readers such as Kindle) and health-care products supplying to above-mentioned electronics giants.[16] In 2013, Foxconn's imports and exports reached US$ 244.6 billion, equivalent to 4.1 per cent of the total trade value of China. Today, Foxconn has *more than 30 manufacturing complexes* in Beijing, Shanghai, Tianjin, Chongqing, Shenzhen and in

16 provinces throughout China. It runs multiple manufacturing facilities in many provinces.[17]

Foxconn currently employs 1.4 million workers in China alone. Out of these, more than 0.43 million (430,000!) workers are engaged in 'state-of-the-art' Longhua campus. The gigantic 1.75 million square metre Longhua complex in Shenzhen city, South China, includes multi-storey factories, warehouses, dormitories, banks, two hospitals, two libraries, a post office, a fire brigade with two fire engines, a kindergarten, an exclusive television network, an educational institute, a book store, soccer fields, basketball courts, tennis courts, track and field, swimming pools, cyber theatres, shops, supermarkets, cafeterias, restaurants, guest houses and even a wedding-dress shop.[18] Later, outpacing this 'campus', a new complex has been built in Sichuan province investing US$2 billion and for that expansion a total of 14 villages in Deyuan had been demolished to create the 15-square-kilometre industrial space designated for a comprehensive Foxconn Living Zone (i.e. approximately five times larger than the Foxconn's flagship Longhua factory in Shenzhen).[19]

The biggest Longhua factory could produce as many as 137,000 iPhones in a 24-hour day, or *more than 90 a minute*. Management used stop-watches and computerized industrial engineering devices to test the capacity of the workers and if workers being tested were able to meet the quota, the target would be increased every day until the capacity of the workers reached the maximum. A group of workers at the Kunshan factory commented, "We cannot stop work for a minute. We are even faster than machines." A young woman worker added, "Wearing gloves would eat into efficiency, we have a huge workload every day.... During really busy times, I do not even have time to go to the bathroom or eat."[20]

In global outsourcing, electronics suppliers are compelled to compete against each other with animal spirit to meet rigorous specifications of price, product quality, just-in-time production, and time-to-market, generating wage pressure as well as health and safety hazards at the factory level while maintaining or increasing profit margins or cutting additional cost transferring the whole burden on to the workers. Apple, the number one brand marketing iPhones and iPads is the frontrunner in putting pressure on the suppliers and thereby squeezing the workers more and more. It obtains products and services 'within tight time-frames' and 'at a cost that represents the best possible value' to its customers and shareholders. Apple's strength is well illustrated by its ability to capture an extraordinary *58.5 per cent* of the value of the iPhone despite the fact that manufacture of the product is entirely outsourced. Particularly notable is that labour costs in China account for the smallest share, *only 1.8 per cent* or nearly US$10, of the US$549 retail price of the iPhone.[21]

Chart 8: Percentage Share of Profits of Apple

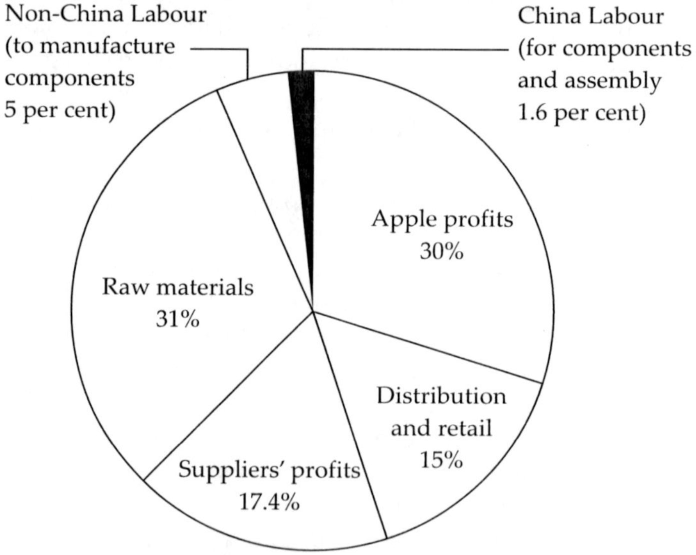

[*Source:* Apple's iPad City: Subcontracting Exploitation in China, Jenny Chan, Pun Ngai, Mark Selden, http://www.ccsp.ox.ac.uk/sites/sias/files/documents/Apples%20iPad%20City.pdf, accessed 17.01.17]

Moreover, Apple is notorious in its last-minute change in orders and designs in products mounting tremendous pressure on the suppliers to squeeze the workers maximum.

The *New York Times* has offered the following story as the Apple redesigned the iPhone's screen at the last moment:

> One former [Apple] executive described relied upon a Chinese factory to revamp iPhone manufacturing just weeks before the device was due in shelves. Apple had redesigned the iPhone's screen at the last minute, forcing an assembly line overhaul. New screens began arriving at the plant near midnight.
>
> A foreman immediately roused 8,000 workers inside the company's dormitories, according to the executive. Each employee was given a biscuit and a cup of tea, guided to a workstation and within half an hour started a 12-hour shift fitting glass screens into bevelled frames. Within 96 hours, the plant was producing over 10,000 iPhones a day.
>
> "The speed and flexibility is breathtaking", the executive said.[22]

Therefore, every second counts for Foxconn. 'Execution is the integration of speed, accuracy and precision', 'Growth, thy name is suffering'—these are the slogans of Terry Gou, the CEO of Foxconn. Division of labour is so detailed in Foxconn that workers see themselves as merely 'a cog in the machine'. Electronics parts are assembled quickly as hands of the workers move faster along 24-hour non-stop conveyor belts. They are forced to work overtime as their wages are paltry. *Overtime hours are 2-4 hours daily, 80-100 hours in a month*, though the Chinese labour law has stipulated it at the maximum of 36 hours in a month. It is reported by Students & Scholars Against Corporate Misbehaviour (SACOM) that in the Chengdu complex of Foxconn, the *workers have to stand 14 hours a day*. The number of employees crammed into a dormitory room is 6-22.[23] Moreover, workplaces in the Foxconn campuses are hazardous, harmful and detrimental to the health of the workers.[24]

Each frontline worker in Foxconn specializes in one specific task and performs monotonous, repetitive motions at high speed. The rotating day and night shift system and extreme work intensity take away any feeling of freshness, accomplishment, or initiative towards work. In the production process, workers occupy the lowest position, even below the lifeless machinery. "Workers come second to and are worn out by the machines," was one worker's insightful summary of the worker-machine relationship. Others shared a sense of low self-worth: "I am just a speck of dust in the workshop." On Foxconn factory floors, conversation on the production line between assembly workers is forbidden. "You will receive a warning letter for breaking the rule," a female worker from Foxconn's Shenzhen Guanlan plant said. Managers enforced a policy of demerit points to drive workers to work harder. A 22-year-old worker explained, "The policy is used to penalize workers for petty offences. You can lose points for having long nails, being late, yawning, eating, or sitting on the floor. There are a whole load of things. Just one point means losing my monthly bonus."[25]

To run the assembly line 24x365 hours the migrant workers and the intern (trainee) workers are packed into dormitories where the workers coming from different provinces and unknown to each other have to live in utter loneliness. It is observed:

> Foxconn provides workers with "conveniences" such as collective dormitories, canteens, services, and entertainment facilities in order *to incorporate the entire living space under the factory's management, serving the just-in-time global production strategy.* To a large extent, *workers' living space is merely an extension of the workshop.* Food and drink, sleep, washing, and other aspects of workers' daily lives are scheduled just like the production lines, with the goal not to satisfy workers' needs as people but rather to reproduce workers' physical strength at the lowest cost and shortest time in order to satisfy the factory's production requirements. But at Foxconn, there is no true rest even after getting off from work. Workers with different jobs and even nightshift and day-shift workers are mixed into the same dormitory. As a result, workers frequently disrupt each others' rest because of different working hours. In addition, random dormitory assignments often break up existing networks of social

> relations, hindering communication and interaction between workers. In this lonely space, workers have forfeited their personal and social lives.
>
> All the Foxconn production sites feature a combination of factories and dormitories—its Shenzhen facilities have the astonishing number of *33 company dormitories with another 120 rented dormitories* in the nearby community... . Most migrant workers live in the dormitories, but they do not have a normal life in their "home"—they are living with strangers, not allowed to cook, and not permitted to receive friends or families overnight. Whether the worker is single or married, he or she is assigned a bunk space for one person. The private space is virtually reduced to one's own bed behind a self-made curtain.
>
> From the perspective of labor control, these factory-provided dormitories mean that production and labor reproduction activities take place in a self-contained, all-encompassing geographical locality. This facilitates flexible production through imposing overtime work, *as the distinction between "home" and "work" is blurred. The lengthening of a work-day to 24 hours* to meet the global production schedule means that the *appropriation of labor surplus is absolute*. Such a socio-spatial arrangement strengthens managerial domination, wherein control over labor is extended from the factory shop floor to the sphere of everyday life. The dormitory labor system is a cost-efficient solution for companies like Foxconn to ensure that workers spend their off-hours just preparing for another round of production.[26]

The workplace and the dormitories are so 'disciplined' that it looks like a 'prison'. In these 'prisons', workers work hard to reproduce their labour power to be expended to multiply the super-profits of the capitalists. While preparing to start work on the production line, the management will ask the workers: "How are you?" Workers must respond by shouting in unison, "Good! Very good! Very, very good!" This militaristic drilling is said to train workers as disciplined labourers.[27] The management has hired more than 1,000 security guards to keep internal order in the Foxconn Longhua plant (no littering, no jay-walking, and so on) and prevent unauthorized persons from entering sensitive areas. Every factory building and dormitory has security checkpoints with guards standing by 24 hours a day. All employees, whether they are going to the toilet or going to eat, must be checked. To thwart rivals intent on industrial espionage, the company bars employees from bringing music players or mobile phones onto the shop floor. Body searches are not uncommon. Men reportedly must take off belts with metal buckles and women their wired bras before they can pass the electronic security systems. Commentators, referring to worker interviews held that *physical and verbal violence is systemic* in the Foxconn system. Workers are *harassed and beaten up* without serious cause.

Factory-floor managers and supervisors often give lectures to production workers at the beginning and the end of the work day. After working a long shift of a standard 12 hours (of which four hours are illegally imposed, forced overtime), workers still have to stand, for often 15 minutes to half an hour, and listen to speeches, although the content of such meetings remains the same: the management evaluates the production target of the previous shift, reminds workers of the tasks they need to pay special attention to, and reiterates work rules and regulations.

In this terrible work atmosphere, several workers in the plants and dormitories attempted suicides (discussed in Chapter I). In fact, the accumulated effects of endless assembly line toil, punishing work schedules, harsh factory discipline, a friendless dormitory and, rejection from managers and administrators, compounded by the company's failure to provide her with income, and then her inability to make contact with friends and family, were the immediate circumstances of their attempted suicide. After the attempts of 18th suicides, Foxconn installed 3,000,000 square metres of safety nets between dormitory buildings to prevent employees from killing themselves by jumping off the rooftop. CEO Terry Gou called them "nets with a loving heart." In fact, the workers now live in "a cage."[28]

When a company like Apple or Dell needs to ramp up production by 20 per cent for a new product launch, Foxconn has two choices: hire more workers or give the workers you already have more hours. When demand is very high, it is very difficult to suddenly hire 20 per cent more people. Especially when you have a million workers—that would mean hiring 200,000 people at once. To meet the demand alongside forcing existing workers to do more overtime, Foxconn, in collusion with the local or provincial administration hires student or interns (trainees or apprentices). Recruitment through vocational schools is an efficient way to pick up tens of thousands of new workers at once, who are purportedly hired in the name of skills training and school-business cooperation. Foxconn in its own report declared that *1,50,000 interns* have been engaged in the production jobs which is approximately *15 per cent of its workforce*. China has more than 13,300 registered vocational schools and colleges. The interns of second and third years coming from these schools/colleges have become a huge source of cheap and disposable labour in Foxconn as well as in China. At Foxconn, *interns* were placed on assembly lines to work illegally long shifts of *10 to 12 hours* (both at day and night shifts), six to seven days a week though the labour law in China clearly mentions that "interns shall not work more than eight hours a day" or "interns shall not work overtime beyond the eight-hour workday". Most of them are 16-18 years of age. A typical comment by interns, their hopes for gaining technical knowledge dashed, underlines the harsh reality of life on the line: "We are sent to do trivial tasks like checking iPad screens and cleaning the product surface ... we are frustrated at repeating the same boring work all day." Another intern said: "I often dream, but repeatedly tear apart my dreams; like a miserable painter, tearing up my draft sketches…I'm not interested in assembling iPhone parts. It is exhausting and boring. I want to quit. But I cannot."[29] Another 17-year-old student intern said, "Come on, what do you think we would have learned standing for more than ten hours a day manning the machines on the line? What is an internship? There is no relation to what we study in school. *Every day is just a repetition of one or two simple motions, like a robot.*"[30]

At Foxconn, as of January 2011, while student interns and entry-level workers had the same starting wage of 950 yuan/month (US$154), only employees could receive a skill bonus of 400 yuan/month (US$65). Interns were not entitled to have their skills assessed in order to qualify for the bonus. Maintaining that student interns are not employees—even when they perform work identical to that of production workers—Foxconn does not enrol interns in government-administered social security, which covers medical insurance, work injury insurance, unemployment benefits, maternity insurance, and old age pensions, nor in a housing provident fund. A quick look at the maths reveals that, in 2015, assuming a total of 150,000 student interns working in various Foxconn factories during one month in the peak season, the savings from not providing them with welfare benefits is roughly 150,000 persons × 300 yuan = 45,000,000 yuan (= 6935400 US dollars at current prices).[31]

The wages received by the workers are so poor that they are forced to do overtime work like other countries in the global supply chain. Jenny Chan and Pun Ngai write about wages received by the workers:

> Under the direct pressure of Apple and other buyers, and the hunger for ever more corporate profit, Foxconn, as of May 31, 2010, paid 450,000 production line workers at its two Shenzhen plants only 900 yuan (US$132) a month for a 40 hour week. In other words, Foxconn has set its maximum base wages at the local minimum wage standard.... *60 per cent* of the monthly total wage is from doing *overtime* work.[32]

In this connection the authors note that in general the Chinese manufacturing wages as a percentage of US wages are abysmally low compared to those of Japan and East Asian Tigers like South Korea and Taiwan in the early years of their economic takeoffs. Economists Erin Lett and Judith Banister (2009) estimated that the average *hourly* compensation costs of China's manufacturing workers in 2006 was only US$0.81. The Economist stated that as of July 2010, the Chinese migrant workforce "is still cheap... *just 2.7 per cent* of the cost of their American counterparts." Based on government statistics, the labour income share of China's GDP declined from 56.5 per cent in 1983 to 36.7 per cent in 2005; by contrast, many OECD countries maintained the ratio of labour returns to GDP at 60 per cent or more for the comparable period of 1978 to 2008. [On the contrary], corporate profits in China have increased rapidly, growing by *20 per cent* between 1978 and 2005, the sole exception being the recession accompanying the 1997-1998 Asian financial and currency crisis. The export sector has turned most of its profits into enterprise savings, dividends, and re-investment, rather than sharing it with workers.... Non-payment of wages and unfair treatment remain commonplace while labour disputes have been on the rise since the 1990s.[33]

Under the protests and mass unrest of the workers in the export-driven industries in China, the China government decided to increase the wage-level. But it will be seen later that the increase in wages cannot keep parity with the inflation; moreover the industrial houses cut back several benefits enjoyed by the workers till 2010.

Under these circumstances, workers in China, particularly in the export-led factories and other utilities became restive and agitation of the workers sometimes rocked the country. But often workers are denied venting their legitimate demands as the sole government- and CPC-backed labour union present in China is used to maintain 'class-peace'. In most cases, particularly in the export-led industries and assembly-hubs, labour unions are either present on paper or totally non-existent.[34] Foxconn, like many other wholly owned foreign-invested enterprises, evaded its legal responsibility to allow a trade union in its complexes. Chinese leaders, in response to mounting worker strikes and other forms of action in an era of super-exploitation, have supported greater participation of workers in union organization in the hope that enterprise-level unions will help to maintain social stability.[35] Under the pressure Foxconn have allowed to form a union in 2006 in its Shenzhen facility. But to establish immediate control over it, Foxconn was CEO Terry Gou appointed his special personal assistant as its chairwomen. Notwithstanding this, the workers in export-led industries in particular have been protesting against the low wages, no-payment of wages and other working conditions in China. Statistics from the latest China Labour Statistical Yearbook show that labour dispute arbitration committee (LDAC) cases in China have been steadily climbing since 2011 and have far exceeded the last climax of dispute cases reached after the global financial crisis of 2008. The number of workers involved in labour disputes also *surpassed 1 million*, nearly equal to the all time high reached in 2008.[36]

After the spate of suicides on Foxconn campuses which rocked the media of the world, the Apple management has decided to relocate some of the iPhone and iPad assembly jobs to another contractor MNC named Pegatron (also based in Taiwan) which manufactures and assembles various electronics goods like Foxconn, Dongguan Meitai, Jabil Circuit, Zhen Ding Technology and so on. Strikingly, the work-conditions in Pegatron are no better, sometimes worse than others. To uncover the work practices going on in Pegatron the undercover filmmakers and journalists pretending to be workers in a factory describe the following horrendous story:

> "*Exhausted workers were filmed falling asleep on their 12-hour shifts* at the Pegatron factories on the outskirts of Shanghai. One undercover reporter, working in a factory making parts for Apple computers, had to work *18 days in a row* despite repeated requests for a day off. Another reporter, whose *longest shift was 16 hours*, said: "Every time I got back to the dormitories, I would not want to move. Even if I was hungry I would not want to get up to eat. I just wanted to lie down and rest. I was unable to sleep at night because of the stress."
>
> "Overtime is supposed to be voluntary, but none of the reporters were offered any choice. In addition to the excessive hours, one reporter had to attend unpaid meetings before and after work. Another reporter was housed in a dormitory where *12 workers shared a cramped room*."[37]

The website quoting China Labor Watch (CLW) further shows that:

> Right now, in Shanghai, China, a factory owned by the Taiwanese Pegatron Group is pushing out millions of units of the iPhone 6s for Apple. There, its young production workers toil six days a week in 12-hour shifts. Each day they are paid for 10 and half hours of work, not counting 15 minutes of unpaid meetings. The mandatory overtime shift runs from 5:30 pm till 8 pm.
>
> Before overtime pay, workers making the iPhone earn only the local minimum wage of $318 per month, or about *$1.85 per hour*. This is not a living wage. Even if the factory did not mandate overtime as it does, workers would still depend on their 60-hour workweeks to get by.
>
> After their long shifts, workers take a 30-minute shuttle bus back to their dorms where up to 14 people are crammed into a room. Mold grows pervasively along the walls. Bed bugs have spread throughout the dorm, and many workers are covered in red bug bites.[38]

When the profits of the Apple declines for the first time in 2013, they are beginning to tighten production cost which means inevitable cuts in payment to the workers and forcing the workers to toil longer. CLW shows one of the reports that Pegatron passes the crisis of the Apple on to the workers by implementing "excessive overtime hours that spanned up to *90 additional hours per month*" and the "overall wage cuts" are "from $1.85 to $1.60 per hour." Interestingly the overtime weekly cap for Apple (as they are forced to stipulate under criticism) is 60 hours per week. But CLW's "latest report claims that these standards have not been met at Pegatron, which employs up to 100,000 workers at peak season to create iPhones and iPads.... [D]uring high volume months, 40 to 70 per cent of factory workers worked more than Apple's standard 60-hour workweek. Workers were often forced to stay overtime and were rarely granted leave. Student interns, though forbidden by law from working overtime, put in an average *additional 80 hours per month*." Moreover, "hourly wages technically were increased in 2016 to meet the new minimum wage of $2 per hour as set by the Shanghai government. But as wages were increased, worker subsidies such as workday meals, medical insurance and retirement were abolished. When accounting for these additional costs, the report found that *wages actually decreased by 25 cents per hour* from 2015 to 2016."[39]

It is notable here that the Apple CEO Tim Cook received one million shares of Apple's stock in 2011, which was worth 376 million dollars at that time, *almost two times higher than the total base wages of 50,000 Pegatron workers in a year.*[40] But after 2013, Apple's profits rebounded and in 2015, Apple's profit was as high as 53.4 billion US dollars, and its cash asset reached up to $206.4 billion, an increase from $155.3 billion in 2014. *Its cash reserve is enough to hire 1.6 million workers to work 33 years.*[41]

Zhen Ding Technology is another subcontracting firm which supplies flexible printed circuit boards and other components for Apple's iPhone, iPad, Mac and iPod. Zhen Ding also produces for the Amazon Kindle and for Xiaomi. Other clients are Motorola, Dell, Nokia, and Sony. It is the second largest manufacturer of flexible printed circuit boards in the world with four production facilities in mainland China, including their Shenzhen factory. It has nearly 15,000 employees out of which more than 10,000 workers are housed in primitive, dark and filthy dormitories, sleeping on plywood, with six to ten workers in each crowded room. Several workers of this company managed to smuggle their testimonies and undercover photos out of the factories. The testimonies of the workers depict a horrible situation:

> "Workers are trapped on the assembly lines along with the parts that keep coming down the line. *They finish each piece in seconds*! If a worker does not move fast enough, products will pile up on the assembly line, and workers will have to bear the cost of the losses."
>
> Employees listen to the managers and they "work their asses off," inserting parts all day or all night long. To avoid being punished, the workers push themselves beyond their limits. Everyone agrees, the work is mind-numbing.

A production manager calculates the time it takes to finish each step in seconds, and then sets the production goals accordingly. Despite the pressure, *production* goals are going up all the time.

"The production goal increases every day. Today we met the production goal, and then it goes up tomorrow. It goes up till we cannot finish the job. On the bulletin board in our workshop, the actual assigned production goal is always higher than what we expected. Our team just broke the record and finished 15,000 pieces! Today the goal becomes 18,000 pieces. They are trying to kill us."

Another worker told us: "It does not take any special technique to be a worker at Zhen Ding. You only need to *repeat simple steps tens of thousands of times. We are just machines.* Our lives are boring. But what can we do?"

"It is very tiring during the peak season. Many workers are *so exhausted that they just do not want to eat*. They would rather sleep at their work station. Many workers try to find a corner in the plant to take a quick nap. We are exhausted."

"The supervisor sniffs around like a mean dog. Once he finds something wrong, he bites. He yells when someone makes a mistake or lets products pile up, or when a worker goes to the bathroom too often....There are no rules about production goals. The supervisor bumps it up whenever he wants to. Workers get yelled at for not being able to meet the goal. Workers might even be fired.... Once the workers finish their production, he raises the production goal the following day."

Each employee has an ID card, which stores information regarding the worker's activities. The workers are watched constantly, entering the workshop or dorm, clocking in and out, and working overtime. The workers have to swipe their cards to enter the plant and start working, and again to enter the cafeteria when they are allowed to eat.

The gates on each floor of the factory have electronic locks. One worker told a researcher that he was constantly made to swipe his ID card... to the point where he "wanted to puke." Surveillance cameras are everywhere, and the workers are constantly monitored. When workers leave their workshops, they are required to pass a metal detector test along with a full body scan. In addition, security guards at the factory gate search the workers' belongings... .

The workers are not allowed to enter the factory carrying their cell phones, cameras or tape recorders. Management hires well over 100 security guards to patrol the premises and watch the workers. According to researchers, "Many workers told us that they have seen *security guards beat the workers*... and not just one guard beating a worker, but rather a group of guards. This happens often."

Day shift: 8 am to 8 pm. Night shift: 8 pm to 8 am. Workers receive four days off a month, but their days off do not always fall on Sunday. Supervisors arrange the workers' days off. Switching shift every month harms the workers' health.

Workers report that their *biological clocks are off and that they are exhausted all the time*. One worker in the flexible printed circuit board workshop told researchers: "I cannot sleep during the day when I am on night shift. Some of the workers cannot stand the hours and quit."

Another worker called "Lee" worked in the assembly workshop. He told us: "Two shifts. The bosses' machines can make money non-stop, 24 hours. As long as the boss makes money, our lives and deaths do not matter."

When they are working the night shift, workers receive a stipend of 6.5 RMB ($1.06) per night. For the month, workers on the night shift can earn a stipend of $28.09... .

Without permission, workers cannot leave their work stations to use the toilet. Workers are *only* allowed to go to the bathroom during their meal breaks and their two ten-minute rest breaks. The workers must "learn to hold their urine as long as they can on the assembly line."

Mr. "A" told us: "My job is to attach stickers to printed circuit boards. I do not dare to leave my position to go to the bathroom. If I leave while there is no one to sub for me, the circuit boards will pile up as they move down the line. I could get a major demerit point for this. Then I am screwed.

> Not only will my performance bonus be affected, but I might be denied overtime.[42]

Moreover, the speed of the work is "mind-numbing". A researcher observes:

> The work and furious pace of an inspector on his assembly line. Using his left hand, the inspector picks up a partially finished PCB (printed circuit board) from the assembly line and places it in the auto-testing equipment (ATE). Then he turns on the ATE with his right hand. He checks all the indicators and places the qualified products back on the assembly line, while flagging the disqualified products with a red sticker and placing them in a bin. The whole process of completing the *four operations is done in five seconds! In a single minute, he finishes 48 operations*. The inspector *completes almost 20,000 operations, inspecting 5,000 pieces in a single day*.[43]

Dongguan Meitai is another subcontractor producing computer equipment like keyboards, printer cases for Hewlett-Packard, Dell, Lenovo, Microsoft and IBM. In this factory two thousand workers, mostly young women, are producing equipment in 12 hours shift, normally from 8 am to 8 pm, seven days a week. All overtime is mandatory. Workers are allowed just two days off a month. Including unpaid overtime—mandatory work meetings and preparations—workers are routinely at the factory 12½ hours a day while toiling 11½ hours. On average, including unpaid overtime, workers are at the factory 81¼ hours each week while toiling 73¾ hours of obligatory overtime, which exceeds China's legal time by *318 per cent!* At the extreme, workers are at the factory 87½ hours a week, while working 80½ hours, which exceeds the legal limit by *388 per cent!* Workers needing to take a day off while the factory is operating on the weekend must apply for permission to be absent. Even if permission is granted, workers are docked 50 RMB ($7.20)—or nearly one-and-a-half day's wages—for taking a Saturday and Sunday off—which are supposed to be their weekend holidays.

Factory regulations spell out very clearly that all workers must arrive approximately 30 minutes early to their shifts for a mandatory 20-minute work meeting with management and to allow ten minutes to clean and prepare their workstations. At the end of each shift, workers must stand at attention as the foreman reviews the day's production, analyzing problems and explaining corrective plans to be implemented the following day. Moreover, workers on each line must take turns joining other 'volunteers' to stay behind approximately once a week to clean the entire factory. This way management does not have to hire and pay for janitorial staff. It is the same with the company dorms. Workers have to take turns sweeping and mopping the dorms and toilets and hauling out the garbage. The routine in the workplace are as follows:

> *The workers sit on wooden stools, without backrests, as 500 computer keyboards an hour move down the assembly line, twelve hours a day, seven days a week, with just two days off a month. Every 7.2 seconds a keyboard passes each worker, who has to snap six or seven keys into place—one key every 1.1 seconds.* The assembly line never stops. The workplace is frantic, monotonous, numbing and relentless. Each worker inserts 3,250 keys an hour; 35,750 keys during the official 11-hour shift; 250,250 a week, performing over *one million operations a month. Workers are paid 1/50th of a cent for each operation they complete.*
>
> Of the 2,000 or so workers at the Meitai factory, the majority are young women, ranging in age from 18 to their mid-twenties. While working, the women cannot talk, listen to music, or even lift their heads to look around. Workers are ordered to "periodically trim their nails"—to facilitate work, or be fined. Workers needing to use bathroom must learn to hold it till there is a break. Security guards spy on the workers, who are prohibited from putting their hands in their pockets and are searched when they enter and leave the factory....
>
> The workers get up around 6 am. When they return to their dorm, sometime between 9 and 9.30 pm—they bathe

> using a small plastic bucket. Summer temperatures routinely reach into the high 90s.
>
> During the winter, workers have to walk down several flights of stairs to fetch hot water in their buckets. Ten to twelve workers share each over-crowded dorm room, sleeping on narrow metal bunk beds that line the walls. Workers drape old sheets over their cubicle openings for privacy.
>
> If a worker steps on the grass on the way to the dorm, she is fined. The workers are locked in the factory compound four days a week and are prohibited from even taking a walk... .
>
> Workers who hand out flyers or discuss factory conditions with outsiders will be fired. Many young workers have *never heard the word union and have no idea what it is*. All the workers know is that they all feel like they are "serving a prison sentence."[44]

These are the conditions of the workers in electronics assembly and manufacturing jobs in the global supply chain. The narrations of the plight of the workers in China (also called 'global workshop') establish the facts that these lead-brands are running their business at the expense of super-exploitation of the workers. Currently, up to 75 per cent of all electronic products are produced globally in a contract manufacturing system, outsourced by brand-names like HP, Dell, Apple, and so on. Electronic products made up 56 per cent of total exports of China in 2006.[45] If we take the example of iPhone marketed by Apple, some revealing facts will emerge. According to iSupply, the retail price of a new iPhone is $600 in 2010. The manufacturing components cost $187.51, which is paid to the processor, flash memory, and other component production companies like Samsung. The assembly cost is only $6.45. Deducting the amount of pure profit from the operational costs borne by the factories, it is clear that *workers earn less than $6.45 per day*. Since most of the materials used in production are specified by Apple and their associated costs are pre-negotiated by Apple and other suppliers, Foxconn can only purchase the production materials at a fixed price and cannot cut costs by purchasing cheaper materials. Therefore it can only profit from the price difference between its assembly revenue and the cost of workers' salaries, thus introducing great incentives for factory management to pay workers as little as possible. As a result, the profit pressure passes down through the supply chain and falls onto the backs of workers.[46]

Because of this, Foxconn should not bear the only responsibility for worker suicides or hazards faced by the workers in the workplaces: Apple, HP, Dell and other international brands or MNCs are also responsible, as their goal of profit maximization succeeds at the cost of subsistence level of workers' wages and sub-optimal working conditions.

Almost similar experiences are observed in garments and toy industries of China where lead firms exploit the labour maximum through the subcontracting practices in the global supply chain.

Garment Workers in China

> I work from the early morning till late 10 pm. I sometimes even work till 11 pm. I have to iron 600-700 pieces of shirts per day, but each of the shirts from UNIQLO is only 0.29 RMB. In the peak season, I can iron 900 pieces of shirts in one day. I sometimes work on Sunday too. The piece rate is really too low for us. But it is very hard to increase.
>
> —A worker from Luenthai, a subcontracting firm attached to UNIQLO.

In 1995 China occupied rank number one in exports of textiles and garments. Though declined to an extent in the recent times as some of the garment manufacturing operations are relocated to Bangladesh, Vietnam, Cambodia, etc. where the labour costs are cheaper, it still maintains its leading position in garment exports owing to its well-developed infrastructural, logistical and supply chain advantage. The clothing exports of China took up almost 40 per cent of the total global clothing exports in 2010. There are more than 100,000 garment manufacturers in China which employ over 10 million people.[47] In recent times some of the factories are relocating from coastal regions to inland (Central and Western) China because of the cheaper labour costs. Even though the minimum wage is increasing in China (particularly in coastal regions) and has surpassed some of the South and South East Asian countries in recent years, it is by no means a 'livable' income. Only by living with minimum wage is never able to make ends meet for the workers in the export-led garment industry. Therefore, as pointed out earlier, *overtime work* is always the key component of workers' monthly salary in all the industries integrated to the supply chain.

China is the production hub of many of the fast fashion brands such as H&M, Zara, Gap and UNIQLO. UNIQLO, the Japanese brand is the new superstar in the global fashion stage and its retail stores are operated in almost all cosmopolitan cities throughout the world, such as France, Germany, Shanghai, UK, US, Australia and Russia. It has 861 stores worldwide and roughly 70 partner manufacturers worldwide; 70 per cent of its products are made in China.[48]

Students and Scholars Against Corporate Misbehavior (SACOM), a Hong-Kong based labour rights group made an undercover survey in two of the supplier firms named Luenthai factory in Dongguan and Pacific Textiles factory in Guangzhou. They revealed some startling facts about the working conditions in these factories where workers are *paid as little as one-third of the average monthly salary of other urban workers* in the province. As a result, most of the workers are forced to do overtime—in Pacific Textiles it is 134 hours and in Luentahi it is *112 hours a month* though in Chinese Law it is stipulated as maximum *36 hours per month*. Moreover, in Pacific, the workers are paid *1.5 times* of their base wage for overtime *work instead of 2 times* as written in the labour law. In addition, workers are paid bonuses by pieces, so most of the workers put in as many as hours as they can in order to earn as much as possible.

Both factories maintain very high temperatures inside their facilities. At Pacific, the average temperatures recorded at the textile workshop is 38 degrees Celsius (100 degrees F) during the summer. The dyeing workshop records temperatures ranging from 38 to 42 degrees Celsius (100-107 degrees F). Workers are also required to stand very close to the dyeing tanks which operate at *100 to 135 degrees Celsius (212-275 degrees F)*. These tanks have no protective enclosures to prevent workers from coming into contact with the chemicals. The workers in the ironing department at Luenthai are required to stand (ostensibly to maintain morale) while *operating irons at 200 degrees Celsius (392 degrees F)*. Male workers are seen working topless in order to deal with the heat. Workers describe the factories as "hell" and said that some of their colleagues "fainted in summer because it is too hot." It is interesting to note that workers are given a high temperature allowance of 7 RMB *($1.11) a day*.

The factory floors are routinely awash in chemical-laden wastewater. Workers report that one of their colleagues was electrocuted at the Pacific factory after machinery came into contact with the water, killing him. The workers are exposed to textile process dusts that can cause byssinosis, occupational asthma and respiratory irritation which can be lethal in the long-term. Even worse, dense concentrations of dust have been known to spontaneously combust under very dry conditions. In 1987, 47 died and 179 were injured in a blast at a linen mill in Harbin in north eastern China. Workers are also allegedly exposed to hazardous chemicals. Pacific's dyeing workshop uses solvents like A569 PTEG and A203 PT200, both of which are irritants to human eyes and skin. Moreover, they have to work under the irritating smell of the chemicals for at least 12 hours per day, without protective measures. Workers in the dyeing department usually wear rain boots for the slippery floor but topless body and work with bare hands.

The factory managers rely heavily on a system of fines to control product quality and to manage workers. Pacific management list *58 different punishments* that can be meted out to workers for violating rules—of which 41 are fines. Any fabric defects produced in the knitting department or even a stain on the knitting machine is punishable with a 50-100

RMB ($7.98-15.96) fine, which is equal to a whole day's bonus. Workers caught napping also forfeit their daily bonus.

Pacific and Luen Thai workers do not have proper representation and thus cannot bargain with the factory managers. At Pacific, the workers' union is led by the factory administrative director, which is illegal under China's workers' union law. At Luen Thai, there is no workers' union at all, just a workers' committee that supplies "entertainment and welfare."[49]

Box: Inside the Global Supply Chains of 50 Top Companies

The 50 top MNCs only employ six per cent of people in a direct employment relationship but they rely on a *hidden workforce of 94 per cent*—a massive convenient workforce hidden in the shadows of global supply chains. Just a handful of these companies could recognize their workforce and change the lives of millions of working people. These 50 companies hold a *combined wealth equivalent to that of 100 nations.*

They have the resources and the reach. Working people pay the price for them—slavery, informal work, precarious short-term contracts, low wages, unsafe work and dangerous chemicals, forced overtime, attacks by governments on labour laws and social protection, inequality—it is all part of a great global supply chain that is today driven by corporate greed with an eternal quest for profit and shareholder value.

Their profits are too often driven by low wage levels that people cannot live on; these profits risk safety with the result of indefensible workplace injuries and deaths; these profits are increased by tax evasion or tragically linked to pollution of community land and water, even while their lobby teams are turning governments against the rule of law that would hold them to account.

These 50 companies occupy combined revenues of $3.4 trillion, with a hidden workforce of 116 million. They are operating in the developing and underdeveloped countries of which 58 per cent of countries exclude groups of workers from labour law, 70 per cent of countries have workers who have no right to strike, 60 per cent of countries deny or restrict workers collective bargaining and 52 per cent of countries deny workers access to the rule of law.

Company profiles of some of the companies are as follows:
Apple Inc
Products: iPhone, iPad, Mac, iPod
Revenue (2014): $183 billion
Country of equivalent value: Ecuador
Company employees: 98,000
Supply chain workers: Between 1.6 and 2.3 million

Apple Inc is the world's largest publicly traded corporation by market capitalization and the world's second-largest information technology company by revenue. Apple sold 74.5 million iPhones during the three months that ended on 31 December in 2015—the equivalent of 34,000 iPhones an hour every day of the quarter—more than the entire population of the UK.

Gap Inc
Products: Clothing, accessories
Revenue (2014): $16.4 billion
Country of equivalent value: Niger
Company employees: 140,000
Supply chain workers: 1 million (2012)

Global retailer Gap Inc. offers apparel and accessories under the Gap, Banana Republic and Old Navy brands. Gap Inc's supply chain operates through 1,000 contractors across 40 countries—almost half of these are in Asia. Up to 98 per cent of the company's purchases are from factories outside the US, in places such as China, Bangladesh, Cambodia, Indonesia and Myanmar.

H&M
Products: Clothing
Revenue (2014): $20.3 billion
Country of equivalent value: Benin
Company employees: 132,000
Supply chain workers: 1.6 million

Its clothing production is outsourced to around 900 suppliers across almost 2,000 factories. Most of these are in Asia, with operations in China, Bangladesh, Myanmar, Cambodia, Hong Kong and Indonesia.

Hewlett-Packard (HP)
Products: Computers, printers
Revenue (2014): $111.4 billion
Country of equivalent value: Ghana

Company employees: 302,000, just fewer than the population of Iceland
Supply chain workers: 661,400

The supply chain includes 63 factories in 16 countries, with almost two-thirds in Asian countries such as Indonesia, Malaysia and the Philippines. HP's major suppliers include Foxconn and Flextronics along with Intel and ADM.

Nike, Inc.
Products: Nike air trainers, sports gear
Revenue (2014): $27.8 billion
Country of equivalent value: Mongolia
Company employees: 48,000
Supply chain workers: 2.5 million

From first selling shoes out of a car boot, Nike, Inc. has grown to be the largest seller of footwear and athletic apparel in the world. The US-based multinational designs, develops and markets Nike, Jordan, Converse and Hurley products and has outsourced production to 709 factories in 44 countries, almost entirely in Asia. There are more than 2.5 million workers across its supply chain including in China, Vietnam, Bangladesh, Cambodia, Indonesia, Hong Kong and the Philippines.

Samsung Electronics
Products: Phones, televisions, components
Revenue (2014): $188.5 billion
Country of equivalent worth: Ecuador
Company employees: 286,000
Supply chain workers: 1.5 million

Samsung Electronics is the world's second largest tech company by revenue and the world's largest smartphone maker. Operations are spread across 220 global sites with almost two-thirds of its labour in Asia.

Walmart
Business: General retailer
Products: Walmart discount department and hypermarket stores
Revenue (2014): $485.6 billion
Country of equivalent value: Vietnam
Company employees: 2.2 million, the population of central Paris
Supply chain workers: 10 million

Walmart is the world's largest retailer, employer and company by revenue. Across more than 11,000 stores in 27 countries Walmart employs 2.2 million employees. The corporation is responsible for its business model, which is reported to destroy independent retail trade in small towns within a few years of a Walmart store opening. Walmart is accused of poverty-level wages, poor working conditions, inadequate healthcare and hostility towards organised labour and unions.

The Walt Disney Company
Business: Media
Products: Toys, apparel, furnishings, entertainment, theme parks
Revenue (2014): $48.8 billion
Country of equivalent value: Cambodia

Disney products are produced in roughly 29,000 factories across more than 100 countries, with just under a third of all factories in China. Disney's vendors have facilities in Hong Kong, Indonesia and the Philippines.

[*Source:* Scandal: Inside the Global Supply Chains of Top 50 Companies, 2016, ITUF, http://www.ituc-csi.org/IMG/pdf/pdffrontlines_scandal_en-2.pdf, accessed 12.01.17]

Workers in Toy Industry

The world of toys is a heaven for children, but it is a world of misery for toy factory workers. These workers make toys such as Barbie, Thomas the Tank Engine and Hot Wheels, Cars Piston Cup racing garage and the Fisher-Price Learn with Me Zebra Walker and so on. The products are sold by Mattel, Hasbro, Disney, McDonald's, Lago, Marks and Spencer, NSI Toys, Walmart and other large American companies. Seventy Five per cent of the global toys are produced in China. According to a report from the US Department of Commerce, 85 per cent of the US toy consumption, worth $22.2 billion came from Chinese imports in 2010. Most of these toy products are sold at US retailers like Walmart. There are more than one thousand toy manufacturers in China.[50] Most of these toys are made in Guangdong Province, where $12 billion worth of toys are produced every year and 1.5 million workers are employed in more than 6000 toy factories.[51]

China Labour Watch and several researchers made undercover reports in some of these toy factories exposing deplorable working conditions. At the Hung Hing factory the researcher found that the 8000 workers put in up to *100 hours of overtime a month,* far in excess of the legal maximum of 36 hours. Workers say they have to sign a document agreeing to work additional overtime on top of the legal maximum. At the On Tai Toy Company the researcher spent three weeks in the factory and found workers put in up to *140 hours of overtime every month,* nearly four times the legal limit. A typical working day during the peak season starts at 8 am and does not end till 10 pm. Workers routinely put in six-day weeks, but if the factory is busy there are no days off.

Box: Walmart in China

Eighty per cent of Walmart's suppliers are located in China. Since because the company is so much bigger than any other retailer, it can dictate its terms. Gary Gereffi, a professor at Duke University, said in an interview broadcast on the PBS show Frontline that "No company has had the kind of economic power that Walmart does, to be able to source products from around the world.... *Walmart is able to transfer whole US industries to overseas economies.*"

Because of its size and its innovation in computerizing its inventory and tightly managing its suppliers, coupled with its willingness to squeeze its suppliers to the exclusion of all other factors, Walmart holds life or death power over manufacturers. Gereffi said:

"Walmart is telling its American suppliers that they have to meet lower price standards that Walmart wants to impose. The implication of that in many cases is if you're going to be able to supply Walmart at the prices Walmart wants, you have to go to China or other offshore locations that would permit you to produce at lower cost.... *Walmart is giving them the clear signal that you can not be a Walmart supplier if you cannot produce at substantially lower prices....* You can go to China, or, in many cases, many US suppliers cannot make that move, and *they just go out of business,* because Walmart is the dominant company for many US suppliers. If they cannot go offshore, those suppliers end up going out of business."

And Walmart leverages this power further by contracting to make products with its own name ("private-label products" in retailing lingo) and undercutting makers of traditional branded products, who cannot survive unless they, too, drive down their costs. This only accelerates the race to the bottom.

Nonetheless, let us not lay all the blame for corporate globalization at the doorstep of Walmart headquarters. The *internal logic* of capitalist development is driving the manic drive to move production to the locations with the *most exploitable labor*, not any single company, industry or country. One company will inevitably become the most ruthless in implementing what companies in a variety of industries are forced to do under the rigour of capitalist competition. Walmart so happens to be it.

Fully *two-thirds* of China's exports are shipped from factories wholly or partially owned by non-Chinese companies. The world's multinational corporations profit immensely from China's low wages and like the current Chinese system just as it is.

[*Source:* Chinese Exploitation and Multinational Corporate Profits, By Pete Dolack, 29.02.12, https://systemicdisorder.wordpress.com/2012/02/29/chinese-exploitation-and-multi-national-corporate-profits/, accessed 28.05.16]

Workers complained that they were banned from talking to one another on the production line and were fined up to £5 if they went to the toilet without applying for an "off-duty" permit. They reported regular burns from soldering irons and electric shocks from old hair dryers used to set glue, along with concerns about the effect on their health of unmarked chemicals they have to work with. Up to 10 workers share each 20 square metres dormitory room, which is fitted with bunk beds. Dozens share the toilet and the outside of the building is piled deep with rubbish, which is home to rats.[52]

In Dongguan, Zhenyang toy factory has over 1000 regular employees and 800 temporary and student workers, many of whom are just 16 years of age. Workers are required to be between 16 and 30 years old and two-thirds are women. Zhenyang mainly manufactures Christmas toys, dolls, infant and baby toys. In peak season, shifts run *12 to 13½ hours*. The Injection Moulding department runs back-to-back 12-hour day and night shifts. Work in all Zhenyang's production departments is constant and fast. Pressure to produce and make quota is enormous: "Both hands must be constantly moving," the workers say. Work areas are very crowded. Workers are not allowed to move from their work stations, or *even to drink water*. They must get a special pass to use the bathroom, and each production line of 35 to 50 workers has only one pass.

Making laser guns and toy cars, the quota for a team of 36 workers is 11,000 pieces a day. So, in essence, each worker must complete 306 toys per day. A worker told that she had to make 2400 Disney doll legs in a day—an average of 218 legs per hour! She said, "You cannot take your eyes off it for a second."[53]

Another subcontracting company named Sunny Toys Co. Ltd located in Shenzhen produces electronic and plush toys and supplies both to Walmart and Disney. In this factory, workers begin to work at 8 am everyday till 12 pm, and work from 1.30 pm to 5.30 pm in the afternoon. Overtime work starts at 6 pm. Overtime work varies in different departments. In peak season, from May to November, workers have to work for very long hours. Workers in sewing department worked till 10 pm for most nights in September, and 10.30 pm in October. Handwork workers worked till midnight in October. The packing workers usually worked till 11 pm and had to work overnight sometimes. Workers reported that on September 30th they worked till 4 am in the morning and continued to start work at 8 am the following day. Workers observed that they were exhausted from work. They usually have only 2 days off in a month and some workers even complained that they worked throughout the month without a rest day. Frontline management was fierce and always scolded workers for low productivity. If workers are late for 3 times in a month, their wages will be deducted. If there are defective products, fines will be imposed. Therefore, workers have to keep working to maintain a high productivity.

In Dongguan Crown-Ace Toys Company Ltd, workers' access to toilet is restricted. Workers need to apply for an "off-duty permit" for toilet break. And workers highlighted that "off-duty permits" are very limited. In some production lines, there is only one permit shared by 60 workers. There is also a security guard at the toilet door. If workers are found going to the toilet without an "off-duty permit", workers will be fined.[54]

Interestingly, while American and European consumers worry about exposing their children to Chinese-made toys coated in lead, the Chinese workers, often as young as 16, face far more serious hazards. In these factories the workers do not use earplugs despite the fact that noise levels are extremely high in some departments. Workers report that some of their colleagues who are longtime employees of the factory have suffered hearing loss. In the spray paint department, the workers do not always have fans. Nor do they have masks. The spray paint and printing work rooms are full of fumes from chemicals including industrial alchohol, phenylenediamine and sodium peroxide. Workers just starting in this department often feel nauseous and dizzy, and have headaches. In the Pearl River Delta region, factory workers lose or break about 40,000 fingers on the job every year, according to a study published a few years ago by the Shanghai Academy of Social Sciences.[55]

Earning paltry wages, toy workers have to depend on overtime. Earlier it is noted that the workers have to work a maximum of 140 hours of overtime in certain factories depending on the orders and festive season. Though 36 hours of overtime work is stipulated in the Chinese Law, 60-80 hours of overtime works are common in many factories. Even with such massive amounts of overtime, a toy worker can only earn 1/2000 of the value of each toy he/she works on. Based on information collected in CLW's investigation, if we combine all wage remuneration a toy worker receives, that worker will earn less than 2 cents US$ for each toy that he/she produces. At Mattel's Shenzhen-based supplier plant Winson, if a worker does 110 hours of overtime a month, working on 40,320 toys, she will earn *$0.016 per toy*. The classic Mattel toy brand Rock 'Em Sock 'Em, which was being produced at Winson, retailed on Amazon at $30 in October 2015. This means that each Winson worker earns *only 0.05 per cent* the market value of the Rock 'Em Sock 'Em toy.[56]

While workers struggle year after year to survive, the corporations above them exploit workers' labour to enlarge the fortunes of shareholders and executives. In 2014, Disney's revenue and profit reached $48.81 billion and $7.5 billion, respectively. That same year Disney CEO Robert Iger's total compensation of $43.7 million made him the twelfth highest paid CEO in America, according to *The New York Times*. This means that a Chinese worker making Disney's toys would need to work 11 hours a day, six days a week for *7,011 years* to earn the annual compensation of Disney's CEO. For Mattel and Hasbro, the comparable figures are *1,534 and 2,466 years*, respectively.[57]

Notes

1. Richard Walker and Daniel Buck in *New Left Review* in 2007, quoted in 'The Global Stagnation and China', by John Bellamy Foster and Robert W. McChesney, *Monthly Review*, February 2012, Vol. 63, Issue 09.
2. China and Socialism: Market Reforms and Class Struggle, Martin Hart-Landsberg and Paul Burkett, *Monthly Review*, July-August 2004.
3. Labour Protests and Trade Union Reforms in China, Jenny Chan, Ngai Pun and Mark Selden, https://www.etui.org/content/download/22940/190872/file/Chapter+10.pdf, accessed 25.05.16.
4. https://tradingeconomics.com/china/gdp-growth-annual, accessed 31.12.17.
5. Capitalist Globalization: Consequences, Resistance and Alternatives, Hart-Landsberg, Update Publications, Kolkata, p. 34.
6. Ibid., p. 43.
7. 'The Global Stagnation and China', by John Bellamy Foster and Robert W. McChesney, *Monthly Review*, February 2012, Vol. 63, Issue 09.
8. Ibid.
9. See Note 5, p. 45.
10. From the Claw to the Lion: A Critical Look at Capitalist Globalization, Critical Asian Studies, Hart-Landsberg, http://www.tandfonline.com/doi/full/10.1080/14672715.2015.997024, accessed 08.12.17.]
    Foster and McChesney have also noted that: "According to a 2006 report by the Development Research Centre of the State Council (China's cabinet), foreign capital (concentrated in the export sector) controlled 82 per cent of market share in communications, calculator, and related electronics; 72 per cent in instrumentation products, cultural, and office machinery; 48 per cent in textile apparel, footwear, and hats; 49 per cent in leather, fur, feather, and related industries; 51 per cent in furniture; 60 per cent in educational and sports products; 41 per cent in plastics;

and 42 per cent in transport equipment." [The Global Stagnation and China, by John Bellamy Foster and Robert W. McChesney, *Monthly Review*, February 2012, Vol. 63, Issue 09]

11. See Note 5, p. 46.
12. "While the reform process has taken an especially heavy toll on state workers, private-sector employment—especially at firms producing for export—has grown" writes Martin Hart-Landsberg ['The US Economy and China: Capitalism, Class, and Crisis', *Monthly Review*, February 2010, Vol. 61, Issue 09]. The private sector now contributes more than 60 per cent of China's GDP growth and provides over 80 per cent of jobs. [02.08.17, http://www.chinadaily.com.cn/business/2017-08/02/content_30328022.htm, accessed 08.12.17]
13. See Note 5, pp. 48-49.
14. Global Capital, the State, and Chinese Workers: The Foxconn Experience, Pun Ngai and Jenny Chen, http://content.csbs.utah.edu/~mli/Economics%205420-6420/Ngai%20and%20Chan-Global%20Capital%20State%20and%20Chinese%20Workers.pdf, accessed 25.04.16.
15. Ibid.
16. Apple's iPad City: Subcontracting Exploitation in China, Jenny Chan, Pun Ngai, Mark Selden, http://www.ccsp.ox.ac.uk/sites/sias/files/documents/Apples%20iPad%20City.pdf, accessed 17.01.17.
17. See Note 3.
18. Ibid.
19. See Note 14.
20. Ibid.
21. The Politics of Global Production: Apple, Foxconn and China's New Working Class, July 2013, Jenny Chen, Ngai Pun, Mark Selden, https://www.researchgate.net/publication/264225687_The_Politics_of_Global_Production_Apple_Foxconn_and_China%27s_New_Working_Class, accessed 25.04.16.
    The authors have noted that: "A cost and profit analysis of an iPad reveals the economics and corporate power relations underlying Apple's global business model. Where profit margins are often in the single digits in the low-end computing market, Apple retains 30 per cent of the sales price of the US$499 iPad, even more if it is sold through Apple's retail outlets or online store. In contrast, labour cost for the iPad in China is estimated at only 1.6 per cent, or US$8. Although Apple does not disclose its contracts with Foxconn, there is no doubt that Chinese workers who assemble much of the iPad receive a small share of the value it generates, while Apple enjoys extraordinary profit margins." [Apple's ipad City: Subcontracting Exploitation in China, http://www.ccsp.ox.ac.uk/sites/sias/files/documents/Apples%20iPad%20City.pdf, accessed 17.01.17]
22. See Note 5, p. 52.
23. Meet the Workers Who Make Your iPad: 100 Hours of Overtime, No-Suicide Pacts, Standing for 14 Hours a Day, 10.05.11, https://

thinkprogress.org/meet-the-workers-who-make-your-ipad-100-hours-of-overtime-no-suicide-pacts-standing-for-14-hours-a-469754e0ab7f#.huogvdx3a, accessed 21.06.11.

24. Hazardous working conditions in Foxconn are described as: "Foxconn's polishing workers are responsible for transforming raw aluminium into shiny stainless iPad casings. Each polishing machine produces metallic dust as it processes and grinds with ever greater refinement. Microscopic aluminium dust clouds the air. It coats workers' clothes. A young female polishing worker described the situation, 'I'm breathing aluminium dust at Foxconn like a vacuum cleaner.' The polishing workshop windows were tightly shut so that workers 'felt as if we were suffocating', 'Some tearing and pain also occur as the tiny solid aluminium particles are rinsed from my eyes by tears', Ma Quan, a 20-year-old worker, explained to us. He added: 'Everyone in the workshop is wearing a thin gauze mask, with a centre section of activated charcoal, but it doesnot have an airtight seal and provides no protection. Some of us are suffering from shortness of breath'. [Ibid]
25. See Note 14.
26. Ibid.
27. Ibid.
28. Suicide as Protest for the New Generation of Chinese Migrant Workers: Foxconn, Global Capital, and the State, Jenny Chan and Pun Ngai, http://apjjf.org/-Jenny-Chan/3408/article.html, accessed 25.04.16.
    The CEO of Foxconn Terry Gou said: "Hon Hai has a workforce of over one million worldwide and as human beings are also animals, to manage one million animals gives me a headache." [Terry Gou: Managing "1 m Animals", *Financial Times*, 20.01.12, http://blogs.ft.com/beyond-brics/2012/01/20/terry-gou-managing-1-million-animals/, accessed 01.06.16]
29. 'Interns or Workers? China's Student Labour Regime', Jenny Chan, Pun Ngai and Mark Selden, 31.08.15, *Asia Pacific Journal*, http://apjjf.org/-Jenny-Chan/4372, accessed 31.05.16.
30. See Note 16.
31. See Note 29.
32. See Note 28.
33. Ibid.
34. The Chinese labour federation had a total membership of 258 million surpassing the ITUC's (International Trade Union Confederation) global membership of 176 million workers in 161 countries and territories excluding China. [Labour Protests and Trade Union Reforms in China, Jenny Chan, Pun Ngai, Mark Selden, https://www.etui.org/content/download/22940/190872/file/Chapter+10.pdf, accessed 25.05.16]
35. In 2013, China spent as much as 769.1 billion yuan on 'stability maintenance', which exceeded the total annual military budget. [Ibid]
36. http://www.clb.org.hk/content/labour-disputes-historic-highs-official-statistics-reveal, accessed 08.12.17.

37. Apple Pays Chinese Workers $1.85/Hour for a 12-Hour Shift, 6 Days a Week, 01.03.16, http://anonhq.com/apple-pays-chinese-workers-1-85hour-to-work-in-unhygienic-conditions-for-a-12-hour-shift-6-six-days-a-week/, accessed 24.05.16.
38. Ibid.
39. As Apple's profits decline, iPhone factory workers suffer, a new report claims, 01.09.16, https://www.washingtonpost.com/news/the-switch/wp/2016/09/01/as-apples-profits-decline-iphone-factory-workers-suffer-a-new-report-claims/?utm_term=.a1aaf69af158, accessed 09.02.17.
Pegatron is located in Shanghai, which is a region with one of the highest wages in China. In other parts of China, whether it is a Foxconn or Pegatron factory, the wages received by the Apple workers can be assumed as the lower and some cases, lowest.
40. During off-season, there were around 50,000 workers, while during the peak season, there were around 100,000 workers. [August 2016, http://www.chinalaborwatch.org/upfile/2016_08_23/Pegatron-report%20FlAug.pdf, accessed 12.01.17]
41. August, 2016, http://www.chinalaborwatch.org/upfile/2016_08_23/Pegatron-report%20FlAug.pdf, accessed 12.01.17.
42. Exhaustion has no limit at Apple Supplier in China, December 2014, http://www.globallabourrights.org/reports/document/1412-IGLHR-China-AppleZhenDingTech.pdf, accessed 29.05.16.
43. Ibid.
44. High-Tech Misery in China, February 2009, http://www.globallabourrights.org/reports/HIGHTECH_MISERY_CHINA_WEB.pdf, accessed 20.05.16.
45. China News Net, December 11, 2006, quoted in The Role of the State, Labour Policy and Migrant Workers' Struggles in Globalized China, Chris King-Chi Chan, Pun Ngai, Jenny Chan, http://sacom.hk/wp-content/uploads/2013/07/2010GlobalLaborJournal-PN.CC.JC_.pdf, accessed 25.04.16.
46. Chinese workers contribute nearly $6.50 to each iPhone, about 3.6 per cent of the total manufacturing cost. If it is assumed that in place of Chinese workers, the US workers work as intensely as the real ones in Foxconn or in other subcontractors and the iPhone is assembled in the USA in place of China, it is calculated that the total assembly cost would rise to $65 (which is $6.50 in China) and still leaves 50 per cent profit for the Apple.... Despite decades of wage stagnation in the United States and of wage increases in China, the ratio between the two, adjusted for purchasing power parity, remain extremely large. One study, based on data from China's National Bureau of Statistics, estimated the difference in 2009 to be around 16-to-1, rising to 37-to-1 if prevailing exchange rates are used to make the comparison—and it is these that matter to US, European, and Japanese firms weighing whether to outsource their production. ['The GDP Illusion: Value Added versus Value Capture', by John Smith, *Monthly Review*, Vol. 64, Issue 03, July-August 2012]

47. Investigative Report on the Working Conditions in UNIQLO's China Suppliers, January 2015, SACOM, http://sacom.hk/wp-content/uploads/2015/01/2014-UNIQLO-Investigative-Report_final_20150109.pdf, accessed 12.01.17.
48. Ibid.
49. UNIQLO, Japanese Fast Fashion Label, Accused of Labour Violations, 13.04.15, http://www.corpwatch.org/article.php?id=16018, accessed 24.05.16.
50. The Other Side of Fairy Tales, 20.11.15, China Labour Watch, http://www.chinalaborwatch.org/report/111, accessed 27.04.16.
51. http://factsanddetails.com/china/cat9/sub61/item358.html, accessed 31.12.17.
52. Revealed: True Cost of the Christmas Toys We Buy from China's Factories, November 2010, https://www.theguardian.com/world/2011/dec/04/chinese-toy-factories-christmas-disney, accessed 03.02.12.
53. Dirty Toys Made in China, 10.12.15, http://www.globallabourrights.org/reports/dirty-toys-made-in-china, accessed 28.05.16.
54. Disney, Walmart and ICTI Together Make Workers' Rights Violations Normal and Sustainable, 22.10.10, http://sacom.hk/report-disney-walmart-and-icti-together-make-workers-rights-violations-normal-and-sustainable/, accessed 26.04.16.
55. In Chinese Factories, Lost Fingers and Low Pay, 05.01.08, http://www.nytimes.com/2008/01/05/business/worldbusiness/05sweatshop.html, accessed 24.05.16.
56. For example, at Mattel's Shenzhen-based supplier plant Winson, one production line maintained a daily quota of 1,600 toys, and each worker on the line will work on each of the 1,600 toys. Working six days a week, 4.2 weeks a month (assuming a 30-day month), a Winson worker will be expected to produce 40,320 toys per month. The worker's base monthly wage (i.e. before overtime) is the local minimum wage of 2,030 RMB ($319). After adding in all other high-season remuneration, including overtime, and before taking deductions, a worker's income may reach 4,060 RMB ($638) per month—this assumes 110 hours of overtime. If we divide monthly income (4,060 RMB) by the number of toys produced (40,320), we reach the conclusion that each Winson worker earns 0.100069 RMB ($0.016) per toy. [The Other Side of Fairy Tales, 20.11.15, http://www.chinalaborwatch.org/report/111, accessed 27.04.16]
57. See Note 50.

4
Working Conditions in Other Asian Countries

> It seems almost impossible to believe that 1,200 finishing section workers could have been kept at the Next Collections factory for nearly 500 hours in the month of June. When we met with several Next Collections workers in a safe location one evening in late June, we could immediately see that these young workers were sick, dazed and exhausted. There were deep shadows under their eyes, which were terribly bloodshot.
>
> —About the garment workers in Next Collections factory of Bangladesh supplying apparels to Gap, a giant MNC

> The prolongation of the working day beyond the limits of the natural day, into the night, only acts as a palliative. It only slightly quenches the vampire thirst for the living blood of labour. Capitalist production therefore drives, by its inherent nature, towards the appropriation of labour throughout the whole of the 24 hours in the day. —Karl Marx, *Capital*

It is observed earlier that the Asian countries have a major share in the global supply chain of various products, such as electronics, automobile, garments, leather products (particularly footwear), toys, and so on. It is also observed that during the last decade, due to the rise in labour costs in China, some of the manufacturing and assembling operations are relocating to 'newly emerging countries' of Asia. These countries are in fact some of the poorest countries of the world like Bangladesh, Cambodia, Vietnam, Pakistan, Myanmar, etc. where particularly the manufacturing and assembling of garments and leather goods are outsourced to subcontracting firms integrated to the MNC-led global supply chains. In addition, there are 'more industrialized' countries in Asia such as Thailand, Malaysia, Indonesia, etc. which are also integrated to the supply chain producing mainly electronics and automobile products. In all these countries, whether forward or backward with respect to each other, the working conditions in different sectors are unquestionably precarious—in some cases the worst. If we take the garment sector, these precarious conditions are vividly exposed by several experiences.

Garment Workers in Bangladesh, Cambodia and Thailand

According to the available statistics, total textiles and garments exports from Asia rose from US$154.3 billion in 2001 to a peak of US$451.5 billion in 2014. More than 60 per cent of the global apparel exports originated from 10 Asian countries, including—in order of market share: China, Bangladesh, Hong Kong, Viet Nam, India, Indonesia, Cambodia, Malaysia, Pakistan and Sri Lanka. With the rise of production costs in China and the relocation of production lines to overseas bases, China's share of Asia's garment exports has declined from a peak of 67.6 per cent in 2011 to 64.9 per cent in 2016. The US and EU remain the largest garment export markets. Together, they absorbed a total of 50.6 per cent of Asia's garment exports in 2016.[1]

In Sri Lanka (5 per cent), Cambodia (12 per cent) and in Pakistan (15 per cent) the garment industry occupies a significant share of the GDP. Bangladesh has the highest dependence on textiles and clothing as a total share of merchandise exports (83.5 per cent), followed by Pakistan (67.2 per cent) and Sri Lanka (47 per cent). In Bangladesh and Cambodia textile and clothing manufacturing together are the largest employer in manufacturing—75 per cent and 90 per cent of all jobs respectively.[2]

Bangladesh is the second largest exporter of ready-made garments in the world, after China. The growth of the industry has been dramatic. In the 1983-84 fiscal year, Bangladesh exported garments worth just over US$31.5 million, and employed 120,000 workers in 384 factories. By 2013-14 it exported garments worth more than US$24 billion, and employed some 4 million workers in 4,536 factories. Garments account for almost 80 per cent of the country's export earnings and contribute more than 10 per cent of GDP. More than 20 million people depend directly and indirectly on the industry.[3]

Bangladesh rose to its position largely because of its lack of regulation and the low wages it pays its garment workers, 80 per cent of whom are women. Bangladesh's minimum wage for the sector is one of the world's lowest—or the very lowest—even after the government raised it in response to fallout from the Rana Plaza disaster. It is noted earlier that wage in Bangladesh is just *14 per cent* of the 'living' wage.

Table 5: Monthly Wages of Garment Workers, Adjusting for Purchasing Power ($)

Country	*Year 2001*	*Year 2011*
Bangladesh	93.67	91.45
Cambodia	161.89	126.26
China	144.86	324.90
India	150.20	169.67
Vietnam	182.43	254.78

[*Source:* http://qz.com/389741/the-thing-that-makes-bangladeshs-garment-industry-such-a-huge-success-also-makes-it-deadly/, accessed 24.04.16]

The size and sophistication of garment factories in Bangladesh varies considerably. At one extreme are the flagships, purpose-built factories that employ thousands of workers and have relatively secure, long-term contracts with foreign buyers. At the other extreme are unregistered, back-street workshops that employ dozens of workers and work on a subcontracted, often short-term basis. There are also many medium-sized factories, employing about 500 workers each. Conditions are worse in the smaller subcontracting factories

Box: How Much Does It Cost to Make a Denim Shirt in Bangladesh, Versus the US?

US		*Bangladesh*	
Industrial Laundry	$0.75	Industrial Laundry	$0.20
Materials	$5	Materials	$3.30
Labour Costs	$7.47	Labour Costs	$0.22

[*Source:* http://edition.cnn.com/2013/05/02/world/asia/bangladesh-us-tshirt/, accessed 06.07.16]

which do not bother with garment brands' codes of conduct since they do not directly interact with the brands.

From the report of Human Rights Watch it is found that: "Workers in almost all of the factories complained that managers did not pay wages or benefits in full or on time. This included pay for overtime, maternity benefits, the Eid holiday bonus, and compensation for working during vacations." Moreover, since the majority of the workers are women, gender discrimination and harassment are common in all the factories. A female worker at a Dhaka-based factory employing over 400 people told Human Rights Watch that women workers there were humiliated when they asked for their benefits:

> In our factory, 80 per cent of workers are female and they will get pregnant, but the managers are not doing anything about maternity leave and bonuses. When we protested about it, our supervisors used really bad words against us, such as: 'If you are all concentrating on fucking, why are you working here? Go and work in a brothel.'

Pregnant women should not, according to the Labour Law, do "any work which is of an arduous nature", but a worker in another factory said that "*pregnant women are given a heavy load* and if they could not do it they are fired."[4]

Workers in most of the factories interviewed by Human Rights Watch said they had witnessed supervisors verbally and sometimes *physically abusing people for not meeting production targets*. In a factory, one worker said he was hit for missing his production target:

> One day I was a bit late for meeting my target and the factory manager came and grabbed my neck, then slapped me twice in front of my fellow workers. After that he took me to the time card section to sign a blank piece of paper, so that he could sack me and say I had resigned. But I did not sign and never got sacked. I could not protest about it, because anyone who does is fired straightaway.

In another factory, one of the workers performing subcontracted work for a US company said that the verbal and physical abuses are common. According to one woman worker:

> The factory working condition was very poor. Whenever someone missed the target bosses started shouting at them. Sometimes they would also beat the workers. One of the supervisors once kicked me on the back just because I was talking to a fellow worker.

In some of the cases documented by Human Rights Watch the abuse was of a sexual nature. Most garment workers are women, while supervisors and managers are mostly men. A worker at one factory, for example, said a colleague was insulted and pushed for not meeting her production target:

> The line supervisor put his hands on [her] and used bad words like, 'You should not be working here, go and fuck outside.' He pushed her off her chair and away from her machine. This was just because she had not fulfiled her target and still had some work left over.

Some interviewees said that workers were verbally abused for using the toilet and thus avoided the toilet as well as drinking anything during the day. Sometimes this verbal abuse also had sexual overtones. The woman quoted above working on products being sold to a US buyer told us: "We were not allowed to spend sufficient time in the toilet. If someone stays a long time in the toilet they use foul language like, 'Did you go to the toilet to make love'?"[5]

Ha-Meem Group is the Bangladesh's second largest garment exporter which owns 26 factories and employs over 30,000 workers. The MNC baron Gap and Old Navy clothing make up about 70 per cent of total production at the Next Collections factory run by this group, one of the subcontracting groups in Bangladesh. In the factory the working conditions are dreadful and the working hours touch the 'maximum' limit. The researchers commenting on this factory observed: "The 3,750 workers at the Next Collections factory work seven days a week, including on Fridays, which is supposed to be their weekly day off. It is typical for the workers to toil from 8 am to 10 pm, 11 pm, 1.00 am, sometimes 3.00 am or even later. *Fifteen- to 17-hour shifts are routine* in the finishing section.... In just 21 days in June, these workers were kept in the factory for a *stunning 334 hours!* When workers ask how long their shift will be, their managers always shout the same answer: "Keep working till it is done!"[6]

One pregnant woman worker narrates her harrowing story:

> In April 2013, I worked *150 hours overtime*. In May, I toiled *160 hours overtime*. And in June 2013, I worked *210 hours overtime*. You know that June 25 was a public religious holiday [Lailatul Barat]... You should know that I had to work from 8 am on June 24 to 7 am on June 25. That is a *23-hour work shift*! We could not say our prayers. I worked a whole night shift on June 24. I was obligated to do that even being pregnant. If we ask our supervisor for leave, it seems that we are committing a crime, despite the fact that we are routinely forced to work extraordinary hours. They have no sympathy toward pregnant women workers at the factory.... On July 3, 2013 I had to work till 1 am despite my pregnancy. In July and during the Ramadan, I worked in most cases till 10 or 11 pm This was strictly obligatory.... [On July 22, Monday] I gave birth at 9.30 am, but the baby was immature and died.
>
> That was my first baby, which I lost. The gruelling hours, constant strain and pressure to reach excessive production goals all led to the death of my baby. For me, it is a loss I will never get over.... After the delivery I have been shaken and physically sick.... I feel feeble and have developed the following complications: I can not sleep at night; I feel weak; if I stand up I feel dizzy; sometimes I have a fever; I have

> low blood pressure; I feel constant nausea and can not eat; I feel no hope.
>
> The company demanded that I return to the factory on July 26 to resume work. But how can I work just four days after the death of my baby? I am sick physically and emotionally. *Management thinks we are machines—that we have no feelings, no sorrows, no hardship. Even after I lost my baby, I can not mourn her.* Management wants the workers to have *no personal emotions, no feelings, no misery*. Our bosses are happy if we behave like machines and accept this as our universal fate.[7]

The researchers also report that:

> Despite the mind-numbing mandatory overtime, if an exhausted worker arrives even a minute late to work, he or she will be docked their entire attendance bonus. If a worker punches his or her timecard out a minute early, he or she will be docked an entire hour's wages. Physical punishment is the norm at Next Collections. No matter how many hours a worker has toiled, if she makes an error in production, *she will be slapped, shoved or even punched.*
>
> Anyone who dares challenge the gross human, women's and workers' rights violations will be immediately fired. When a young woman helper makes a mistake, the management humiliates her in the presence of all her co-workers, forcing her to stand in front of her sewing line for one-and-a-half hours.
>
> Young women are routinely robbed of their legal, paid maternity leave. Once a woman is six months pregnant, management begins to harass and bully her to "get out." These women are fired (or forced to resign) with nothing—denied their maternity benefits, paid vacation days they have earned, their severance pay and sick days.[8]

The workers of this factory subcontracted by Gap live in horrible places and denied any required facilities. The researchers said:

> When you look at the hip, feel-good Old Navy clothing, it is hard to believe that Gap workers live in some of the poorest

> hovels in the world. It is common for two, three, or even more Gap workers to share a small six-by-nine-foot room. In one home we visited, workers spread out a blanket to sleep on the concrete floor. They cannot even afford a makeshift wooden bed. Their primitive bamboo roof is torn. They have tried to repair it with cardboard, but the rain still pours in. Other Gap workers rent small one-room "homes" with walls and roofs of corrugated sheet metal. They heat up like ovens when the sun shines.[9]

After the inhuman treatment at the workplaces and the gruesome incident of Rana Plaza where more than thousands died, workers became restive and demanded higher wages and rights to organize in unions. As the demonstrations of the workers are building up, the leaders of the workers are targeted by the management and hired goons in collusion with the government and administration of Bangladesh. *Violations include physical assaults on union organizers* by both managers and thugs acting at their behest, threats and *multiple forms of harassment, and dismissal of union members*. The union organizer said that when the workers tried to set up a union, organizers were brutally assaulted and scores of workers fired. Women workers were beaten while pregnant, forced to work at night, and eventually fired, without receiving all their arrears. One of them said:

> I was beaten with metal curtain rods in February when I was pregnant. I was called to the chairman's room, and taken to the 3rd floor management room which is used by the management and directors—and there I was beaten by the local goons… There were other women who were called at other times, and they were beaten the same way as well. They wanted to force me to sign on a blank piece of paper, and when I refused, that was when they started beating me. They were threatening me saying, 'You need to stop doing the union activities in the factory, why did you try and form the union. You need to sign this paper.'[10]

With this struggle the workers have achieved some of the demands partially met by the Bangladesh government and the management. Wages have improved but still lie far below the 'living' wage. Some of the workers achieved their unions but still less than 10 per cent of garment factories in Bangladesh have unions.[11]

Cambodia is another 'emerging' country in Asia manufacturing garments for the world markets. In 2013, garments accounted for 13 per cent of the Cambodian GDP. Cambodia's global exports reached $6.5 billion in 2013, with $4.96 billion (76 per cent) coming from the garment and textile industry. The garment sector figure rose to $5.7 billion in 2014.12 An estimated 85 per cent of garment factories located in Cambodia are foreign-controlled, predominantly by investors from China, Hong Kong, Malaysia, Singapore, South Korea and Taiwan. Foreign-owned companies have kept the production processes within Cambodia limited. The majority of factories undertake "cut-make-trim" production functions—manufacturing clothes from imported textiles based on designs provided by international buyers.

Women between the ages of 18 and 35 dominate the Cambodian garment production sector, comprising an estimated *90-95 per cent* of the industry's estimated 700,000 workers. These numbers do not, however, include women engaged in seasonal, home-based garment work. Most of the garment industries recruit young women migrating from rural areas.[13]

All garment and textile products made in Cambodia are exported, of which in recent years the United States accounted for 67 per cent, the European Union 22 per cent and Canada 6 per cent.[14] International brands like Gap, Marks and Spencer, Nike, Puma, Joe Fresh, Adidas, and H&M are the garment barons subcontracting their production facilities in Cambodia. Like other countries in the global supply chains, the garment workers of Cambodia face immense pressure from their employers to meet just-in-time and quotas and/or rush orders from the international brands.

Owing to exposure to high temperatures and high levels of chemical substances, exacerbated by poor ventilation systems and nutrition among workers, episodes of *mass fainting* are a regular occurrence in Cambodian garment factories. According to reports by the Cambodian government, in 2015, 1,806 workers fainted in garment and footwear factories—the same number as in 2014. These 2014 and 2015 numbers mark a 109 per cent increase in the number of people who fainted in 2013.[15] In fact, *malnourishment and poor working conditions have resulted in episodes of mass fainting in the factories*. Human Rights Watch also noted in a report released in March 2015 that: "Malnutrition, due to low wages and time poverty, is endemic in Cambodia's garment workers. This has led to a

Chart 9: International Comparison of Hourly Labour Costs in Textile Industry, 2011 (in US$)

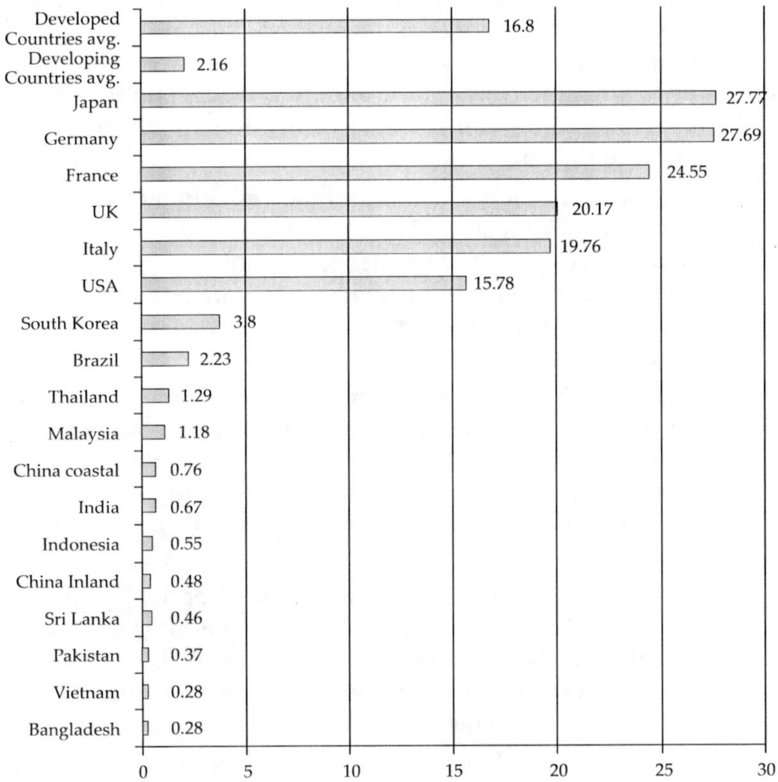

[*Source: Southern Insurgency: The Coming of the Global Working Class*, Immanuel Ness, Pluto Press, p. 10]

situation where workers producing high street fashion for Western markets are constantly weak and prone to collapse."[16]

But for a football shirt (used by the world famous football clubs) of international brand, the workers get the proportion of sale price of just *0.6 per cent*, while the *shops take away 59 per cent* and the *brands 12 per cent*.[17]

The general working conditions of garment workers in Cambodia in brief are as follows:

> Although Cambodian law limits the work week to 48 hours, with a maximum two hours overtime per day (for a six-day work week), they often far exceeded the 12-hour overtime weekly limit. The demand to meet production targets meant that workers are pressured not to take bathroom or rest breaks, and special bonus incentives to meet targets are often unpaid. Workers technically have the right to refuse overtime hours, but that in practice they could not refuse because they are afraid of dismissal from their work.
>
> Sixty per cent of Cambodia's 400 garment factories utilise short-term contracts. The *casualization* of the workforce (mainly women) over recent years enables employers to *hire and fire more easily*, and provides fewer benefits to workers. Workers who have worked for less than a year are not entitled to maternity benefits.
>
> While the minimum monthly wage for footwear and garment factory workers approved by the Labour Advisory Group in 2010 was $61, workers are able to earn around $80-90 during the peak season with two hours or more of overtime every day. However, they have to work long hours and eat less, with little time to rest.
>
> Many *under-age children*, between 12 and 14 years old, driven by the lack of educational access and/or the need to supplement their family's income are engaged. Often they are paid less than the minimum wage and are instructed to hide from view when "visitors" visit the factory.
>
> Although the law in Cambodia provides for three months of maternity leave and maternity pay if employed for one full year (without interruption), the pervasive use of short-

> term contracts often thwarts any meaningful enforcement of these protections for pregnant employees. These workers are particularly vulnerable to exploitation. Their condition meant that denial of bathroom and rest breaks could easily lead to dismissal for failure to meet production targets. One Phnom Penh factory worker told Human Rights Watch: *"It does not matter whether you are pregnant or not—whether you are sick or not—you have to sit and work.* If you take a break, the work piles up on the machine and the supervisor will come and shout. And if [a pregnant] worker is seen as working 'slowly' then her contract will not be renewed." *Sexual harassment is common,* with an ILO survey showing that 20 per cent of women report sexual harassment leading to a "threatening work environment."
>
> There are *concerted efforts to break unions* of the workers on behalf of the government and management. As soon as workers have initiated union-formation procedures, factory management would dismiss union officer-bearers or coerce or bribe them to resign, thwarting union formation. Since December 2013 Cambodia's Ministry of Labor introduced new obstacles to licensing unions, delaying the certification of unions and allowing management time to use retaliatory measures against union leaders. Additional measures to raise the threshold for the number of workers required to gain recognition.[18]

Cambodia's Constitution vows to guarantee the right to strike and the right to non-violent demonstration. The 1997 Labour Law 'guarantees' workers the right to form unions of their choice and 'protects' workers against interference from employers and discrimination on the basis of union membership. Although union membership is significantly higher in the garment industry than in other industries in Cambodia, with at least 37 garment union federations in existence as of 2014, many garment workers remain unrepresented. Union leaders are often targeted by factory owners, and *violently beaten* by law enforcement officials *while striking outside the workplace.* Many have faced dismissal or have been fired due to their activities.

In late December 2013 and early January 2014, more than 200,000 Cambodian garment workers took to the streets to demand a new minimum wage of $160/month. The strike closed the industry for one week. In response, armed soldiers chased and attacked workers with slingshots, batons, and metal pipes in front of a garment factory in Phnom Penh. On January 3, 2014, police and military personnel *shot and killed* at least five striking workers during a renewed mobilization. Those killed by the Cambodian security forces were employed at factories producing clothing for several major multinational corporations, including Puma and Adidas. An additional 38 people were hospitalized during the attack, 25 suffering from bullet wounds, and many were arrested. Immediately following the strike, the government instituted an interim ban on freedom of assembly prohibiting gatherings of 10 people of more which lasted around three months. Further, the government instituted an interim ban on union registration that lasted for most of 2014.[19]

Box: Adidas Exploitation Chain

Around the world 775,000 workers, mainly women, in 1,200 factories across 65 countries make Adidas products. Almost all the jobs are outsourced to factories in poorer countries, particularly in Asia.

In Indonesia, workers are paid as little as *34 p an hour*, with some factories not even the legal minimum wage. As a result, workers said they skip meals to save money and that every day someone in their factory passes out because they are exhausted or unwell. In the Philippines, workers said that their basic wage does not cover their families' minimum needs; more than half those interviewed said that they are forced to pawn ATM cards to loan sharks for high-interest loans.

None of the workers interviewed in China, Indonesia, Sri Lanka or the Philippines are paid a living wage—a wage that covers the cost of basic necessities such as food, housing, clothing, healthcare and education. Faced with such low pay, *workers often have little choice but to work excessive hours just to scrape together enough to get by*. Researchers found workers in China work from 8 am to 11 pm, regularly working overtime in excess of the legal limit. In Indonesia, Sri Lanka and the Philippines workers all reported that overtime is compulsory in order to meet their production targets.

Long hours are not the only problem workers face—in China, workers live in a *state of permanent uncertainty with little job security.* The majority of workers are employed on temporary contacts—and their contracts state that they have two places of work over 120 miles apart. The workers say that if they disobey their managers they fear being transferred, effectively dismissing them. Workers also face an *appalling lack of basic dignity and respect at work. In Indonesia workers need their managers' permission just to go to the toilet. Workers reported being verbally abused, having shoes thrown at them or being slapped across the face.*

In Indonesia the trade unions that do exist are not given bargaining rights by the factory management. Workers also *face individual harassment and punishment for union organizing;* at one factory in Indonesia supplying Adidas 10 workers were suspended earlier this year and face losing their jobs—believed to be as a result of their union activism.

At Adidas' Chinese suppliers trade union activities are even more repressed. Researchers found that the staff manual in one factory makes clear that any activity to educate or organize the workers to secure improvements in working conditions is a punishable offence; *if workers hand out leaflets they will be fired immediately.*

[*Source:* https://waronwant.org/sites/default/files/Adidas%20briefing.pdf, accessed 08.12.17]

In essence, the working conditions in Cambodia are similarly precarious like all the other countries of 'developing' Asia. Thailand, a more developed country than Bangladesh or Cambodia exhibits no other different experiences for the garment workers.

Textile and garment manufacturing continues to be one of Thailand's largest industries, employing more than one million people and bringing in over $7 billion annually through exports. Thailand exports 38 per cent of its textiles and garments to the USA, 30 per cent to the European Union, 7 per cent to ASEAN countries, 6 per cent to Japan and the remaining 19 per cent to Africa and the Middle East. Well known brands sourcing garments from Thailand include Adidas, Reebok, Nike, Levi Strauss, Timberland and Benetton.[20]

Thailand's expanding garment sector is constantly seeking sources of cheap labour. Neighbouring poorer countries supply this much needed cheap labour coming from Myanmar, Cambodia and Lao PDR. It is estimated that around *2.5 million migrant workers live and work in Thailand. Around 50 per cent of all migrants are women.* Owing to the political situation in their home countries, almost all migrants crossed into Thailand without any documentation and therefore *without any employment benefits* and facilities. Many garment factories in Thailand are located along the Thai-Myanmar border in mountainous areas recruiting exploitable and cheap migrants from Myanmar.[21]

Thailand's Labour Protection Act (1998) regulates working conditions and limits a working day to eight hours, or 48 hours a week. After eight hours, overtime should be paid at the rate of 1.5 times the normal wage. However, in reality this is far from the case. In Mae Sot, on the Thai-Burma border, the women *averaged 11 working hours a day with an unpaid hour off both at lunch and at dinner*. Some factories gave an unpaid day off every Sunday; some only twice a month. Overtime payment only starts after these 11 hours, and overtime is mandatory, not optional.

The legal minimum wage in Mae Sot is 153 baht (£3.10) a day. But the women working in garment factories in Mae Sot received only 69 baht a day *(£1.40) for a 10 or 11 hour working day*. In busy times with overtime, the workers may get 100 baht per day (roughly £2.00), still far below the minimum wage. In addition, wages are rarely paid on time.[22] Migrants commonly have deductions made for food and lodging by the factory, resulting in very little left over, most of which is either saved or remitted back home. About half the workers live in dormitories in the factory grounds. All the workers live in one hall, a common experience for migrant workers in factories. Conditions in these dormitories are often crowded and unsanitary, with the management doing little to improve things.

In fact, most factory workers live on factory compounds the entire time and are restricted to their immediate surroundings. They have *little contact with family, are isolated from the community,* and enjoy minimal if any access to medical services, although they do find time to socialize with colleagues on and off the compound. Migrant women are *denied paid maternity leave.* If the woman does decide to return to the factory after giving birth, commonly she will find that her position has been given to someone else, and has effectively been turned away from her former job without severance pay.[23]

Workers in the Electronics Industry in Malaysia

Malaysia has become a major global manufacturing hub for the electrical and electronics industry in the last decades of the 20th century. It is Malaysia's leading manufacturing industry and a key driver of the Malaysian economy, contributing 32.8 per cent of exports and 27.2 per cent of employment in 2013. Several MNCs from the USA, Japan, Europe, Taiwan and South Korea have chosen Malaysia as their manufacturing base outsourcing to different subcontracting firms. The industry is characterized by high foreign investment holdings, with 86.5 per cent (approximately US$2.68 billion) of investment in the industry originating from foreign sources in 2013.[24] Major companies investing in this sector in recent years include USA MNCs Dell, Intel, Motorola, Seagate; Asian MNCs Fujitsu, Sony, Panasonic, Hitachi, Toshiba, Sanyo, Canon, Konica-Minolta, Samsung, Sharp, Mitsubishi; and European MNCs Bosch, Osram, Siemens, Alcatel, Philips, etc.

Jobs in the electronics sector in Malaysia are primarily low-wage and low-skilled. Low-wage, low-skilled factory jobs are increasingly performed by foreign (migrant) workers in the country, One report has estimated *1.9 million documented and at least 2 million undocumented foreign workers in Malaysia in 2010,* comprising approximately *25 per cent to 30 per cent of the total workforce* in Malaysia.[25] Around 300,000 workers are employed in Malaysia's electronics industry, of which *70-80 per cent are women.*[26] These migrants come mainly come from countries like Indonesia, Nepal, Bangladesh, Burma, the Philippines, Vietnam, India, Cambodia and Thailand.

> Box: Nike in Vietnam
>
> In the year 2014, Nike produced over 365 million pairs of athletic shoes, while at the same time refusing to make a single sneaker in the United States. Meanwhile, they are making these shoes at a tremendous profit while paying their overseas workers pennies. In fact, Nike's largest production centre is Vietnam, where more than 330,000 workers, mostly young women, toil in 67 factories making goods for Nike. Everyone knows that Nike shoes do not come cheap, selling in the U.S. from $60 to $120 to well past $200. In February 2015, we looked at a sampling of ten shipments of Nike sneakers from Vietnam destined for the U.S. market. It did not take long to find that the average customs value of the Nike sneakers was just $5.27 per pair.
>
> Meanwhile, Nike's presence in Vietnam led to a continuation of *wages as low as 27 cents an hour* in 2012, with a slight increase to *48 to 69 cents an hour* in January 2015, which is well below subsistence levels.
>
> Nike's revenues for the year ending February 2015 totalled $30.3 billion.
>
> [*Source:* http://www.globallabourrights.org/reports/a-race-to-the-bottom-trans-pacific-partnership-and-nike-in-vietnam, accessed 29.05.16]

Electronics facilities, along with most other manufacturing companies in Malaysia, are primarily located in and around over 200 industrial estates or parks and 18 Free Industrial Zones (FIZs). Apart from duty free import of raw materials, tax breaks, advanced infrastructure, and IT, these zones are attractive to foreign investors, amongst others, because of its *low-cost workforce, low levels of unionization and weak labour rights*. Malaysia maintains a highly restrictive labour legislation, which, amongst others, limits collective bargaining rights and the right to strike. Malaysia's Industrial Development Council (MIDA) advertises its special economic zones (Free Industrial Zones) with "no minimum wage legislation", "minimum conditions of employment" and "responsible trade unions and harmonious industrial relations."[27] As a result of the anti-union measures specifically in Malaysia's electronics industry, the workforce is less able to defend its rights. This is reflected in the industry's working conditions. Factory workers are paid little and obliged to perform repetitive, tedious tasks for long exhausting hours. MNCs play an influential role in determining labour relations in the regions and industries they invest in. Indeed, in Malaysia, firms are known to threaten to leave Malaysia if their demands are not met, and the manufacturing industry has successfully lobbied for the liberalization of foreign worker recruitment to meet their labour demands. In 2008, the then head of the enforcement unit of the Immigration Department, Datuk Ishak Mohamed, was quoted in a national newspaper as follows:

> "Outsourcing is good as it will attract foreign direct investment. *Investors will not want unions to be formed in their establishments*. Through outsourcing, it would be difficult for unions to be formed as the outsourcing company, and not the factory, would be the employer."[28]

Thus these foreign/migrant workers, being denied the basic rights, become the major source of super-profits for the world-famous international brands.

Box: Slave-Like Conditions—Shrimp Workers in Thailand

Every morning at 2 am, they heard a kick on the door and a threat: Get up or get beaten. For the next 16 hours, No. 31 and his wife stood in the factory that owned them with their aching hands in ice water. They ripped the guts, heads, tails and shells off shrimp bound for overseas markets, including grocery stores and all-you-can-eat buffets across the United States.

After being sold to the Gig Peeling Factory, they were at the mercy of their Thai bosses, trapped with nearly 100 other Burmese migrants. Children worked alongside them, including a girl so tiny she had to stand on a stool to reach the peeling table. Some had been there for months, even years, getting little or no pay. Always, someone was watching.

No names were ever used, only numbers given by their boss—Tin Nyo Win was No. 31.

Pervasive human trafficking has helped turn Thailand into one of the world's biggest shrimp providers. Despite repeated promises by businesses and government to clean up the country's $7 billion seafood export industry, an *Associated Press* investigation has found shrimp peeled by modern-day slaves is reaching the US, Europe and Asia....

US customs records show the shrimp made its way into the supply chains of major US food stores and retailers such as Walmart, Kroger, Whole Foods, Dollar General and Petco, along with restaurants such as Red Lobster and Olive Garden.

It also entered the supply chains of some of America's best-known seafood brands and pet foods, including Chicken of the Sea and Fancy Feast, which are sold in grocery stores from Safeway and Schnucks to Piggly Wiggly and Albertsons.

Inside the large warehouse, toilets overflowed with faeces, and the putrid smell of raw sewage wafted from an open gutter just outside the work area. Young children ran barefoot through suffocating dorm rooms. Entire families laboured side-by-side at rows of stainless steel counters piled high with tubs of shrimp.

Tin Nyo Win and his wife, Mi San, were cursed for not peeling fast enough and called "cows" and "buffaloes." They were allowed to go outside for food only if one of them stayed behind as insurance against running away.

But escaping was all they could think about.

Shrimp is the most-loved seafood in the US, with Americans downing 1.3 billion pounds every year, or about 4 pounds per person.

The Thai Frozen Foods Association lists about 50 registered shrimp sheds in the country. However, hundreds more operate in Samut Sakhon, the country's main shrimp processing region. Here the humid air hangs thick with the smell of dead fish. Refrigerated trucks with seafood logos barrel down streets straddled by huge processing plants. Just as ubiquitous are the small pickups loaded with migrant workers from neighbouring Cambodia, Laos and Myanmar being taken to gut, fillet, de-vein and peel the seafood that fuels this town's economy.

Abuse is common in Samut Sakhon. An International Labour Organization report estimated 10,000 migrant children aged 13 to 15 work in the city. Another U.N. agency study found nearly 60 per cent of Burmese labourers toiling in its seafood processing industry were victims of forced labour.

Tin Nyo Win and his wife peeled about 175 pounds of shrimp for just $4 a day, less than half of what they were promised. A female Thai manager, who slapped and cursed workers, often cut their wages without explanation. After they bought gloves and rubber boots, and paid monthly "cleaning fees" inside the trash-strewn shed, almost nothing was left.

"We had to get up at 3 in the morning and then start working continuously," said Eae Hpaw, 16, whose arms were a patchwork of scars from infections and allergies caused by the shrimps. "We stopped working around 7 in the evening. We would take a shower and sleep. Then we would start again."

Former employees told the AP they had been locked inside and forced to work long hours with no days off and little sleep.

The conditions they described inside were horrific: A woman eight months pregnant miscarried on the shed floor and was forced to keep peeling for four days while haemorrhaging. An unconscious toddler was refused medical care after falling about 12 feet onto a concrete floor. Another pregnant woman escaped only to be tracked down, yanked into a car by her hair and handcuffed to a fellow worker at the factory.

"Sometimes when we were working, the tears would run down our cheeks because it was so tiring we could not bear it," said the worker who ran away. His name is being withheld due to concerns about his safety.

"We were crying, but we kept peeling shrimps," he said. "We could not rest. ... I think people are guilty if they eat the shrimp that we peeled like slaves."

[*Source:* Global Supermarkets Selling Shrimps Peeled by Slaves, 14.12.15, http://bigstory.ap.org/article/8f64fb25931242a985bc30e3f5a9a0b2/ap-global-supermarkets-selling-shrimp-peeled-slaves, accessed 23.04.16]

The majority of these migrant workers are not hired directly by the factories, but by outsourcing agents, which manage not only the bureaucratic aspects of the recruitment and migration process, but increasingly the payment of workers; they have become direct employers. There are 227 labour contractor firms/agents in Malaysia which are legal and recruit foreign/ migrant workers charging large 'fees' from these workers. In many cases migrant workers are forced to take debt from these agents to pay the 'fees' and thus *become bonded* till they are able to repay the debts. Undocumented stay was made a punishable offence in 2002, with up to five years' imprisonment, whipping, and fines of MYR 10,000 (around 2,500 EUR). So, these workers have no other avenue other than bondage to these agents or to be documented ('legal'). Migrant workers are routinely harassed by RELA—an armed paramilitary civilian volunteer corps with nearly 4 million members nationwide—who are granted "certain powers" by the government to tackle illegal immigration.[29] Given workers agree to high loans and interest rates (up to 25 per cent) on the basis of promised salaries, this can throw workers effectively into debt bondage. According to a 2010 Amnesty International report, many enter the workplace at least $1,000 in debt, after being charged high fees by recruitment agents.[30]

The migrant workers fall outside collective bargaining agreements and are not entitled to bonuses or allowances. They also cannot join unions, or be represented by unions when it comes to disputes between workers and employers. Some outsourcing agent practices also include paying workers only for the day or hours that they work, without granting regular labour rights such as a paid rest day per week, paid annual leave, paid public holidays, paid sick/hospitalization leave, maternity leave and benefits. Most workers found their passports were being held by the outsourcing agents, *some received threats of deportation when they complained about working conditions*. Workers are not supposed to talk about non-work related subjects during their shifts. Workers reported if they come late or if they are absent the factory will inform the agency. The agency will deduct part of the worker's salary, also when absent due to illness. These workers have to work 12-hour working days on most days, and 6 work days a week. On top of that migrant workers are expected to perform three to four hours of overtime work on a daily basis. Refusing overtime is reportedly very difficult. Workers also reported that occasionally they have to work more than twelve hours a day to complete their targets. A female Vietnamese worker in Penang says:

> Our employer forces us to work seven days a week. *I am exhausted. I stand for 12 hours every day. If we do not work, our employer beats us.* I have seen a Nepalese worker beaten. The employer also beat a Vietnamese worker and cut her hair.[31]

Most of the workers are crammed into a small dormitory like structure. Workers narrated their experiences in the following words:

- The whole house has three rooms. There are over 40 people living there. It is overcrowded. There is no place to even walk around.—Female Burmese worker in Klang Valley
- We all live in a hallway, no bedrooms, no privacy. There are too many people, 26 in all, but only one toilet. It is also very hot.—Male Nepalese worker in Johor
- The room is very crowded and noisy. Workers stay in the hallway, without proper bedrooms. There is no drinking water, only tap water from the bathroom.—Male Nepalese worker in Johor
- Every month, I pay levy and debt. By the end of the month, I have nothing left to save.—Male Bangladeshi worker in Klang Valley[32]

In the standard annual medical check-up, women have to undergo a pregnancy test. *They have to agree in the signed contract not to become pregnant during their employment term* and interviewed women said that the agency frequently reminded them that they may not have sexual relationships because it could lead to a pregnancy. All women workers reported that if they were to become pregnant, then they would immediately be sent back to their home countries.[33]

*****

We have observed so far that the imperialist capital in the present stage of capitalism are pushing into the Asian developing and underdeveloped countries where the reserve army of labour is abundant and the cost of production, particularly the cost of labour is much cheaper than (often fractions of) the advanced countries. The imperialist capital is outsourcing the production of commodities to the subcontracting firms in search for super-profits. The subcontracting companies, under the cost-cutting pressure of the lead MNCs, pass the burden on to the workers giving incredible lower wages compared to the advanced countries. In other words, the expropriation of the surplus value of labour power is absolute in the global value/supply chain.

In most of the developing and underdeveloped countries of Asia, integrated to the global supply chain, the 8-hour working day is beginning to be a thing of the past. Working hours become 12 hours as a general norm. In many cases the working day is now much longer as it is stretched to '16-17 hours', even to '24 hours'. Workers are forced to do 100-120 hours or more hours of overtime job (even at a single rate) per month which is far above the stipulated labour law of the countries (in Bangladesh, women workers are confined in the factory for a stunning 334 hours)! They are denied any moral, intellectual and recreational enrichment or leisure time. It is reminiscent of the 'industrial age' of England where the working class, including the children of the workers were forced to toil for prolonged working hours and denied the basic necessities. Observing this phenomenon in England, Marx wrote in *Capital*:

> [I]t is self-evident that the labourer is nothing else, his whole life through, than labour-power, that therefore all his disposable time is by nature and law labour-time, to be devoted to the self-expansion of capital. Time for education, for intellectual development, for the fulfiling of social functions and for social intercourse, for the free-play of his bodily and mental activity, even the rest time of Sunday (and that in a country of Sabbatarians!)—moonshine! But in its blind unrestrainable passion, its were-wolf hunger for surplus-labour, *capital oversteps not only the moral, but even the*

> *merely physical maximum bounds of the working-day. It usurps the time for growth, development, and healthy maintenance of the body*. It steals the time required for the consumption of fresh air and sunlight. It higgles over a meal-time, incorporating it where possible with the process of production itself, so that food is given to the labourer as to a mere means of production, as coal is supplied to the boiler, grease and oil to the machinery. It *reduces* the sound sleep needed for the restoration, reparation, refreshment of the bodily powers to just so many hours of torpor as the revival of an organism, *absolutely exhausted*, renders essential. It is not the normal maintenance of the labour-power which is to determine the limits of the working-day; it is the greatest possible daily expenditure of labour-power, no matter how diseased, compulsory, and painful it may be, which is to determine the limits of the labourers' period of repose. Capital cares nothing for the length of life of labour-power. All that concerns it is simply and solely the maximum of labour-power, that can be rendered fluent in a working-day. It attains this end by shortening the labourer's life.[34]

Marx observed these conditions of the workers in the seventeenth to nineteenth century England where the working day was extended to the "maximum bounds". Two centuries later the lengthening of working days in the Asian developing and underdeveloped countries in the global supply chain is strikingly similar to that Dickensian age. Workers in the present ages are similarly "absolutely exhausted", working days are lengthened usurping the "time for growth, development, and healthy maintenance of the body". Still it is observed in these countries that "time for education, for intellectual development, for the fulfiling of social functions and for social intercourse, for the free-play of his bodily and mental activity, even the rest time of Sunday" is robbed.

The overall working conditions in these countries are absolutely deplorable in general. The workers are forced to toil in wretched workplaces, in a horrid environment, in filthy and suffocating workshops, in a hazardous, dangerous conditions and unhealthy atmosphere; their children are born and brought up in this putrid environment and often are forced to work in the same conditions as their adult counterparts. Capitalism brings more and more women into the active labourforce in an increasing rate, but at the same time these women workers—whose 'nimble' hands work faster, who are proclaimed as 'docile' and 'pliant' and who are often seen as 'reluctant' in joining unions—are denied any maternal and necessary benefits. When pregnant, they are thrown out of the factories mercilessly denying any compensation. Even the basic physical necessities (such as drinking of water, going to toilets) of the workers are suppressed resulting in serious health problems. In these factories every second counts. The owners do not waste even a second to maximize profits. Often the workers are beaten by the supervisors or thugs hired by the management for not complying with the management orders and failing to meet the high production target. They are greatly unrepresented or denied to be organized in unions. There are very few opportunities to vent or redress grievances.

Even in the highly modernized factories of the 'flagship' companies, operating as subcontractors run by the multinationals such as Foxconn, Pegatron, Flexitronics, Bosch etc, and at the conveyor belt of the assembly chains, the conditions are no better. Workers are moulded to act like 'machines', like 'robots', they are made appendages to the fast moving conveyor belt. Virtually they must have no emotions, no joy, no personal feelings other than run faster with the speed of the machines to fulfil the targets. They are tied to exhausting, tedious, routine and monotonous jobs so tightly and caged in stringent discipline of dormitory life or slum life so rigidly that they have no personal life, no pleasure to enjoy, no communication with the loved one, no freedom of leisure, no time to spare for intellectual development. They are, in fact, *slave-labour* bonded tightly with the hankering capital serving the riches by satisfying their desires. These acts of barbaric exploitation and dehumanization of the workers, which often leads to suicides or mass fainting are seen all over the developing and underdeveloped countries of Asia.

Though the workers are striving to work hard, work harder to make commodities that will satisfy the consuming strata of the rich countries, they have no job security; once the demands plummet, or if the lead MNCs cut the production quota, the workers are thrown out of the factories. Never since the end of the Second World War, has workers' job security been reduced to such a flexible and vulnerable one. Understandably, most of these workers are denied any social security like pension, medical benefits, insurance, etc. Accumulation of capital in very few hands at the one pole creates accumulation of misery, exhaustion, ignorance, poverty and destitution at the other pole. One hundred and fifty years ago, Marx observed in *Capital*:

> [W]ithin the capitalist system all methods for raising the social productiveness of labour are brought about at the cost of the individual labourer; all means for the development of production transform themselves into means of domination over, and exploitation of, the producers; they mutilate the labourer into a fragment of a man, *degrade him to the level of an appendage of a machine, destroy every remnant of charm in his work* and turn it into a hated toil; they estrange from him the intellectual potentialities of the labour process in the same proportion as science is incorporated in it as an independent power; they distort the conditions under which he works, subject him during the labour process to a despotism the more hateful for its meanness; they transform his lifetime into working-time, and drag his wife and child beneath the wheels of the juggernaut of capital. But all methods for the production of surplus-value are at the same time methods of accumulation; and every extension of accumulation becomes again a means for the development of those methods. It follows therefore that in proportion as capital accumulates, the lot of the labourer, be his payment high or low, must grow worse. The law, finally, that always equilibrates the relative surplus population, or industrial reserve army, to the extent and energy of accumulation, this law rivets the labourer to capital more firmly than the wedges of Vulcan did Prometheus to the rock. It establishes an accumulation of misery, corresponding with accumulation of capital.

> *Accumulation of wealth at one pole is, therefore, at the same time accumulation of misery, agony of toil slavery, ignorance, brutality, mental degradation, at the opposite pole,* i.e. on the side of the class that produces its own product in the form of capital.[35]

Marx's observation is widely relevant in present-day capitalism also—in the global-supply-chain-type model of 'development'. Here the "agony of toil slavery, ignorance, brutality and mental degradation" is part of the life of the working class—the descendants of the English working class of the seventeenth to nineteenth century. In the present stage, capitalism changes in form, but not in content.

Notes

1. Changes in Asia's Textiles and Garments Supply Chain, 06.10.17, http://hkmb.hktdc.com/en/1X0ABIVN/hktdc-research/Changes-in-Asia%E2%80%99s-Textiles-and-Garments-Supply-Chain, accessed 31.12.17.
2. Emerging Trends in Factory Asia, Surendra Pratap, Asia Monitor Resource Centre, http://www.amrc.org.hk/sites/default/files/Emerging%20Trends%20in%20Factory%20Asia.pdf, accessed 12.01.17.
3. 'Whoever Raises Their Head Suffers the Most', Human Rights Watch, April 2015, https://www.hrw.org/report/2015/04/22/whoever-raises-their-head-suffers-most/workers-rights-bangladeshs-garment, accessed 05.03.17.
4. Ibid.
5. Ibid.
6. Gap and Old Navy in Bangladesh, Institute for Global Labour and Human Rights, October 2013, http://www.globallabourrights.org/reports/document/1310-IGLHR-GapOldNavyinBangladesh.pdf, accessed 29.05.16.
7. Ibid.
8. Ibid.
9. Ibid.
10. See Note 3.
11. Ibid.
12. Cambodia: Worker Rights Abuses in Garment Industry, May-June 2015, http://maryknollogc.org/article/cambodia-worker-rights-abuses-garment-industry, accessed 24.04.16.
13. Precarious Work in Gap Value Chain, www.ituc-csi.org/IMG/pdf/afwa_gap_may_23-2.pdf, accessed 05.07.16.
14. Restricted Rights: Migrant Women Workers in Thailand, Cambodia and Malaysia, www.waronwant.org, accessed 24.05.16.

15. See Note 13.
16. Work Till You Faint, http://sportexecutive.dk/work-til-faint/, accessed 23.04.16.
17. Ibid.
18. Cambodia: Worker Rights Abuses in Garment Industry, May-June 2015, http://maryknollogc.org/article/cambodia-worker-rights-abuses-garment-industry, accessed 24.04.16; Restricted Rights: Migrant Women Workers in Thailand, Cambodia and Malaysia, www.waronwant.org, accessed 24.05.16.
19. See Note 13.
20. Ibid.
21. Ibid.
22. Ibid.
23. Ibid.
24. Forced Labour in the Production of Electronic Goods in Malaysia: A Comprehensive Study of Scope and Characteristics, 2014, http://www.verite.org/wp-content/uploads/2016/11/VeriteForcedLaborMalaysianElectronics2014.pdf, accessed 08.12.17.
25. Ibid.
26. See Note 14.
27. The Life of a Migrant Worker in Malaysia, 23.01.13, http://evertiq.com/news/23693, accessed 08.12.17.
28. Outsourcing Labour: Migrant Labour Rights in Malaysia's Electronics Industry, January 2013, https://www.somo.nl/wp-content/uploads/2013/01/Outsourcing-Labour.pdf, accessed 08.12.17.
29. Malaysia: Forced Labour Casts Dark Shadow Over Electronics Industry, 21.11.16, https://www.theguardian.com/global-development/2016/nov/21/malaysia-forced-labour-casts-dark-shadow-over-electronics-industry, accessed 08.12.17.
30. Modern-Day Slavery Rife in Malaysia's Electronics Industry, 17.09.14, https://www.theguardian.com/global-development/2014/sep/17/modern-day-slavery-malaysia-electronics-industry, accessed 08.12.17.
31. See Note 24.
32. Ibid.
33. See Note 27.
34. *Capital*, Vol 1, Chapter X, Section V, *italics* added.
35. https://www.marxists.org/archive/marx/works/1867-c1/ch25.htm, *italics* added.

5
Concluding Remarks

> A study of the struggle waged by the English working class reveals that, in order to oppose their workers, the employers either bring in workers from abroad or else transfer manufacture to countries where there is a cheap labour force. Given this state of affairs, if the working class wishes to continue its struggle with some chance of success, the national organizations must become international.
>
> –Karl Marx, Speech to the Lausanne Congress of the First International in 1867

In the period of globalization the imperialist capital is making deeper inroads into the developing and underdeveloped countries with a specific model of 'development'. Under this model of 'development', thousands of EPZs/SEZs have been set up in these countries, mammoth projects of development of infrastructure are taken such as sea-ports, airports, power stations, connecting railway tracks and roads, bigger cities equipped with modern amenities such as shopping malls, recreation centres, etc. The ruling classes of these countries set up scores of industrial zones/parks or economic corridors for quicker delivery of finished goods to the foreign countries. It is observed that these projects are destined to serve the imperialist capital which is outsourcing many of the products to the subcontracting companies or enterprises integrated to the global supply chain reaping super-profits by exploiting the burgeoning reserve army of ('surplus') labour in these countries. This venture of modern capitalism not only helps the giant MNCs to make lucrative profits, but also helps the capitalist subcontractors (in many cases they are also MNCs, such as Foxconn, Pegatron, Bosch, etc) to make huge fortunes.

It is also noted that even UNCTAD equivocally terms this model of 'development' as "enclave-like growth". This is in fact a newer form of colonial subjugation by which a creamy layer of the society by serving the MNCs and big corporate houses (who are in many cases acting like managers of the imperialist capital) is making enormous fortunes, whereas the vast lower strata of people remains languishing in utter poverty and misery. In fact, in this pompous endeavour of 'development' there are no places of the millions of poor people toiling in agricultural activities as poor peasants or landless labourers who can hardly make ends meet; there are no places of millions of artisans, fishermen, Adivasis (tribal), Dalits, and economically backward people toiling for a paltry income. There are no shares of multitude of workers who are forced to sell their labour power at rock-bottom wages and under precarious conditions. It is an inequitable distribution of wealth where the majority of fortunes are concentrated in few hands; it is sheer exploitation and rejection of billions of working people cornering them at slums and ghettos outside the glittering cities and export-led zones keeping for them meagre opportunities to earn below subsistence level of wages. A recent report says:

> Globally, 82 per cent of the wealth generated last year went to the richest one per cent of the global population, while 3.7 billion people that account for the poorest half of the world saw no increase in their wealth.
>
> It takes just four days for a CEO from one of the top five global fashion brands to earn what a Bangladeshi garment worker will earn in her entire lifetime. In the US, it takes slightly over one working day for a CEO to earn what an ordinary worker makes in a year. It would cost $2.2 billion a year to increase the wages of all 2.5 million Vietnamese garment workers to a living wage. This is about a third of the amount paid out to wealthy shareholders by the top five companies in the garment sector last year.

And in India,

> 73 per cent of the wealth generated last year went to the richest one per cent, while 67 crore Indians who comprise the poorest half of the population saw one per cent increase in their wealth.
>
> In the last 12 months the wealth of this elite group increased by Rs. 20,913 billion. This amount is equivalent to the total budget of the central government in 2017-18.[1]

It is the true nature of the model of 'development' prescribed by the imperialist capital where billions of working people are excluded and sidelined. Under this model in the global supply chain of production, the MNCs are making super-profits by super-exploiting the huge masses of the reserve army of labour available to work at paltry wages and worst working conditions. In fact, never in history, have workers to face such atrocious attacks of the imperialist capital and their national partners. Each worker toiling in front of the running conveyor belt, each worker at tiny and ghastly workplaces, each worker at the crammed dormitories, in the filthy ghettos or slums, even household workers—making parts of the shoes or garments for the rich world—are facing similar onslaught of the imperialist capital. In advanced countries jobs are squeezing and are outsourced to the developing and underdeveloped countries making them most insecure. Moreover benefits enjoyed by these workers are fast depleting. On the other hand, the hapless workers of the developing and underdeveloped countries—who are numerous in numbers and where the wages are incredibly low compared to the advanced countries—have to bear the brunt of the super-exploitative capital that are observed in our earlier discussion.

A truth may have been haunting any conscious being. With the defeat in the international working class movement—which has occurred due to the internal weakness of the world proletarian struggle—has not only incapacitated the working class of the globe and but also made the working class largely divided, disorganized and dispersed all over the world. Overall, the working class has lost its battle against the imperialist capital; they have lost its organizations also once built with tireless and heroic efforts. Hence the cleavages between the workers of the advanced countries and backward countries are deepened. In India, the workers not only divided as permanent and contract/casual workers, as 'formal' and 'informal' labour, as resident and migrant labour, but they are also divided along the lines of religion, caste, race, creed, sex, and nationality to a large extent.

Thus incapacitated and divided by the internal weakness of the working class, the march of imperialist capital becomes so aggressive and atrocious. Hence a pertinent question arises: how will the workers make resistances against this aggression of the imperialist capital? How can they be prepared to wage forward marches against the onslaught?

It is observed that the workers in some Asian countries are trying their best to resist these onslaughts, trying to stage sporadic protests and build up struggles, somewhere wild-cat strikes against the attacks on their rights, and in some cases workers are able to achieve some of the demands (some increase in wages, formation of unions in a few cases, etc); in India, particularly in the automobile sector, workers are somewhat successful in uniting the permanent and contract labour demanding regularization of the contract labour. But on the whole, these strivings or economic struggles of the workers are in fact largely defensive, these strivings are just to build desperate resistances against the snatching away of the age-old rights; nay, these are, in the main, strivings for a mere 'survival', striving for maintaining 'existence', striving to make just two meals a day, for a shelter, for clothing—in fact, it is a desperate striving for any kind of job, striving for a 'subsistence wage', just to reproduce the labour power to be expended at the factories or workshops the next day. At the most, through these struggles, say in China, where workers are on the move on a larger scale than other Asian countries, workers can build 'embryonic trade union consciousness', but not 'class consciousness'.[2] They are now more aware about their legal rights, but not aware of their 'class interests'. In this context we would like to quote the once famous, but now almost forgotten words of Marx:

> Economic conditions first transformed the mass of the people of the country into workers. The combination of capital has created for this mass a common situation, common interests. The mass is thus already a class as against capital, but not yet *for itself*. In the struggle, of which we have noted only a few phases, the mass becomes united, and constitutes itself as a class for itself. The interests it defends become class interests. But the struggle of class against class is a political struggle.[3]

When the workers are able to "defend" their "class interests", when the workers are organized as a "class", then they are able to wage a political struggle against the capital as "the struggle of class against class is a political struggle". When they can organize themselves as "class for itself", then they are transformed into a truly "working class" capable of waging class struggle. Therefore they must be able to forge unity of the "class struggle" or "political struggle" against the capital as a "class" not only on a national scale, but also on an international scale. In this context, the excerpt of Karl Marx's speech to the Lausanne Congress of the First International in 1867 is remarkable. Marx said:

> The power of the human individual has disappeared before the power of capital, in the factory the worker is now nothing but a cog in the machine. In order to recover his individuality, the worker has had to unite together with others and create associations to defend his wages and his life. Untill today these associations had remained purely local, while the power of capital, thanks to new industrial inventions, is increasing day by day; furthermore in many cases national associations have become powerless: a study of the struggle waged by the English working class reveals that, in order to oppose their workers, the employers either bring in workers from abroad or else transfer manufacture to countries where there is a cheap labour force. *Given this state of affairs, if the*

> *working class wishes to continue its struggle with some chance of success, the national organisations must become international.*[4]

So, the "working class ... organizations" must be "international". What is the meaning of working class organizations? What is its significance in the present time? Does it sound like any type of 'organizations'? Are the economic organizations, i.e. the trade union organizations 'capable' to build unity of the working class on an international scale and 'capable' to defend the "wages and life" of the working class not only on a national level, but also on an international level?

If we comprehend with deeper insight the words of Marx—the "working class organizations" will be nothing but political organization of the working class. Since the character of capital is international and the working class in each country is facing the aggressive march of imperialist capital, the duty of the working class cannot be limited in forming only economic organizations, but it must build also the political organizations on a national level; and thus they will be capable in paving the way for broader unity among these political organizations against the onslaughts of imperialist capital.

Moreover, learning from the defeat of the international working class movement, the conscious section of the working class must prepare themselves not to lose the leadership and control of the movement and organization that occurred before.

In fact, we have to recognize that the strivings of the workers at the national level are *in essence* the striving for a "working class organization" in that country. Moreover, these strivings at the national level are *in fact* linked with the strivings of the working class in other countries; therefore these strivings are international *in content*. The duty of the workers is to build a class-struggle and political (class) organizations against the offensive march of the capitalist class not only in one country, but also they have a bounden duty to make contacts and forge unity of struggles and (class) organizations among the workers of other countries.

"If the working class wishes to continue its struggle with *some chance* of success, the national organizations must become international"—such is the call of Marx 150 years ago. This call is now *more* relevant in the present stage of capitalism.

Notes

1. Richest 1 per cent bagged 73 per cent of wealth created last year—poorest half of India got 1 per cent, says Oxfam India, 22.01.18, https://www.oxfamindia.org/pressrelease/2093, accessed 23.01.18.
2. Chinese Migrant Workers: Factors Constraining the Emergence of Class Consciousness, Anita Chan and Kaxton Siu, http://psc.bellschool.anu.edu.au/sites/default/files/IPS/PSC/CCC/publications/papers/Anita-Kaxton-Migrant-workers.pdf, accessed 17.02.17. The excerpts read like: "Using the Marxist-Leninist theoretical schema, we conclude that migrant workers in South China as a class are at the level of 'embryonic trade union consciousness'. Breaking down the development of consciousness into stages and phases since the mid-1990s, we can see that their consciousness has been hovering at the rights-based level. The workers' main concern is still their own personal and immediate economic conditions, and only occasionally is there a breakthrough into the interest-based level. At times sparks of union consciousness might flicker."
3. *The Poverty of Philosophy*, Karl Marx, Progress Publishers, pp. 159-60, *italics* added.
4. Speech to the Lausanne Congress of the First International in 1867, Marx and Engels, *Collected Works*, Vol. 20, London: Lawrence and Wishart, p. 422, *italics* added.